TEACHING
That Makes a
DIFFERENCE

HOW TO TEACH *for* HOLISTIC IMPACT

DAN LAMBERT, Ed.D.
ASSOCIATE PROFESSOR OF YOUTH MINISTRY
JOHN BROWN UNIVERSITY

YOUTH
SPECIALTIES
ACADEMIC

WWW.ZONDERVAN.COM

YOUTH
SPECIALTIES

ACADEMIC

Teaching That Makes a Difference: How To Teach for Holistic Impace
Copyright © 2004 by Youth Specialties

Youth Specialties Books, 300 South Pierce Street, El Cajon, CA 92020, are published by Zondervan,
5300 Patterson Avenue SE, Grand Rapids, MI 49530

Library of Congress Cataloging-in-Publication Data

Lambert, Dan, 1962-
  Teaching that makes a difference : how to teach for holistic impact /
by Dan Lambert.
     p. cm.
  ISBN 0-310-25247-4 (hardcover)
 1. Church work with youth. 2. Christian education of young people.
I. Title.
  BV4447 .L332
  268'.433--dc22

2004008613

Editorial and art direction by Rick Marschall
Editing by Doug Davidson
Proofreading by Joanne Heim
Cover and interior design by Mark Arnold
Printed in the United States of America

04 05 06 07 08 09 / DC / 10 9 8 7 6 5 4 3 2 1

TABLE OF CONTENTS

Acknowledgements 6

A Note about the Web site 8

Read This First! 9

Chapter 1) WHAT IS HOLISTIC TEACHING? 11
    1) The Current Climate of Religious and Biblical Understanding in Youth Culture ——————— 12
    2) The Biblical Basis for Holistic Teaching ——————— 17
    3) How Holistic Teaching Prepares the Way for Lifelong Spiritual Growth ——————— 21
    4) The Role of Teachers in the Teaching-Learning Process ——————— 22
          a. The Characteristics of Teachers ——————— 23
          b. The Tasks of Teachers ——————— 24
          c. Other Tidbits from Scripture ——————— 27
          d. Warnings to Teachers ——————— 28
    5) The Role of the Holy Spirit in Teaching ——————— 32
    6) For Discussion ——————— 35
    7) Activities ——————— 36

Chapter 2) WHO ARE ADOLESCENTS ANYWAY? 37
    1) A Brief History of Adolescence ——————— 38
    2) Physical Development ——————— 40
    3) Intellectual Development ——————— 42
    4) Emotional Development ——————— 43
    5) Social Development ——————— 44
    6) Brain Development ——————— 45
    7) Identity Development ——————— 47
    8) Vocational Development ——————— 49
    9) Moral Development ——————— 50
    10) Spiritual Development ——————— 51
    11) Teaching Implications ——————— 53
    12) For Discussion ——————— 56
    13) Activities ——————— 57

Chapter 3) WHO ARE THE KIDS YOU TEACH? 59
    1) Defining "Cultural Exegesis" ——————— 60
    2) Why Doing a Cultural Exegesis is Essential ——————— 61
    3) Getting Started ——————— 61
    4) Doing Some Homework ——————— 67
    5) Analyzing What You've Found ——————— 70
    6) Applying the Conclusions to Your Teaching ——————— 72
    7) For Discussion ——————— 73
    8) Activities ——————— 74

Chapter 4) HOW DO KIDS LEARN? **75**

    1)   Our Senses and Learning   76
    2)   A Variety of Theories   77
            a. The Sensory Model   77
            b. Bi-polar Models   80
            c. The 4MAT ® System   87
            d. Multiple Intelligences   89
    3)   Information Overload   91
    4)   For Discussion   92
    5)   Activities   93

Chapter 5) WHAT SHOULD YOU USE TO TEACH? **96**

    1)   Curriculum Defined   96
    2)   Curriculum Theories   100
    3)   Commercial Curriculum   109
    4)   Choosing Curriculum   111
    5)   Scope and Sequence   115
    6)   For Discussion   117
    7)   Activities   118

Chapter 6) HOW CAN YOU PREPARE TO TEACH? **119**

    1)   A Step-by-Step Guide   120
    2)   The Details   121
    3)   For Discussion   136
    4)   Activities   136

Chapter 7) WHAT TEACHING METHODS SHOULD YOU USE? **138**

    1)   What is a Teaching Method?   139
    2)   How to Choose a Good Method   139
    3)   The Discussion Monster   140
            a. Advantages of Discussion   140
            b. Potential Problems with Discussion   141
            c. Types of Questions   142
            d. Bloom's Taxonomy and Discussion Questions   143
            e. Tips for Leading Great Discussions   147
    4)   The World's Longest List of Teaching Methods   149
    5)   For Discussion   165
    6)   Activities   165

Chapter 8) HOW CAN YOU KNOW IF YOU'RE MAKING A DIFFERENCE? 167

1) Why Evaluate? 168
2) What to Evaluate 170
3) How to Evaluate 171
    a. Formal Evaluations 172
    b. Informal Evaluations 174
4) What to Do with Evaluations 174
5) Making Changes 175
6) Continuing to Improve 177
7) For Discussion 179
8) Activities 179

Chapter 9) HOW MIGHT JESUS TEACH TEENS TODAY? 181

1) Some Observations about Jesus' Teaching 182
    a. Whom Jesus Taught 183
    b. What Jesus Taught 184
    c. How Jesus Taught 189
    d. Where Jesus Taught 192
    e. When Jesus Taught 192
    f. How People Responded 193
2) Some Mistakes to Avoid When Trying to Teach like Jesus 193
3) So How Might Jesus Teach Today's Teenagers? 196
4) The Ultimate Reward 202
5) For Discussion 203
6) Activities 203

Chapter 10) WHAT OTHER TEACHING TIPS SHOULD YOU KNOW? 205

Read This Last! 217

Glossary 218

References 227

A Note from the Author about the Pink Ribbon on the Back Cover

During the writing of this book, my family was devastated by breast cancer. One of my uncles died from complications related to breast cancer. An aunt had a radical mastectomy. And my only sister was diagnosed with the disease and underwent surgery plus aggressive chemotherapy and radiation treatment. Because this is an issue in my family, I want to use this book to raise awareness. The pink ribbon ON THE BACK COVER is a symbol of the fight against breast cancer. To learn more, please visit www.pinkribbon.com. A portion of the proceeds from this book will go toward the fight against breast cancer.

ACKNOWLEDGEMENTS

I had no idea how difficult it would be to write a book when this process began. Even more difficult is making sure that what I want to say is said well, and that those whom I need to thank get mentioned. Here goes:

To my mom, SHIRLEY LAMBERT, who instilled in me at a very early age a love for learning by getting me books with math games when my friends were getting train sets and BB guns.

To my dad, DICK LAMBERT, whose very life is a witness and encouragement to me.

To my TEACHERS AT ADAMS CENTRAL SCHOOLS in Monroe, Indiana, who modeled holistic teaching to me from kindergarten through twelfth grade.

To those who have encouraged, discipled, mentored, and taught me in college, in seminary, and in my youth ministry experience. Thanks especially to DOUG, BRAD, DAVE, NORM, AND MYRON.

To FORT WAYNE YOUTH FOR CHRIST, where I got my start in youth ministry with the best group of examples an ignorant youth ministry neophyte could have had.

To PLEASANT DALE CHURCH, where I found a church family and had my views of youth ministry profoundly changed and sharpened.

To CLOVERNOOK CHRISTIAN CHURCH, where I was encouraged and challenged as never before.

To ALEXA, CALEY, AND CAMERON, my own kids and most important youth group, whom I love very much and who are now learning from their own youth pastor and ministry team.

To BECKY, my wife of twenty years. There is no way to express the thanks I need to. I am fortunate to have married the perfect woman who is also a great copyeditor.

To THE LORD, JESUS CHRIST. Thank you for the gifts you have given me and the unspeakable privilege of working with adolescents. I pray that you are pleased with this work and that it enhances your kingdom in some small way.

SPECIAL THANKS

As I was preparing the manuscript for this book, I asked some trusted colleagues and friends to give me their feedback on the first draft. Thank you to Terry Linhart, Pamela Erwin, Brad Edwards, and Sam Hannon for your time and terrific ideas. Also, during the spring semester of 2003, my Christian Education with Adolescents class at John Brown University used the manuscript for this book as their primary reading. Part of their assignment was to critique and make suggestions for improvements to each chapter, which they did with relish. What I initially hoped would be a good idea turned out to be an invaluable help. The comments and suggestions of these students, whose names are listed below, turned this book into an excellent text. I am deeply indebted to them.

Adam Butler
Allison Johnson
Brandon Norrell
Brandon Wimberly
Caleb Summers
Chase Willsey
Chris Borkert
Evan Gundy
Johnny Knox
Jonathan Snyder
Kim Peabody
Kristin Snyder
Luke Davis
Meghann Wharton
Nick Ballard
Mike Stuckey
Molly Schulte
Nate Bishop
Noah Mitchell
Paige Canfield
Pearl Vazquez
Ryan Hawk
Steven Victor Amos
Tim Wiley
Tyler Carroll
Virginia Moor

The information in this book is intended to be dynamic. To help keep the information in these pages up to date and to further enhance the benefit of *Teaching That Makes a Difference*, we have created a supplemental Web site on which you can find:

- Up-to-date reference material for each chapter
- Web links for related information
- A searchable database of teaching methods
- Interactive discussions and chat rooms
- Additional teaching tips
- Power Point outlines for teaching
- Test bank for professors
- Ideas for using this book to equip your ministry team
- Much more

I would like to thank Jess Elmquist and the staff at TrueWell (www.truewell.com) for their assistance in creating this Web site. If you are looking for a tool to help you design and maintain your ministry's Web site, I highly recommend them to you.

To get to the Web site for this book, just type *www.teachingyouth.com* in the address bar of your Web browser.

A GREAT TOOL FOR EQUIPPING YOUR
YOUTH MINISTRY TEAM TO BECOME GREAT TEACHERS

Our Web site also includes several very practical ideas for using each chapter of this book to equip youth ministry volunteers to teach well. These include handouts, Power Point slides, meeting outlines, and several other helpful resources—all free!

CHAPTER 1

WHAT IS HOLISTIC TEACHING?

(And Why Teaching Well Matters)

"[My Christian friends would] say they're Christians because they say they believe in God, and they go to church usually. And I say, 'That doesn't make you a Christian. What makes you a Christian is believing all that and living it out.' They don't live it out. They do far worse things than I do and that makes them hypocrites."
—CLAIRE, A COLLEGE FRESHMAN[1]

"I think a lot of people are losing their religion. Definitely. Even me, I know that when I grew up I used to go to church every Sunday, and now it's become holidays. But I think as long as you have your own thing, whether it's meditation—anything that centers you in life is good. Do I pray? Yeah, I do."
—ACTRESS KIRSTEN DUNST[2]

*   *   *   *   *

The future of the church is in trouble, and those of us who teach youth need to step up and accept our share of the blame. God has entrusted us with a high and holy calling, but we've treated it like it's just another chore in life. We rarely take the time to do it well, and often would prefer not to do it at all. We wait until the last minute to get ready (if we take the time at all), and only put in the effort to do it right when we know something special is happening, like visitors or evaluation.

THE CURRENT CLIMATE OF RELIGIOUS AND BIBLICAL UNDERSTANDING IN YOUTH CULTURE

Our sloppiness in teaching God's Word haunts us with the maturing of the young people we typically call Generation X. Witness the incredibly high number of public figures between ages 20 and 35 who either grew up in the church or call themselves Christian, but use that term very differently than most of us might. Here are a few quotations from or about some well-known performers:

JESSICA SIMPSON *is "a minister's daughter, a poor kid who moved seven times before she was eight as her father, Joe, sought work as a youth minister and therapist for abused kids in Baptist parishes around Dallas."* [3]

"The Bible. That's my favorite book. I was an usher in church; my grandmother played the piano. And my father's a deacon now."
—**SKINNY DEVILLE** (REAL NAME WILLIAM HUGHES) OF THE GANGSTA RAP GROUP **NAPPY ROOTS**[4]

"I have an intense history with Christianity."
—**BEN MOODY,** WHOSE BAND, **EVANESCENCE,** HAD THEIR ALBUMS PULLED FROM CHRISTIAN BOOKSTORES WHEN IT WAS DISCOVERED THAT BAND MEMBERS DRANK AND SWORE.[5]

"I love the teachings of Christ, but I don't think of myself as a Christian by anyone's conventional understanding."
—**MOBY**[6]

"I'm a believer in Jesus Christ."
—**TOM DELONGE OF BLINK-182**

"I pray before we go on stage and I pray at night."
(EXPLAINING THAT HE ABSOLUTELY BELIEVES IN GOD, BUT HOPES THAT GOD IS NOT JUDGMENTAL ABOUT HIS BEHAVIOR.)
—**MARK HOPPUS OF BLINK-182,** KNOWN FOR THEIR PROFANITY-LACED LYRICS, CONCERTS IN THE NUDE, AND VIDEOS FEATURING PORN STARS[7]

NO DOUBT LEAD SINGER **GWEN STEFANI** *"was raised in a Christian family, which is what she blames for her worst faults—namely that she is too judgmental and not open enough."* [8]

"I was angry. I was battling myself in my brain. I was kind of tormented by it because I was dealing with guilt issues about all the Ten Commandments and all the other things the Bible says I wasn't living in my life...[But now] I'm at peace with it. There's no guilt anymore."
—CREED'S SCOTT STAPP[9]

"I mean, all three of us have faith, and I think we all believe there is a God...but it's not a Christian God or a Buddhist God or a Muslim God. It's the God I see when I look at my little boy. It's the God I see in nature...It's the God that is revealed to me through the world around me."
—CREED'S SCOTT STAPP[10]

"We continuously surround ourselves with spiritual people, and give God our praise...It's a great thing that we speak up for our Christianity, and nobody's gonna tell us to stop."
—BEYONCE KNOWLES OF DESTINY'S CHILD[11]

"I'm a Christian. I go to church."
—BRITNEY SPEARS[12]

"I can honestly say that I'm a Christian, but my spirituality has been developed on the road and is based on my experiences with God."
—JUSTIN TIMBERLAKE, WHO GREW UP IN A BAPTIST CHURCH WITH WHAT HE CALLS FROWNING, JUDGMENTAL ELDERS.[13]

"Sure," you might be thinking, "but these are famous people. We shouldn't expect them to reflect the experiences and attitudes of the typical kids in our churches." Yet all of these now-famous people once *were* youth in our churches and have since formed less-than-biblical, or at least radically nontraditional, views of God, Christianity, and personal faith. These are some of the gifted, talented, and driven kids that God created to be singing his praises and serving his kingdom.

They're no different from the "regular" teens we see every week at school, in our neighborhoods, and in our ministries.

Still not convinced? Then take a look at what some other, non-famous young people say about their experience growing up in church.

Amazing Conversions is a terrific book by Bob Altemeyer and Bruce Hunsberger (Amherst, NY: Prometheus Books, 1997) that chronicles the stories of forty-six college freshmen they called "Amazing Apostates." That is, these students were identified in a survey of more than 2,000 college freshmen as being among those who were raised in church-going, Christian families but had abandoned their faith by the time they reached college. Consider the following excerpts:

> Anne says she was very devout all the way through high school, until age 17, when she started seeing things differently. *"I just started making up my own mind, and stopped believing basically about the church"* (p. 39). *"I didn't like being told how you should interpret different readings. Why can't you make up your own mind?"* (p. 41).

> Bill thinks it very unlikely that he will ever return to religion. *"Those things aren't nearly as important to me as freedom of thought and freedom of expression"* (p. 44). *"I am a lot stronger than I would be if I had let Christ control my life instead of making my decisions"* (p. 45).

> Dwight expressed concern that *"you don't have a choice. They only give you one side and that's what you have to believe in"* (p. 50).

> [Eleanor] also hunted for answers in the Bible, which she read every evening before she went to bed…But they were answers she could not accept (p. 54).

These examples could go on and on, but you get the gist. The authors make several interesting conclusions and observations based on their study. They note that several of the young people compare the religious teaching of their youth to Santa Claus: "My parents told me *that* was true, too," remarked one student. "What is the evidence for God, really?" (p. 111, emphasis original).

The authors conclude that the "nuclear" cause of the amazing apostasy they uncovered originates with this issue: Can you believe in the Bible, and its story of the existence of God? (p. III). When youth struggled with questions of belief, the church offered them little support. Those participants who went to pastors with their questions said that clergy offered reasoned answers to the questions more often than parents, but failed to convince. "I couldn't get a straight answer," said Chuck (p. 112). The authors concluded that "Traditional religious teachings would 'come up short' in the truth department more often in bright minds, *if* the teachings did not make sense" (p. 121, emphasis original).

I doubt it would take much effort for you to think of people you grew up with or teenagers you've taught in church who would say many of these same things. A lot of the youth growing up in our churches now are developing similar attitudes. It's time to get serious about addressing the problem.

More evidence comes from a company called Highway Video in Mountain View, California (www.highwayvideo.com), that has produced a series of film shorts over the past few years with some very disturbing content. Among their great products are some "person on the street" interviews asking basic religious questions. Prayer, truth, death, and going to church have all been subjects. The comments of these anonymous interviewees indicate an alarming lack of understanding about the God of the Bible, even among those who grew up in the church.

All of this leads to the inescapable conclusion that the church has done a very poor job of making disciples of most of the teenagers God has put in our care.

So what does that mean for those of us who are called to teach youth? After reading this chapter, one of my students at John Brown University commented, "I think the church not only does a very poor job of teaching, but an even worse job of bringing up effective teachers." I agree, but this doesn't have to be the case. We can teach teenagers not just what the Bible says, but why we trust the Bible and how the Bible should make a difference in our everyday lives. And we can equip almost any willing Christian to be a very good teacher.

Both anecdotal and statistical evidence indicates that we are losing our youth, especially the older, brighter ones. Kids who are expressive, inquisitive, artistic, MARGINALIZED, or doubting have an exceedingly difficult time finding teachers who connect with them in our churches. Rather than challenging students to excellence in a variety of ways, we are in the midst of a youth ministry culture

CHECK THE GLOSSARY

If the words in SMALL CAPS are new to you, the glossary at the end of the book may be helpful.

where we are attempting to "Love them into the kingdom." Anybody can do that, right? Evidently not. Somehow we're falling short. Just loving them is *not* enough. The world loves them too. Most kids know just as many non-Christians who love them as Christians. And non-Christians are rarely seen as hypocrites, which is a very big deal to teens.

There was a lot of speculation that the terrorist attacks of September 11, 2001, would spark a spiritual revival in America's churches. Just six months later, most churches (except the largest megachurches) were back to their pre-9/11 attendance levels.[14] Christians keep waiting for something to happen that will shake people into revival. But until we do a better job of teaching God's truth and making disciples, external events will never bring sustained change.

While many public polls have shown an increase in spirituality in North America, they have also shown a marked decrease in people, including teens, who identify themselves as evangelicals. One research report summarized the trend in this way:

> *The percentage of teens who are evangelicals—i.e., those who are not only born again but also believe in the accuracy of the Bible, personal responsibility to evangelize, believe in salvation by grace alone, and possess orthodox biblical views on God, Jesus, and Satan—has declined from 10 percent in 1995 to just 4 percent today.*[15]

WHAT HAVE WE BEEN TEACHING KIDS, ANYWAY?

If the numbers in this report are even close to being accurate, it is pretty damning evidence that the church has been doing an exceedingly pathetic job of teaching youth.

This is also reflected in research that indicates declining attendance at youth group meetings.[16] We who are youth ministry leaders have been largely blinded by the apparent growth in attendance at megachurch youth events. We need to keep in mind that these churches represent a tiny percentage of churches in America. Even if these congregations are growing (and some reported attendance numbers have been called into doubt recently),[17] there are tens of thousands of other North American churches in which youth participation is declining.

It isn't that God is no longer important to young people. In fact, more youth say they think about God and the meaning of life regularly than ever before. They just aren't doing it in Christian churches or in evangelically ORTHODOX ways as much.[18]

To stop this bleeding, we must do a better job of passing on the faith. We can't just tell kids what they are to believe—as indicated above, that strategy doesn't work well. And we have to do more than just make sure kids feel close to God. That tends to leave them questioning in those moments when they don't feel close to him.

The best way to raise the next generation of Christian believers is to teach holistically. Feed their souls, challenge their minds, strengthen their emotions, and guide their actions. This is the type of HOLISTIC teaching we see in Scripture.

THE BIBLICAL BASIS FOR HOLISTIC TEACHING

To teach holistically is to touch every part of who the student is. This includes the physical, mental, emotional, social, and spiritual realms. The idea is to teach individuals in the way God has created us, as whole beings made in his image, rather than fragmented parts.

Somehow, over the past several decades, teaching in the church has become dominated by several troubling tendencies. In some congregations, teaching is focused entirely on memorizing portions of Scripture. In others, ill-educated lay people facilitate discussions for groups of other lay people—which too often amounts to the blind leading the blind. Other churches feature teachers who talk for the entire class time, what Lois LeBar calls, "Teaching that is only poor lay preaching."[19]

None of these strategies affects the head, heart, and hands of students. What the church needs are teachers who understand the mandate to share knowledge, motivate students, and lead them to become radical world-changers for Christ.

There is ample biblical support for the idea that humans are whole persons and should be taught as such. Often called the *SHEMA*, Deuteronomy 6:4-9 says it this way:

> Hear, O Israel: The LORD our God, the LORD is one. Love the LORD your God with all your heart and with all your soul and with all your strength. These commandments that I give you today are to be upon your

hearts. Impress them on your children. Talk about them when you sit at
home and when you walk along the road, when you lie down and when you
get up. Tie them as symbols on your hands and bind them on your fore-
heads. Write them on the doorframes of your houses and on your gates.

This passage calls us to teach so that people (specifically the younger generation) will love God with every bit of who they are. The words *heart, soul,* and *strength*
convey the idea that loving God is not just a mental activity or just an emotional
activity or just a physical activity. Indeed, loving God requires all of us. Our teaching should reflect that same principle.

Elsewhere in Deuteronomy, God makes a related declaration to Israel. "For I
command you today to love the LORD your God, to walk in his ways, and to keep
his commands, decrees, and laws" (30:16). Notice how God addresses his people
as whole beings. He addresses the intellect by telling them to know and understand
his commands (a necessary precursor to keeping them). God addresses the heart by
telling them to love him. And he addresses their lifestyles by commanding them to
walk in his ways and keep his commands.

We see this same holistic understanding reflected in the Psalms as well. Psalm
78:1-8 reads like this:

> O my people, hear my teaching;
>   listen to the words of my mouth.
> I will open my mouth in parables,
>   I will utter hidden things, things from of old—
> what we have heard and known,
>   what our fathers have told us.
> We will not hide them from their children;
>   we will tell the next generation
> the praiseworthy deeds of the LORD,
>   his power, and the wonders he has done.
> He decreed statutes for Jacob
>   and established the law in Israel,
> which he commanded our forefathers
>   to teach their children,

so the next generation would know them,
    even the children yet to be born,
    and they in turn would tell their children.
Then they would put their trust in God
    and would not forget his deeds
    but would keep his commands.
They would not be like their forefathers—
    a stubborn and rebellious generation,
whose hearts were not loyal to God,
    whose spirits were not faithful to him.

> **"TEACHING IS NOT ABOUT PEOPLE FEELING MOVED IN CLASS; IT IS ABOUT PEOPLE MOVING WHEN THEY GET OUT OF CLASS."** —Josh Hunt
> *Disciple-Making Teachers*

God's view of us as holistic creations is reflected in many ways in this passage. The psalmist speaks of what we know (God's statutes and deeds), what we feel (trust, loyalty), and what we do (teach, keep God's commands).

In the New Testament, holistic growth is evidenced, appropriately enough, in the life of Christ. After Jesus' parents thought they had lost him, only to find him in the temple, Gospel writer Luke records: "And Jesus grew in wisdom and stature, and in favor with God and men" (2:52). Here, we see that the Lord, himself, matured holistically. Jesus grew intellectually, physically, socially, and even spiritually. (Consider how that is possible—God in the flesh grew spiritually!) God believed this fact was important enough to inspire Luke to include it in this holy record.

Jesus also makes this connection several times in his own teaching. For example in John 14:15, the Lord says, "If you love me, you will obey what I command." Here Jesus again brings together what we know (what he has commanded us), what we feel (our love for him), and what we do (obey him). This speaks to the holistic nature of what it means to follow Christ.

Other examples are found in Matthew 7:20, Mark 7:20-23, Luke 6:47-49, Luke 8:21, and Luke 11:28. In each case, Jesus emphasizes to the disciples that hearing (intellectual growth) is important, but not enough. The doing of the Word is what makes his teachings complete.

The early church followed this model. Acts 2:42 tells us, "They [the Christians] devoted themselves to the apostles' teaching and to the fellowship, to the breaking of bread and to prayer." Notice the holistic aspects of this passage.

There is intellectual, social, and spiritual growth happening here, in the individual as well as in the church body as a whole.

Paul's writings also reflect this idea. Consider 1 Corinthians 13:11, for example: "When I was a child, I talked like a child, I thought like a child, I reasoned like a child. When I became a man, I put childish ways behind me." Again, we see a holistic growth process.

Another example is found in Ephesians 4:14-15:

> Then we will no longer be infants, tossed back and forth by the waves, and blown here and there by every wind of teaching and by the cunning and craftiness of men in their deceitful scheming. Instead, speaking the truth in love, we will *in all things* grow up into him who is the head, that is, Christ (emphasis added).

Philippians 2:1-2 is another good example:

> If you have any encouragement from being united with Christ, if any comfort from his love, if any fellowship with the Spirit, if any tenderness and compassion, then make my joy complete by being like-minded, having the same love, being one in spirit and purpose.

The apostle addresses intellectual, emotional, spiritual, and social aspects of the Christian life. He never indicates that any one aspect is more important than another; indeed, all are equally important. If any are neglected, a Christian, and the body of Christ, is incomplete.

In the general epistles, James 2:14-17 makes this connection as well. This too often misunderstood passage states:

> What good is it, my brothers, if a man claims to have faith but has no deeds? Can such faith save him? Suppose a brother or sister is without clothes and daily food. If one of you says to him, "Go, I wish you well; keep warm and well fed," but does nothing about his physical needs, what good is it? In the same way, faith by itself, if it is not accompanied by action, is dead.

James' meaning really is not such a mystery. If you have faith, either that of the head (by knowing Christ as Lord) or of the heart (by feeling it), then what you do will automatically reflect that faith. Those with true faith in Jesus as Lord will reflect that in their actions in the same way that an apple tree cannot produce any other fruit but apples. The knowing and the feeling are, by nature, accompanied by the doing.

I can think of many churches that do a great job of encouraging their teens to memorize Scripture, but the attitudes of the kids is horrible or unfriendly. Others spend a lot of resources in providing great worship and prayer time, but their youth turn that "spiritual feeling" off as soon as they walk out the church doors. In either case, the result is a COMPARTMENTALIZED view of faith that sees Christianity as a series of activities that fill certain time periods without permeating every aspect of life.

HOW HOLISTIC TEACHING PREPARES THE WAY FOR LIFELONG SPIRITUAL GROWTH

Life is a whole. We live every minute of every day as a whole person. From work to family to shopping to playing, we use our minds, feelings, relationships, and experiences to take it all in and have the rich and abundant life Christ desires for us. (See John 10:10.)

Think about it like a basketball team. What kind of players would a coach have by lecturing to his team all the time? Imagine the first game of the season. This team would be full of players who have learned the rules and maybe even saw the coach draw plays on the board. Perhaps they even prayed that God would make them good players. But if those players were never motivated to excel or given opportunities at practice to develop skills and run plays, that first game would be a disaster.

Or what if the coach spent every practice sitting around and talking with the players about how they felt about basketball? Maybe they'd discuss great players of the past or classic books on basketball theory. As long as the discussion centered on basketball, the coach could think he was making basketball players.

A third setting might see the coach throw basketballs onto the court and let the players do whatever they want during practice. As long as they're having fun and bringing other potential players with them, everything is fine. They get a lot of scrimmaging done. No one complains about how practice is boring or about having to do those difficult dribbling or rebounding drills.

Yet another strategy might be for the coach to spend all his time giving motivational speeches and showing terrific basketball movies such as *Hoosiers*. If the coach is a good speaker, the players are always fired up, always ready to take on the opponent. There's a lot of motivation here.

Unfortunately, this is how the typical youth teaching setting operates—by emphasizing, even if unintentionally, only one aspect of the person. It's safe to lecture all the time and control the CLASSROOM ENVIRONMENT. It's easy to sit around and talk about God and just let the questions and comments flow. It's popular to just have fun times with games and activities, and throw a brief talk in at the end. But God calls us to much more.

To develop great basketball players, a coach must teach the rules and theories of the game. Players also need a coach who can create practice drills and activities that allow them to hone their skills, and can challenge and motivate them to go beyond where they ever dreamed they could. In the same way, teens need Christian teachers who can touch them on all those levels.

Young people growing up in the church need to learn about God and his relationship with people in history, about his laws and plan for our redemption. (Some would call this a "personal theology.") They also need to learn to experience God's love and to feel God's presence with them. And they need opportunities to share God's love, to serve others, and to be pushed further in their faith than they ever dreamed possible. Our calling as teachers is to "coach" teens to develop in all these areas, so they might truly integrate their faith with all of life.

THE ROLE OF TEACHERS IN THE TEACHING-LEARNING PROCESS

In his wisdom, God has chosen to use people to teach others about him. He could have created other ways for us to learn (or made us OMNIPOTENT; he has that ability), but he chose not to. Since God decided to use us to teach each other, there must be some important information in Scripture that helps us learn who we should be as teachers, what we should teach, and how we should teach it.

The Characteristics of Teachers

They are given the ability to teach others (Exodus 35:34, Matthew 23:34, Ephesians 4:11-12). God has chosen to give some of his people the special gift of teaching. Those who have this gift are to use it, not neglect it. But this does not mean that only those given this special gift can be good teachers. The Great Commission commands all believers to teach, even those who do not have the special spiritual gift.

They are filled with the Holy Spirit (Exodus 35:30, Romans 12:6, I Corinthians 12-14). It is essential that every teacher be filled with the Holy Spirit. This implies, most importantly, that those teaching in Christian settings must be Christians themselves. I have too often seen people put in church teaching positions, not because they were good teachers (or even believers), but because someone thought teaching would be good for them—and might even lead them to make a commitment to Christ. Scripture clearly indicates that only believers are to teach other believers in spiritual matters.

They know God's Word well (Ezra 7:6; Matthew 22:16; Colossians 1:28, 3:15; I Timothy 1:3-7, 2:7; 2 Timothy 1:13; Titus 2:1). This is one of the most often mentioned attributes of teachers in the Bible, but one of the most overlooked in the church. If churches were to expect a high degree of Bible knowledge from their teachers, then I fear most would have far too few teachers to meet their needs.

This creates a spiraling challenge on two fronts. First, if churches expect a high degree of biblical literacy of all their teachers, there may not be enough teachers. The second issue is even more significant. If ill-equipped teachers continue to be the norm, then Bible knowledge and good teaching will continue to decline. This crisis of biblically illiterate teachers raising up new generations of even more biblically illiterate believers will bring demise to the church infinitely faster and more completely than will any outside, secular force.

Their teaching brings life (Proverbs 13:14). Good teachers communicate God's Word in such a way that students want to obey it. They inspire their students to want to have an intimate relationship with Christ. This does not take away from free will nor does it mean that good teaching brings salvation. Much like the parable of the sower in Matthew 13, though, good teachers bring life to students whose attitudes are like good soil. Furthermore, great teachers will motivate others to become like good soil.

They live with integrity (Matthew 22:16, Titus 2:7). God desires teachers who "walk the talk"—who live out what they say they believe and what they teach others to believe and do. The integrity that God expects of us is the opposite of hypocrisy—which, as we will discuss later, Jesus railed against more often than anything else.

They are not impressed with nor intimidated by the status and positions of individuals (Matthew 22:16). If you have ever noticed that an elder's daughter got extra time to earn her way onto the missions trip or that a certain deacon had more say about church activities than anyone else, then you've seen this principle violated. Teachers are not to pay attention to the status of the people or families they teach. The truths of God's Word apply equally to everyone; the Lord expects no one to get special treatment.

They will face opposition because of their teaching (Matthew 23:34, Acts 4:1-3, Titus 2:7-8). If we dedicate ourselves to teaching others to obey God's Word, we will face opposition. Argumentative people, disgruntled students, broken down cars, health problems, and financial issues all can be the direct result of teachers doing what God asks of them. Satan will do all he can to frustrate, torment, discourage, and thwart excellent teachers. This should be expected.

They understand that their teaching comes from God, not from themselves (John 7:16-18). There is no room in the church for arrogant, pompous, self-righteous teachers who act as if their ability and words should be credited to them. Good teaching, and the changed lives that result from that teaching, are to God's credit and God's alone. Remember that God has chosen to use us to teach, but we are the vehicles for his Word. We are the messengers, and should never become the focus. All this comes through the ministry of the Holy Spirit (whose role will be discussed in more detail later).

They are in high demand because they are good teachers (2 Timothy 3:10). Great teachers are like bright beacons of light. People know they are good and want to hear them. Scripture says this is to be expected. Jesus was drawing crowds because they were amazed at his teaching. This is a good thing. Teachers should desire to be like a city on a hill that cannot be hidden (Matthew 5:14).

The Tasks of Teachers

Teach what God's Word says (Exodus 18:20, Leviticus 10:11, Deuteronomy 6:1). This should be obvious, but is too often ignored. The Bible must be at the center of Christian teaching. I have seen many teachers talk about a topic and never use any Scripture to explain, support, or clarify their understanding. Teaching topically is fine, but the Bible must be an integral part of every lesson, not merely a starting point or supplement.

Be an example of how to live (Exodus 18:20, Titus 2:7). I can remember several teachers I've had over the years whose lives I wanted to emulate. I might even be able to remember specific lessons some of them taught. What sticks out in my mind, though, is that these people were not only teaching me about God, but were also showing me how to live out the faith. As a youth pastor, professor, dad, and coach, it has been both a blessing and a curse to know that dozens of young people were watching my actions, listening to my words, and noting my attitudes. Being conscious of that has often helped me have confidence in the choices I have made and helped to convict me when I have sinned. This is how it should be.

Teach others how to obey God (Exodus 18:20, Deuteronomy 6:1, 1 Samuel 12:23, Matthew 28:20, 1 Timothy 4:6). In the same way that having a mastery of the Bible is the most often mentioned attribute of teachers in Scripture, teaching others to obey is the most often mentioned task. Our primary calling as teachers is not to help people memorize verses, understand difficult passages, or even feel like the Bible makes a difference in their lives. No, teachers are called primarily to help believers obey all of God's commands.

Our teaching is for nothing if life-changing action does not follow. Teaching that emphasizes increased Bible knowledge is incomplete. Teaching that focuses on good group discussion is inadequate. Even teaching that includes profound EXEGE-SIS is lacking. Changed lives through obedience to God's Word is what Christian teaching is all about. Period.

Teach the younger generations (Deuteronomy 4:9, Titus 2:1-6). One of the most important roles of a teacher is to disciple younger believers. This is God's prescribed way of passing on the faith through generations. Unfortunately, too many wise and experienced teachers hit retirement age and retire from church teaching as well. Our youth are losing a wealth of experience and knowledge by never sitting at the feet of godly men and women who have been through life's skirmishes. Even a battalion of energetic 23-year-olds can't match the impact that one 70-year-old can have in the life of teens.

Teach all the time, not just in class (Deuteronomy 11:19, Acts 5:42, 1 Timothy 4:11). Really, teaching is not just something we should do; it must be part of who we are. Whenever a "TEACHABLE MOMENT" occurs, we should be ready to take advantage of it. Jesus was an absolute master at this. Consider all the times in the Gospels where Jesus and his followers are going somewhere and he teaches a lesson using a tree, a blind man, a storm, a Pharisee, a leper. Jesus didn't rely on classrooms, handouts, electricity, or tables to teach the disciples. We shouldn't be tied to them, either.

Teach even non-Christians so they will come to know God (Psalms 51:13, Acts 17:19-20). People in the church do not often consider teaching non-Christians about Christ. Preaching at them, probably. Inviting them to church, maybe. Condemning their sinful ways, usually. But intentionally teaching them about the things of God, rarely. I do think youth ministry tends to be an exception to this rule. We do a pretty good job of talking with kids who don't go to church about who God is. We encourage teens to bring their non-Christian friends to Bible studies or Sunday school. This is great. Youth ministries—and the entire church—should create even more ways for this to occur.

Bring out "new treasures as well as old" (Matthew 13:52). When you go shopping and find a great shirt on sale, how often do you wear it compared to your old shirts? How do you feel about it? This kind of excitement is what Jesus was referring to in Matthew 13:52, when he compares a teacher of the Law to a land owner who brings out new treasure from his storehouse. A teacher should bring out of God's truth new insights and fresh concepts that bring excitement. We cannot settle for looking at passages the same way we always have. No matter how many times you teach about David slaying Goliath, there are new insights to glean and share.

Stir people up (Luke 23:5). Does anyone ever get fired up when you teach? Does your teaching inspire students to want to change the world? It should. The Word of God is a radical, world-changing message! Truly teaching it cannot result in teenagers nodding in passive assent. Your students should be stirred to action. When that happens, though, be ready for attacks, criticism, and questions.

Prepare others to do something for the kingdom of God (Ephesians 4:11-12). Teaching should prepare students for works of service for God's kingdom. Simply doing "good things" is not enough; actions should clearly have a biblical purpose. A lot of youth ministries work hard at keeping kids busy. Few of them have a clear reason for it.

Help make believers complete (Colossians 1:28). The Greek word *teleion* used in this verse is translated mature, complete, or perfect in most English Bibles. The idea of the word means "brought to completeness." This assumes a holistic approach toward teaching and implies that teachers have an important task in helping disciples mature in their lives. To be complete does not mean that we never make any mistakes, but that we are maturing in all aspects of our lives. Teachers are to facilitate this.

Confront false teaching (1 Timothy 1:3-7, 2 Timothy 1:13). Paying attention to what others are teaching in the church is another aspect of a teacher's ministry. Those who know the Truth and have been entrusted to share it with teens are also called to recognize false teaching and do something about it.

Look for others who will make great leaders and teachers (2 Timothy 2:2). In every group of students, there are some who stand out. Maybe they ask great questions or share unique insights. Sometimes they intuitively know what Scripture says and how to apply it. These youth should be recognized and equipped as leaders in the church—not just leaders in the youth group, but in the whole church. One reason gifted teenagers are leaving churches is because we stunt their growth. If the church does not provide opportunities for involvement and service, those whom God has gifted will find ways to express themselves outside of Christendom. Identifying these kids early and helping them develop the skills and abilities God has given them will help mature them in the faith.

Other Tidbits From Scripture

Teaching seems to be an expectation of mature believers. The writer of Hebrews expresses his disappointment that Christians in that church have not grown to the point where they are teaching yet. We do not know how long they have been believers, but it is long enough that the author chastises them for their spiritual immaturity. Hebrews 5:11-13 reads like this:

> We have much to say about this, but it is hard to explain because you are slow to learn. In fact, though by this time you ought to be teachers, you need someone to teach you the elementary truths of God's word all over again. You need milk, not solid food! Anyone who lives on milk, being still an infant, is not acquainted with the teaching about righteousness.

Evidently God expects his people to be discipled, to grow in maturity, and then to begin to teach others. In this passage, the writer bemoans that while the Hebrew Christians "ought to be teachers," they still have not learned the "elementary truths of God's word." Could it be that all Christians are expected to grow to the point where they can teach others?

Teachers will be judged more strictly. Teaching brings with it a high degree of responsibility. Anyone who teaches teens about the kingdom of heaven is held to a very high level of expectation. James 3:1 reads, "Not many of you should presume to be teachers, my brothers, because you know that we who teach will be judged more strictly." With so many passages in the Bible explaining the expectations of who a teacher is to be and what a teacher is to teach, there is no room to plead ignorance. Those who have been called to teach have a certain level of excellence to reach. To be satisfied with less is to fall short of the calling. This is quite likely what will lead to a harsher judgment.

Teachers can't hide from maturing disciples. John 7:17 says, "If anyone chooses to do God's will, he will find out whether my teaching comes from God or whether I speak on my own." A false or a poor teacher cannot fool students who are intentionally growing in their faith. (Also see Acts 17:11.) If a teacher is a maturing Christian who is making disciples as she is supposed to, students will know. On the other hand, students also can detect bad teaching, false teaching, and disingenuous teaching.

WARNINGS TO TEACHERS

In Matthew 23, Jesus addresses the Pharisees and other teachers of the Law with several warnings of special relevance to teachers. These statements, often referred to as "The Seven Woes," paint a pretty ominous picture of what the Lord thinks about those who abuse their teaching position or do not take their responsibility seriously enough. Check these out. Jesus warns teachers about many specific issues:

Against being hypocrites (Matthew 23:13,15,25,27,29). This seems to be Jesus' biggest problem with the religious leaders of his day. He hated that they were teaching things they did not do themselves. They taught the letter of the Law, but did not live out—or likely even understand—the spirit of the Law. The harsh verbal exchanges between Jesus and the Pharisees over pharisaical prohibitions against healing on the Sabbath or socializing with the imperfect show Jesus' disdain for how these leaders separated their teachings from their lives.

Against not really believing what they teach (Matthew 23:13). Being a Pharisee was considered a pretty good job in the first century. Better than average pay. Good housing benefits. The automatic respect of most Israelites. Oddly, though, there was no prerequisite that they actually had to believe all that God stuff. They probably had a solid cultural-historical religious belief system, but few likely believed that God's deliverer was going to show up in person and not kick some Roman tail. They seem to have been long on DOGMA and short on real spirituality.

This may seem unfathomable, but I have often seen similar dynamics in today's churches. Teachers who don't really believe what they teach typically become teachers in one of three ways:

One possibility is that Joe and Mary Schmoe have been teaching the seventh-grade Sunday school class since 1906. He has been president of the church board several times, and she has been head of the Missionary Society. They have five children and twenty-six grandchildren who still go to the same church. Never mind that he has had two affairs, that they have personally led the ousting of three pastors (and constantly oppose the current one), or that they only tithe when they are perfectly happy with everything. They take the summer off from attending church (even though they don't go anywhere), write the pastor grammatical critiques of his sermons and prayers, and protect the Family Pew like a mama lioness protects her den. Few people think they are good teachers, but everyone is afraid to say anything.

Or maybe Joe and Mary have been a part of the church for more than ten years. Lately they have had marital problems. In fact, Joe moved out a couple of times. Their friends in the church suggested to the pastor that maybe teaching a class would help them refocus their relationship. Joe and Mary accept the opportunity, seeing it as a way to keep connected. A couple of years later, Joe has left Mary again, filing for divorce this time. Mary wants to continue to teach because it gives her something to do. She has been treated for depression and often cries when she teaches. The high schoolers feel sorry for her and don't want to say anything, fearing that teaching their class is the only reason she keeps attending church at all.

Then there's Joe and Mary as new attenders. The church strategy is to get new folks who come to church into ministry as soon as possible. Church-growth theory states that people are more likely to keep attending if they get involved. Joe grew up in a nominally Catholic home but hasn't attended regularly since eighth grade. Mary grew up with hippie parents who worshiped nature but not God *per se*. This is their first time to hear about Jesus since they were married. After administering the mandatory spiritual gift inventory, the Assimilation Committee decides Joe and Mary would be great middle-school youth sponsors. This ministry would be good for their seeker mentality, they reason.

Scripture says those who teach God's Word should believe it. *No* exceptions for longevity, faltering marriages, seeker ministries, or any other seemingly legitimate reason. When we compromise these standards, the whole church suffers.

Against keeping people from entering God's kingdom (Matthew 23:13). It seems as if the Pharisees were intimidated by people who appeared more spiritual than they were. From what Jesus says about them, we can assume they mocked and ridiculed those whose lives actually reflected God's teachings. Perhaps they even discouraged people from taking the religion thing too seriously.

I see it in today's churches as well. Teens are mocked by other churchgoing youth for carrying their Bibles in school, beginning a prayer meeting before school, or for skipping band camp to spend two weeks at an orphanage in Guatemala. Their teachers and youth leaders at church question their motives and ask if they maybe they aren't taking things too seriously. Kids like that make the faith of many other church members look weak by comparison. We wouldn't want that. By the time these spiritual go-getters reach age 16, they doubt themselves and wind up looking like everyone else.

Against leading followers astray (Matthew 23:15). I once had a college student who told me unbelievable things about his home church's youth group. His youth leader taught him to smoke pot, bought beer for youth outings, and set up couples who needed to lose their virginity at church camp. I might not have believed him if I hadn't met two other teens from that same church who corroborated everything he said. I have also seen youth workers teach their kids to worship angels, pray for the souls of dead relatives, and meditate to find their true inner selves.

Adolescents are highly impressionable and curious about spiritual matters. We must not allow unbiblical teaching to influence them inside the church. We don't know much about how the religious leaders of the first century were leading people astray, but they clearly were. And Jesus was ticked about it.

Against emphasizing the wrong beliefs (Matthew 23:16-24). My eyes were really opened one Sunday when my seven-year-old left Bible school crying because she hadn't been baptized and was going to hell. Her teacher had told the class that Jesus said everyone needed to be baptized to be saved. A discussion with the teacher confirmed what my daughter said. "Does a second grader have the capacity to understand sin, repentance, and forgiveness?" I asked. "Doesn't matter," was the reply, "Jesus said it, so I have to teach it."

This is a pharisaical attitude that Jesus "woed" against. Knowing what to teach to whom and when to teach it is part of the responsibility of a teacher. Sometimes I hear Christian leaders say things like, "In the essentials, unity; in everything else, liberty."[20] Of course the trick is agreeing on what's essential and what's not. Certainly the Pharisees believed they were focusing on the essentials of being Jewish at that time. Jesus tried to set them straight, but they would not hear it. Woe to the teacher who emphasizes what the Bible does not.

Against emphasizing outward appearances and neglecting the inside (Matthew 23:25-28). In the 1984 movie *Footloose*, John Lithgow plays a legalistic town preacher, the keeper of all that is righteous, who has a sudden change of heart about his religious standards. After a discussion with his rebellious daughter, Ariel, and a confrontation with a band of impromptu book burners at the local school library, the pastor realizes, "The devil's not in these books. He's in your hearts."

Up to this time, he had opposed classic literature, most types of modern music, and all forms of dancing. It takes his daughter's confession that she is not a virgin to show him that all the rules and prohibitions he had created failed to keep even his own family, let alone the whole community, from sin.

Jesus railed pretty regularly against religious leaders who concentrated on what people wore and did while neglecting the heart and soul. Unfortunately, we seem to be no better off some 2,000 years later.

Against harshly judging others (Matthew 23:29-32). This woe is uncomfortably tricky to unpack, but I believe it is relatively simple to understand. Jesus' concern here is not that Christians judge other Christians, but that we are way too harsh and self-righteous when we do it. The New Testament is filled with instructions on how to tell an actual apostle from an imposter, a true teacher from a false teacher, and a real believer from an unbeliever. The fruits of the Spirit, Christian love, hospitality, and orthodox beliefs are all litmus tests for that.

The problem comes when we set the bar unreachably high or when we hold others to a different standard than ourselves. In fact, I am afraid that the modern church has become so shy about this that we have stopped judging all together, which has resulted in a pendulum swing in the opposite direction. Christians are called to judge behaviors and attitudes of the world and of each other, but we are to do it by scriptural standards, not our own.

THE ROLE OF THE HOLY SPIRIT IN TEACHING

Fortunately God has provided the Holy Spirit to help us in our teaching. It is not totally up to us to change students. Really that is God's role. Here are a few things that the Spirit does in the teaching-learning process:

The Holy Spirit does the teaching (John 14:26; 1 Corinthians 2:12,14). While God has clearly chosen to use people to teach, it is the role of the Holy Spirit to work in the lives of believers to give that teaching impact. No matter how great my teaching may be, if the Spirit does not bless it, interpret it, and grow it in the minds, hearts, and lives of the students, it will be for nothing.

I grew up in the fertile farmland of northeast Indiana. Every year I would watch my farmer neighbors work the soil by planting, fertilizing, and harvesting. No matter how hard those farmers worked, all their efforts were for naught if it didn't rain enough. In the same way, all my teaching efforts amount to nothing if the Holy Spirit doesn't rain in the lives of those whom I teach.

The Holy Spirit guides and protects the Truth (John 16:13, Ephesians 1:17, 1 Corinthians 1:18-25). One of the most amazing things about the Bible to me is how God has preserved it for thousands of years. Protecting the Truth is the role of the Holy Spirit. Throughout the centuries, as preachers preached and teachers taught, the Spirit was there to make sure the Truth was communicated clearly and accurately.

This should be a huge comfort to those of us who teach youth. There have been times in my teaching when I was absolutely sure that nobody was hearing what I was saying and that I was just wasting good breath, only to have a teen ask a deeply profound question or make an amazingly insightful comment after class. I am so glad we're not in this alone.

The Holy Spirit gifts teachers (Romans 12:3-8, 1 Corinthians 12:27-31, Ephesians 4:7-13, 1 Peter 4:10-11). As mentioned earlier, God not only takes teaching very seriously, but has seen fit to bestow certain believers with unique gifts that allow them to teach with special insight, clarity, and impact.

My college students often ask me if we should allow people who do not have this special gift to teach. I believe we should, unless their teaching is detrimental in some way. Occasionally we actually fight against the Spirit's efforts to gift us. Sometimes we don't recognize the gift or are afraid of it for some reason. Often it takes patience, time, and experience for some folks to realize they are gifted as teachers. Other times a teacher's gift may be in some other area, but students learn from that teacher's life and attitude. This seems perfectly legitimate. To say otherwise would also mean that only those who are gifted as evangelists should ever bring someone to Christ, or that only someone gifted with mercy should ever show mercy.

The Holy Spirit works in the life of the disciple (John 3:3,5-6; 16:7-8; Romans 8:1-13; 1 Corinthians 6:19; 2 Corinthians 3:18; Galatians 5:19-21; Ephesians 5:8; 2 Timothy 1:16; Titus 3:5; 1 Peter 4:12). As we teach teenagers, we should be comforted to know that the Holy Spirit is delivering the message and changing the students. The Spirit's work of convicting, changing, comforting, filling, growing, ministering, and so on, is the impetus youth need to mature in Christ. Without the Spirit's work in the student, we might as well be teaching in a foreign language.

While there are clearly specific roles the Holy Spirit does play in the teaching-learning process, there are also common misconceptions about the work of the Spirit. Here are a few roles the Spirit does not fill.[21]

The Holy Spirit is not a Lone Ranger. As stated earlier, God has chosen to work through people to do his teaching (Matthew 28:19-20; Acts 5:42,18:11; Romans 12:6-7; Ephesians 4:11; 2 Timothy 2:2). I often hear college students lament that they are still in school when they ought to be out in the real world doing ministry. "After all," they reason, "God can teach me anywhere I am. I don't need college."

While God can work in that way, he typically doesn't. God uses the Holy Spirit to work through wiser, more experienced and mature believers to teach us. He doesn't work alone, and that is his choice. Believers need teachers to help them grow and mature.

The Holy Spirit is not a Puppet Master. The Spirit does not mystically take over the mouth and body of the teacher and use her like a public address system. However, it is this false view of the Spirit's role in teaching that often is used as an excuse for poor preparation. "It doesn't matter if I study or prepare. The Holy Spirit does the teaching anyway," is the erroneous attitude here.

The fact is that God expects teachers to work hard in preparation to teach. It is part of our duty to study. Teachers are also to be personally involved in students' lives (Acts 20:27-37; 1 Timothy 4:12-16, 5:1-3,17-18). Setting an example, being an encourager, showing genuine concern, and investing personally are all a part of being a teacher.

The Holy Spirit does not exist to save the butts of lazy youth workers.

The Holy Spirit is not merely the Active Ingredient. Some people see the Spirit as acting only after the human teaching is done. This is kind of like when a baker mixes the bread dough, but has to wait for the yeast to make it rise. There is no automatic time delay with the Spirit. God works directly through the teacher's words even as they are spoken. Many are uncomfortable with the idea that human teachers can be an active ingredient as well, but, again, that's how God created it to be (Philippians 2:12-13).

The proper view is that, while the teacher teaches and the learners learn, the Spirit is working in everybody at the same time. The Spirit uses the teacher to influence the students while working in the minds and hearts of the students.

The Holy Spirit is not a Disinterested Spectator. The success of teaching is never up to the teacher alone. Diligent studying, great methods, a clever delivery, and brilliant insights will not be enough. The inevitable outcome of this mistaken image of the Spirit's role will reveal a person's fallibility and incompleteness without the Spirit (1 Corinthians 2:14, 3:1-3).

God cares deeply that we teach well and has assigned the Holy Spirit to be personally involved every step of the way.

As you can tell, holistic teaching is a very important concept in Scripture. From the life and duties of the teacher to the maturing student to the work of the

Spirit, the Christian teaching-learning process touches every part of the believer's life. Because teens are rapidly developing in so many ways, our job as teachers is even more difficult—and more important.

The quotes and examples from the beginning of this chapter tell a tale of failure on many fronts in church ministry to youth. This book will help you better understand both scriptural mandates and good practice when it comes to teaching teens. The chapters that follow will discuss issues that, when understood, put into practice and melded together, will help you make a more profound impact on the lives of more youth through your teaching.

For Discussion

Think of the youth with whom you were in middle school and high school. How many of them are still active in church? Why do you think they are or aren't?

Who were some of the best teachers you have had in various settings (e.g., church, school, teams, clubs, etc.)? What was it that made them so good? What can you remember about their dependence on the Holy Spirit in their teaching? How, specifically, did they have an impact on your life?

Explain holistic teaching in your own words. How would your ministry be different if you approached it this way?

Holistic teaching is compared to coaching a basketball team in this chapter. What other appropriate metaphors can you think of?

Which of the teacher tasks discussed earlier did your home church do well? Which ones were weak or absent? How can a youth worker help a ministry improve in these areas?

Do most Christian teachers you know take the seven woes from Matthew 23 seriously? How can you help them understand the emphasis Jesus put on teaching?

ACTIVITIES

Do a survey of churches in your area to find out how many students who grew up there in the past 10 or 15 years are still actively involved there.

Watch some of Highway Video's candid interviews. Recreate some of them in your city. How do your own results compare with those on the video?

Do an exhaustive Bible study to find all the places that some or all of the words *mind, heart, soul, spirit, know, obey, do*, and so on, appear in the same passage. What conclusions do you draw?

Make a list of the characteristics of a teacher as discussed in this chapter. Rate yourself on a scale of 1-10 for each. What do you need to do to improve in your weaker areas?

ENDNOTES, CHAPTER 1

1. Altemeyer, B., & Hunsberger B. (1997). *Amazing Conversations.* Amherst, NY: Prometheus Books, p. 48.
2. *RollingStone* (2002, May 23). Issue 896, p. 69.
3. *RollingStone* (2003, November 27). Issue 936, p. 66.
4. *RollingStone* (2002, June 6). Issue 897, p. 41.
5. *RollingStone* (2003, June 26). Issue 925, p. 41.
6. *Blender* (2000, June/July). p. 50.
7. *RollingStone* (2000, January 20). Issue 832, p. 35.
8. *RollingStone* (2002, January 31). Issue 888, p. 40.
9. *RollingStone* (2002, February 28). Issue 890, p. 40.
10. *USA Today* (2001, November 27).
11. As quoted in youthculture@today, Fall 2001, the newsletter of the Center for Parent and Youth Understanding.
12. As quoted in youthculture@2000, Spring 2000, the newsletter of the Center for Parent and Youth Understanding.
13. *RollingStone* (2003, January 23). Issue 914, p. 38.
14. *New York Times* (2001, November 26). New York, p. A1.
15. Barna Research Group, April 23, 2002, news release.
16. Johnston, L. D., Bachman, J. G., O'Malley, P. M., & Schulenberg, J. (1996). *Monitoring the Future: A Continuing Study of American Youth (8th- 10th- and 12th- Grade Surveys)*, [Computer file].
17. Marler, P. L., & Hadaway, C. K. (1999, Summer). Testing the attendance gap in a conservative church. *Sociology of Religion*, Washington, pp. 175-186.
18. *American Demographics.* Ithaca; March 2000, pp. 14-16.
19. LeBar, L. E. (1995). *Education that is Christian.* Colorado Springs: Chariot Victor, p. 26.
20. I have seen this quote attributed to the leader or founder of almost every major denomination. I have a feeling we might find out who wrote Hebrews before we know who said this originally.
21. Adapted from Graendorf, W. C. (1981). *Introduction to Biblical Christian Education.* Chicago: Moody Press, pp. 111-112.

CHAPTER 2

WHO ARE ADOLESCENTS, ANYWAY?

(A Very Brief Survey of Adolescent Development)

"Our youth love luxury. They have bad manners and contempt for their elders and love idle chatter in place of exercise...They contradict their parents, chatter before company, gobble up their food, and tyrannize their teachers."
—SOCRATES, C. 450 B.C.

*　　*　　*　　*　　*

MY ENIGMATIC TEENAGER

She hates me and she loves me with all sincerity.
She wants to hang out with friends as often as can be.
She wants to know I love her, but not in public places.
She needs me to understand all of her many faces.

She asks for money to spend each day, but doesn't want to work.
She keeps her bedroom cluttered, which drives her mom berserk.
She's addicted to the telephone, computer, and TV.
She thinks that curfews and bedtimes are things that shouldn't be.

She believes procrastination is a gift from God.
She eats more than a Sumo champ, but doesn't think that's odd.

She has a personality I barely recognize at all.
She's made my darling little girl appear to go AWOL.

She wants my praise and my advice, but doesn't want to ask.
She thinks becoming an adult is quite a grueling task.
She's an independent thinker, which was my goal from birth.
She's my enigmatic teenager, a gem of boundless worth.

Twenty years of ministry have allowed me to get to know thousands of adolescents. My studies have taken me through centuries of research and observation. My travels have taken me to a wide variety of countries and cultures. And I have reached the conclusion that, at their cores, teenagers are basically the same regardless of era, culture, or ethnicity. Without a doubt differences exist, and some are more subtle than others. But the fact remains that Socrates' lament written almost 2,500 years ago could have been uttered by parents, educators, and community leaders throughout the world in every time period since.

Somehow we black out the memories of our own adolescent experiences as we age. We forget that we, too, loved luxury, had bad manners, disrespected those in authority, preferred socializing over work, talked back to our parents, spoke without being spoken to, scarfed down our meals, and caused trouble in school.

In the study of ADOLESCENCE, it is important to keep in mind that today's American teenagers are both very much the same as, and very much different from, Socrates' Greek youth of centuries ago. This chapter will help you better understand some of the key factors in adolescent development and how they should shape the way we teach students.

A BRIEF HISTORY OF ADOLESCENCE

While Socrates' rant about youth might parallel our own in many ways, do not assume he was addressing adolescence in the same way we know it today. Adolescence is a relatively new phenomenon and, many would say, an artificial construct of modern Western civilization.

Throughout history, and in a great many cultures that exist today, society recognized that children became adults at about age 12 or 13. Various RITES OF PASSAGE existed to mark this transition. When a boy came of age, he learned a trade, started his own family, and became an independent contributor to society. When a girl experienced MENARCHE, she got married and began having children. People went from childhood to adulthood with no intermediate step.

This began to change with the advent of the Industrial Revolution in Europe and America. Factories became a new source of income, and cities grew as large numbers of families, previously dependent on the agrarian economy, moved to where the jobs were. Children and teenagers found jobs outside the family farm for the first time.

The most significant shift occurred, though, after the end of World War II. During the war, the need for military supplies, coupled with the need to keep the regular economy going, created jobs for any man, woman, and child who was not enlisted in the service. When the war ended, millions of servicemen and women were discharged and needed jobs. The solution to that dilemma ultimately created what we know today as adolescence.

The government enforced compulsory education for everyone through age 16. This opened up millions of jobs previously held by youth. With high school graduation occurring for most students at age 18, and marriage being delayed until at least then in most cases, a gap was created between the end of childhood and the beginning of adulthood. When the federal government helped make college education more affordable, marriage was delayed four more years for a large percentage of the population.

> **BUILDING ASSETS**
>
> Any doubt that a holistic youth ministry can help parents in raising healthy teens might be erased by reading *What Teens Need to Succeed* (Benson, P.L., Galbraith, J., and Espeland, P. [1998], Minneapolis: Free Spirit Publishing). Based on a national survey of over 270,000 young people in over 600 localities in the United States, this book details 40 essential "assets" for developing well-adjusted kids. A great youth ministry can enhance most of them.

The result has been a dramatic increase in the average age at which people get married. The 2000 United States census revealed that the age of first marriage was 25.1 years for women and 26.8 years for men.[22] This has created a roughly ten-to-twelve-year gap between PUBERTY and marriage.

By delaying young people's entry into the full-time job market and making a college degree the typical experience for many Americans, society has created a developmental stage that is not biologically necessary. With the responsibilities of beginning families, establishing a career, and contributing to the community artificially delayed, some negative consequences are inevitable.

In addition to creating more free time and frustrated hormones, this change has confused family and social roles. Think about how many young people you know who have graduated from college but still do not know what to do with their lives. Many have moved back in with their parents. This extended period of transition from childhood to adulthood is not a naturally occurring developmental stage. It is a cultural and sociological creation of contemporary western society.[23] It is also a reality that we need to learn about.

So how do adolescents develop? For the purposes of this discussion, we will briefly discuss several different aspects of human growth as they relate to youth, beginning with physical development.

PHYSICAL DEVELOPMENT

At a certain point in time for each human being, the body begins producing increased amounts of certain hormones that prompt a series of changes. The timing of these changes is determined by a complex interaction of genetic codes and cultural factors.[24] Adolescence triggers the various systems in the body to change in many ways.

The most obvious changes an adolescent experiences are physical. Dramatic height changes typically occur during early adolescence in what most people refer to as the ADOLESCENT GROWTH SPURT. Sometimes it seems as if a kid leaves seventh grade at 4'9" and begins eighth grade at 5'6". My oldest daughter grew nearly 9 inches over 18 months during junior high.

Usually girls mature physically much more rapidly than boys. Who can forget those self-conscious years when most of the girls were taller than most of the boys? This is because females usually begin their physical changes 18 to 24 months earlier than males. This is true not only of changes in height, but also of the onset of puberty.

WHEN DOES ADOLESCENCE BEGIN AND END?

Technically, adolescence can begin or end at an amazingly wide variety of ages for many reasons. Practically, though, this chapter deals with ages 10 to 19, which is when most youth workers are highly involved with ministry to adolescents.

EARLY ADOLESCENCE roughly corresponds to the middle school years, MIDDLE ADOLESCENCE is typically the high school years, and LATE ADOLESCENCE is recognized as the college years up to about age 22.

Most of this book deals with the early and middle stages. That is not because ministry with college-aged students is unimportant. Far from it. In fact, ministry with 18-to 24-year-olds may be the most important and overlooked aspect of ministry in the American church today.

Puberty marks the biological transition period, which often lasts five to seven years, during which young people become able to reproduce. Shoulders broaden, hair begins to grow darker and more rapidly under the arms and in the pubic area. Girls develop breasts and broader hips, while guys show signs of facial hair and a more muscular build. Romantic and sexual urges also emerge at this time—and teaching about this aspect of development should not be discouraged or avoided.

One difficult aspect of puberty for youth workers to deal with—and one that is rarely discussed—is menstruation. Since most youth ministers are male, and many youth ministries are more than half female, the onset of a girl's period can create an awkward or uncomfortable moment for both youth and their leaders. This is just one of the many reasons why female leaders should be involved in any activity when female youth are present. I can't count the number of times a female leader has whispered in my ear, "We need to stop at the next drugstore," while on a trip. Maturity and sensitivity are called for at such times.

Some pain and awkwardness may accompany various aspects of growth. As bones and muscles grow rapidly, many youth have a difficult time performing tasks and athletic feats that previously came easily. When their shoes are a size 12 but their muscles are still childlike, some embarrassing moments are inevitable. This ASYN-CHRONICITY IN GROWTH is typical—and is not limited to physical changes.

Obviously, individual guys and girls mature at different rates. You should keep in mind that early maturing girls and late maturing boys are especially self-conscious, and may be more vulnerable than other youth. Those of us who desire to share Christ's love with teens need to be especially sensitive to the fact that these

> **A WORD ABOUT EATING DISORDERS**
>
> I strongly recommend that you learn all you can about ANOREXIA NERVOSA and BULIMIA. These are eating disorders in which teenagers either starve themselves or overeat and then force themselves to throw up (known as bingeing and purging). These disorders usually have psychological causes related to body image and are much more prevalent in girls than guys. Finding Christians in the community who have recovered from eating disorders and are willing to be resources for you is an excellent idea. These people can be invaluable in helping a young person who is struggling with an eating disorder, and can be a great source of information. Some resources to consider: *Diary Of An Anorexic Girl*, by Morgan Menzie; *Dying to Be Thin: Understanding and Defeating Anorexia Nervosa and Bulimia: A Practical, Lifesaving Guide*, by Ira Sacker & Marc A. Zimmer; *Starving: A Personal Journey through Anorexia*, by Christie Pettit.

young people value what we say. A thoughtless comment said in jest often hurts more deeply than we know.

INTELLECTUAL DEVELOPMENT

Adolescence marks the beginning of the intellectual transition from childlike, CONCRETE, black-and-white thinking to more ABSTRACT, possibility thinking. Conceptualizing ideas, relationships, solutions, and so on, are all evidence of a marked shift in mental ability.

During their teens, youth develop the ability to think about their own thinking and explain why and how they perceive what they do. This is called METACOGNITION. These abilities also allow young people to become introspective. As they consider themselves, their existence, and their relationships with others and the world around them, a few interesting dynamics take place.

One, called IMAGINARY AUDIENCE, typically occurs as youth begin to wonder how much attention others are paying to them. This egocentrism can result in a heightened sense of paranoia about what they are saying, doing, and wearing. This is what a kid is experiencing when she wonders who else noticed the new zit on her forehead, the tiny spot of ketchup on her jeans, or the fact that she got a C on her last math test.

A related experience is known as PERSONAL FABLE. Simply stated, this is an adolescent's belief that his or her experiences are unique. This is what a young man is expressing when he tells a teacher or parent, "You have no idea what I'm going through." While the personal fable can result in a false sense of reality in many ways, some psychologists believe it also can help teens develop a healthy sense of SELF-ESTEEM and self-importance.

Yet another aspect of increasing intellectual capacities is the ability to think in multiple dimensions. This allows people to consider someone else's point of view

TEENS AND FAMILIES

Entire books have been written about adolescents and their families, so any discussion of them here will be inadequate. But here are a few facts that social researchers find over and over again in their studies:

- Family, not peers, is still the most important influence in the lives of teens, and remains so through the college years.
- Even as youth seem to be pushing parents away, they desperately want their approval and advice.
- A father, when present, is the most influential person in a teenager's life.
- The natural quest for independence and autonomy is the source of conflict between most youth and their parents, not a conspiracy of rebellion.

or to consider multiple factors in a problem. For example, if you ask an eight-year-old why Judas betrayed Jesus, she might say it was because he was a bad person or because Satan made him. Ask that same question to a 16-year-old, and she would be more likely to mention the political and social expectations of Messiah in the first century, as well as the more obvious possibilities.

This change often means that teenagers begin to question everything they previously accepted as truth—which frustrates many Christian adults. This RELATIVISM is sometimes seen as an incursion of secular thinking by a liberal media or educational system. In reality, it is just a reflection of the natural intellectual growth process. As we've noted earlier, the church often does a very poor job of addressing the intellectual concerns of maturing youth.

The obvious challenge for those of us who teach teenagers is to be aware of these changes, and take advantage of the opportunities they present as we disciple young people into a deeper intellectual relationship with Christ.

EMOTIONAL DEVELOPMENT

Although teenagers often seem to be an emotional mess, research does not really support the idea of STORM AND STRESS adolescence. While it is true that young people experience a lot of internal changes that require some type of emotional response, most kids handle it remarkably well. One of the realities of the teen years is that each kid is coming to grips with being a unique person. This process, called either DETACHMENT or INDIVIDUATION (depending on if you see it in a negative or positive light), defines how youth experience their own realities apart from those of family and friends. It is the progression of becoming less dependent on others— for everything from fixing meals to fixing mistakes.

Healthy individuation occurs when close parental relationships exist and maturing is encouraged.[25] If parenting is too distant, then individuation happens prematurely. If parenting is too smothering or protective, then individuation is discouraged and delayed. An observant youth worker can spend a little time with the family of a high school senior and discover how well the parents have encouraged this process.

Emotional maturity also shows up in the degree of SELF-RELIANCE in teens. This simply means that they see themselves as being able to make more decisions on their own, or at least without their parents' help. As their decision-making becomes more self-reliant, youth gain more confidence, report higher self-esteem, and have fewer behavioral problems.[26]

SOCIAL DEVELOPMENT

Social development is concerned with the question of who adolescents are in relationship to the world around them. Maturing from childhood to adulthood includes many times of transition in various societies. From participating in "big church" to taking communion, from getting a driver's license to voting in elections, there are a wide variety of ways teenagers begin to see themselves as adults.

The onset of puberty itself is often the beginning of social redefinition for teens in America. While menarche is one clear sign for females, males have less obvious milestones. Getting taller, developing a deeper voice, and becoming physically stronger are all changes that earn males new roles in society. While most cultures worldwide have some formal or ceremonial rites of passage, most Western cultures do not.

Getting a job, going to high school, driving a car, attending college or joining the military, and spending more time with friends away from home are all ways that American youth experience maturity and independence. While not exactly rites of passage, these are somewhat tangible signs of AUTONOMY and maturity.

Society has both embraced and embattled adolescents in many ways. Recognizing that teens can hold jobs and contribute economically to their communities, civic leaders work at building some level of mutual acceptance and trust. At the same time, though, curfews and anti-loitering laws aimed at controlling the social lives of teens often communicate a message of mistrust and fear.

Even as they are interpreting what adults think of them, inwardly, teens are beginning to consider what their roles in society should be. Thoughts of jobs, family, and status, occur more frequently as they get older. Decisions about how hard to work in school, what college to attend, and the social circle to identify with all have immediate and future impact.

Another fascinating aspect of social development has to do with the impact of peers. Early in my ministry I spent a lot of time trying to eliminate CLIQUES from the youth group. My assumption was that they were unnecessary and unhealthy. I have since learned, however, that it is only when cliques become exclusive that they are problematic.[27] Kids, and in fact all humans, tend to gather with others who are most like them. Social standing, race, special interests, and intellectual ability are but a few of the ways groups identify themselves, even if unconsciously.

That is not a problem to overcome, but a reality to capitalize on in ministry. You should definitely teach teens that having friends from a variety of social groups is good, but you should also help them learn how to evangelize and disciple friends in their closest peer groups. They will be much more effective in bringing their friends to Christ than you will be.[28]

Brain Development

One of the most rapidly growing aspects of research in adolescent development is in the area of brain development. It seems that the teenage brain has several unique traits that may help explain why youth behave the way they do.[29] The forgetfulness, extreme mood swings, lack of planning, and feelings of invincibility often associated with youth appear to be explainable, at least in part, by how the brain changes during adolescence.

There are two major brain growth spurts in the typical life cycle. The first one occurs between birth and age two. The second one occurs at the onset of puberty. It shouldn't be a surprise that teens and toddlers share so much in common! The "terrible twos" may parallel the limit-pushing of early adolescence. The PREFRONTAL CORTEX experiences tremendous growth during this time. This part of the brain (often referred to as the brain's CEO) is involved with decision-making, controlling moods, and evaluating situations.

One possible implication of this is what researchers call the "use it or lose it" principle. That is, whatever aspects of the brain are used during puberty become hard-wired for life. Parts of the brain that are not actively used may become ineffective due to lack of use. For example, a boy who is involved in band during middle school and high school is likely to develop a lifelong aptitude for music. If that same boy is never exposed to auto mechanics, though, he may never be able to understand how his car works. This could be because the part of his brain designed for mechanical understanding was underutilized during puberty.

COGNITIVE FLEXIBILITY, the function of the brain that develops strategies and organizes information, is also underdeveloped among adolescents. This often leads to teen participation in high-risk activities, because they feel invulnerable to injury. The immature prefrontal cortex of teenagers is also extra sensitive to chemical influences. Substance abuse can be especially cruel to kids, because drugs seem to stunt the growth of this area of the brain.

Another aspect of adolescent brain research has involved comparing brain activity in reading emotions. Studies done using magnetic imaging have shown that teenagers use a more emotional, gut-level part of the brain to interpret emotions expressed on human faces, while adults use a more analytic portion of the brain. This may indicate that a young person's inability to discern when someone is angry doesn't stem just from inexperience in human interaction, but that there is a very real difference in brain function that influences a young person's interpretation of others' moods.[30]

Another area of extreme change during adolescence is the CEREBELLUM, which is located toward the back of the brain and was previously thought to mainly control motor skills. Even into a person's early twenties this part of the brain experiences significant growth and change. The cerebellum works much like a central processing unit for information. When it is less mature, it only receives information and does little organizing or analyzing of it. As a person goes through adolescence, the cerebellum becomes more effective in making sense of information, and even cross references it with other knowledge that has been previously received. Researchers believe that the functioning of the cerebellum may not be essential to any specific task, but that all tasks are enhanced by it.

One of the main influences on brain development is sleep. The typical teen should be getting 9 or 10 hours of sleep each night. Most get only seven and a half hours or less. This may not be a big deal for short periods of time, but when such sleep deprivation occurs over weeks, months, or even years, a negative impact on brain development—and all the aspects of physiological growth that go with it—is inevitable. The brain also has a feature known as the CIRCADIAN CLOCK that helps to regulate the body's function in relationship to its sleep. When youth are used to staying up late and getting up late, this clock adjusts the body's functions to match that sleep pattern.

Sleep has a significant impact on learning. A specific aspect of sleep known as RAPID EYE MOVEMENT (REM) is especially helpful to the brain in retaining information. When the brain gets sufficient REM sleep, learning is much higher. The less REM sleep, the less information the brain retains. Research is showing that the number one predictor of college achievement is not COGNITIVE ability, socioeconomic status, high school GPA, or SAT/ACT scores, but the amount of REM sleep a student gets.[31]   In recognition of this, some researchers and educators are suggesting that high schools and colleges delay their start times until as late as noon and offer more evening classes to compensate for late-sleeping teens.

This brain research is significant, because it helps explain what parents and others who work with youth have known for centuries. Teens are different than adults. Puberty affects more than just physical growth. Moods swings, ambivalence, paradoxical behavior, lack of thinking about the future, and so on, all may have legitimate physiological explanations, thanks to what researchers have learned about the way the brain functions and develops.

IDENTITY DEVELOPMENT

How a person perceives himself or herself is referred to as SELF-IDENTITY. Identity is shaped throughout the life cycle to a certain extent, but identity development is particularly important during adolescence. The depth and complexity of how a young person sees himself grow during this time. For example, a child might respond to the question, "Are you usually a happy person?" with a yes or a no. A maturing teenager would be more likely to respond by explaining that she is sometimes happy and sometimes sad, depending on what is happening in her life.

Even though teens are increasingly aware of who they are and how they are growing, that often does not translate into consistent patterns of behavior. Those who spend a lot of time with youth can easily observe this phenomenon, known as FALSE-SELF BEHAVIOR. Kids just tend to behave more true to who they really see themselves to be when they are around their closest friends, and more likely to be "fake" or "wear a mask" around parents, other peers, or dates.[32]

One of the aspects of youth identity development most often discussed among youth ministers is self-esteem. While identity is how a teen *sees* himself or herself, esteem is how young people *feel* about themselves. During the 1970s and 1980s, discussion and research about adolescent self-esteem peaked as society became concerned about growing trends in youth violence, teen pregnancy, and adolescent suicide. The church reacted by incorporating teaching about self-esteem into Sunday school and youth group. In the 1990s many churches shifted their attention away from focusing on the importance of improving self-esteem and began teaching about what became known as "GOD-ESTEEM"— how God feels about each young person.

Although self-esteem continues to be a primary problem for youth in specific demographic groups (e.g., low socioeconomic status) or with specific personal issues (e.g., abusive parents), the most recent research shows that self-esteem is not really the problem for most teens that society once thought it was.[33] That is not to say that self-esteem should be ignored, but being purposeful about encouraging kids in the things they do well and helping them succeed in school seem to be the most important contribution youth workers can make.

Other aspects of identity development involve both intellectual and social factors. For more than 40 years, Erik Erikson's psychosocial theory of personal growth has dominated developmental thought. He defines a series of crises that people must navigate in each phase of life.[34] For adolescents, the crisis is IDENTITY VS. IDENTITY DIFFUSION. The task is for a young person to come to understand that she is a unique individual with a specific personality and set of thoughts and ideals. The more successful she is at seeing her thoughts and decisions as her own, and not dependent on others, the more appropriately balanced she becomes—and is then ready to tackle the crisis of the next phase of life.

Regardless of how much you buy into Erikson's theory, it is clear that identity development in adolescence is a vital and complicated task. The energy required to resolve the identity crisis often results in a series of other issues. For example, PSYCHOSOCIAL MORATORIUM results when a teen puts his development on hold. Many of the world's educational systems seem perfectly designed for this. The years spent in junior high, high school, and college offer an ideal hiding place for those who are not ready to grow up into adulthood.

Another issue, called IDENTITY CONFUSION, occurs among youth who are unsure of who they are. This can be mild or severe depending on a variety of factors. IDENTITY FORECLOSURE, another potential problem, results when young people decide prematurely on who they are and what they will do as adults. Rather than exploring opportunities, they skip the typical identity crisis of adolescence.

Sometimes youth will purposefully settle on an identity that is at odds with who they are naturally or what societal norms allow. This is called NEGATIVE IDENTITY and often occurs when a teen feels she is unable to realistically establish an acceptable identity. If her parents or others she admires continually fail to acknowledge who she is becoming, she may decide she would rather be somebody with the wrong crowd than nobody at all.

Few teens go through all of these phases before reaching IDENTITY ACHIEVE-MENT. There is no typical flow to these stages. Some teens will navigate adolescence without ever dealing with moratorium, foreclosure, or confusion. Others will have mild bouts with all of them. There is no right or perfect way to experience adolescence, and that is especially true in identity development.

VOCATIONAL DEVELOPMENT

As teens get older, work becomes more and more a part of their lives. Around 80 percent of students have held a job outside of the home before they graduate from high school.[35] Most of these adolescents begin such work at the age of 15 or 16, when they have a driver's license and become more mobile. The summer employment market is especially suited to teenagers. Over 80 percent of high school students plan to get jobs each summer.[36] From fast food to babysitting, construction to retail, nearly any job has a variety of benefits for youth. Or does it?

Some studies have shown that a student's reason for working has a large impact on what he or she gains from the experience. For example, if the job is more to earn extra spending money than to help the family, then teens tend to take it less seriously and act less responsibly.[37] Other research has found that the reason for working, the type of work environment, and the number of hours worked can have a negative impact on an adolescent's attitudes toward work and others—and even their attitude about life. Even money management issues are more problematic for teens with jobs.

So what do we make of such findings? It seems to go back to parental responsibility. What moms and dads teach their kids about the nature of work, their responsibility as an employee, and money management makes a big difference. As youth workers, we can help by teaching biblical principles of labor and finances.

MORAL DEVELOPMENT

Building on the foundational works of Jean Piaget, other researchers, most notably Lawrence Kohlberg and Carol Gilligan, have developed a very strong body of evidence to explain how adolescents grow in moral reasoning. Three primary stages have been identified:

PRECONVENTIONAL MORAL REASONING is predominant through late childhood or early adolescence and is characterized by linking moral choices to physical events. For example, decisions about right and wrong are typically linked to the types of punishment or consequences that might result.

CONVENTIONAL MORAL REASONING, which usually develops during early adolescence and may predominate throughout a person's life, depends on societal norms for determining moral choices. This is evidenced in teens when they use the "everybody's doing it" argument to justify an attitude or behavior. Cheating on tests, drug use, sexual activity, and attitudes toward authority are often defended using conventional moral reasoning.

The final stage may never be reached by most people, according to research. POSTCONVENTIONAL MORAL REASONING interprets society's laws, rules, and norms as relative depending on human needs. This is not to be confused with the postmodern relativism that shapes much contemporary thought. Postconventional moral reasoning values all of humanity more than the individual, so the apparent subjectivism of this stage is not shaped by personal selfishness but by a greater sense of right, wrong, and fairness.

Research also shows that youth who exhibit evidence of advanced moral thought tend to come from family structures "in which parents encourage their child to participate in family discussions, in which the level of conflict in family discussions is neither extremely low nor extremely high, and in which parents expose the adolescent to moral arguments that are fashioned at a higher stage than his or her own."[38]

One of the most frustrating aspects of working with adolescents is their tendency to express their morality so firmly yet often behave in ways inconsistent with their expressed beliefs. A possible explanation for this is that the factors that shape our individual moral choices are more complex than we are able to articulate or recreate in a discussion.

For example, if you try to teach a lesson on physical standards for dating relationships, it will be fairly easy to get most students to agree with you on what is acceptable and what is not. You might use a series of hypothetical situations and even share some of your own experiences to help students to think practically. But even the most realistic group discussions of such circumstances are artificial, and such hypothetical discussions may seem a long way from what two young people with hormones experience when they are together. That is not to say that trying to teach moral reasoning is hopeless. It does seem, though, that very real, personal sharing or the use of case studies to create a realistic scene is the most effective approach.

SPIRITUAL DEVELOPMENT

One reason many of us get into youth ministry is the fact that teenagers are growing spiritually and want answers to their emerging questions. Youth focus less on rituals and traditions of religion and more on actual matters of faith and IDEOLOGY. As youth develop a growing sense of being unique individuals, they also want a faith that is their own. Often various stages of faith development occur during adolescence.

Philip Rice has identified five major dimensions of adolescent religion.[39] He describes the *ritualistic, experiential, ideological, cognitive,* and *consequential* dimensions as ways to understand how teens understand and interpret spirituality. Within each of these aspects, faith develops differently.

James Fowler has identified seven stages of faith development that have served as the focal point for discussion on this issue. Fowler's stages, as he explains, have to do with how people make meaning out of human existence.[40] He has identified the following stages of faith development:

Stage 0: PRIMAL FAITH (birth to age 2 or 3) during which trust is given to loving caregivers, including parents.

Stage 1: INTUITIVE-PROJECTIVE FAITH (ages 2-8) in which imitation of others and acting out religious behaviors is dominant.

Stage 2: MYTHIC-LITERAL FAITH and the Imperial Self (childhood and beyond) is the stage in which the concept of God takes on human ideas. All things good are associated with God.

Stage 3: SYNTHETIC-CONVENTIONAL FAITH (adolescence and beyond) begins the phase of connecting God with a relationship. Spiritual identity is a key quest at this stage.

Stage 4: INDIVIDUATIVE-REFLECTIVE FAITH (young adulthood and beyond) is the stage in which personal ownership of faith occurs and the direct influence of others is decreased.

Stage 5: CONJUNCTIVE FAITH and the Interindividual Self (mid-life and beyond, if at all) witnesses the ability to see multiple sides of issues simultaneously and objectively. Also, a sense of responsibility for others grows at this stage.

Stage 6: UNIVERSALIZING FAITH occurs when one determines to live her life for the sake of others and to reach for higher, selfless ideals.[41]

While Fowler's work has been widely accepted and supported, it is not without its critics. Some contend that the scientific research method cannot be applied to such a delicate and SUBJECTIVE experience as faith. Others believe it impossible to even attempt to explain faith in stages. I believe Fowler's work is helpful, but not flawless. For example, I think identifying the stages of spiritual growth in general rather than by specific ages may be more helpful. It is even conceivable that someone may be raised in one religion, experience a conversion, and begin at Fowler's Stage 1 all over again.

Regardless of the accuracy of various faith theories, the fact remains that teenagers grow at different spiritual rates. Practically speaking, as early adolescents decide about their own individual commitment to their faith or their church, they are deciding how what they believe is different from or similar to the faith of their parents. For some youth, it may be the social aspect that keeps them coming to church activities. They attend Sunday school and youth group events because that is where their friends are. Teens whose closest friends go to another church often want to attend with them.

During middle adolescence, faith becomes even more individualized. As kids get driver's licenses and jobs, and are involved in more extracurricular activities connected with school, they make conscious decisions about their priorities. If making money or playing basketball meets their needs more than attending a weekly youth group meeting, then they have no qualms about skipping youth group. This does not typically reflect a declining interest in spiritual matters as much as it reflects youth ministries that are more attuned to younger teens rather than older ones.

Ministry to older adolescents, those ages 18 to 24, has proven to be very difficult for today's churches. The questions and doubts these young people have are often threatening to established church members. They want their spirituality to be intense, real, open, and life-changing. What too many churches offer is an opportunity to join the adults in their spiritual civic-club environment, which is typically devoid of spiritual challenge, vibrancy, or real meaning. Rather than embracing the challenge of college-age ministry, most churches are content to let this age group go elsewhere, praying that when they are married and have children, they will return to their spiritual roots and be less of a challenge. This is why I refer to ministry among this age group as the black hole of today's Christian church.

This is precisely why colleges are full of energetic and enthusiastic alternative religions, such as Islam, Mormonism, the NEW AGE MOVEMENT, WICCA, and HEDONISM. These movements have little trouble harvesting former churchgoing proselytes who are eager to find meaningful spirituality.[42]

TEACHING IMPLICATIONS

In all of the aspects of adolescent development, there are differences between younger teens and older teens. Teaching must be informed by the developmental realities of the age group. For this reason, teaching settings with narrower age groups of adolescents are often easier and more effective than teaching settings with a wide variety of ages.

Developmental differences are very real. It is vital for teachers to understand and deal with these differences.

With so many aspects of adolescent development to consider, it is easy to get lost in the details. Connecting the developmental dots in ways that enhance holistic teaching takes some intentional thought. The tables on the next two pages should help you think further about how this information should shape your teaching. Table 2.1 illustrates some of the key variations in development between older and younger teens. Table 2.2 will help you consider some of the teaching implications suggested by the adolescent developmental stages discussed in this chapter.

TABLE 2.1

18-24

SOME CHARACTERISTICS OF OLDER ADOLESCENTS	SOME CHARACTERISTICS OF YOUNGER ADOLESCENTS
Physically	**Physically**
• They look like adults.	• Their bodies are changing rapidly.
• They are capable of adult physical activities.	• Girls reach puberty faster than boys.
• They are outgrowing their clumsiness.	• These changes can be a source of stress for many teens.
• Their appetites tend to decrease as they get older.	• They can be physically awkward.
	• Their stamina is increasing but not unlimited.
Mentally	**Mentally**
• They are capable of critical thinking.	• They are creative and inventive.
• They enjoy debating.	• They are learning to think abstractly.
• They enjoy creative problem solving.	• They understand consequences.
• They can make and carry out plans.	• They can think independently and like to show it.
• They can plan for the future.	• They can conceptualize time and space.
	• They enjoy adventure and discovery.
Socially	**Socially**
• They can purposely improve themselves.	• They want to belong.
• They are concerned about relationships with the opposite sex.	• They increasingly want adult status.
• They seek adult status.	• They want adults to accept them.
• They belong to a social group.	• They enjoy competition.
• They seek social approval.	• They can be very self-conscious.
• They like being busy.	
Emotionally	**Emotionally**
• They can control their emotions better.	• They are like roller coasters.
• They can still be moody.	• They easily feel misunderstood.
• Males tend to be more aggressive than females.	• They can have difficulty expressing how they really feel.
• They are looking for security.	• They tend to want to "rebel."
• They are accepting their sexuality.	• They can be very loyal.
	• They are developing independence.
	• They may have difficulty controlling their emotions.
Spiritually	**Spiritually**
• They question adult value systems.	• They are idealistic.
• Their philosophy of life is maturing.	• They are experiencing doubts.
• Their faith is becoming more personal.	• They are ready for deep challenges and encounters.
• They can express faith in their own terms.	• They think about death.
• They can make lifelong commitments.	• They can smell dishonesty and hypocrisy.
• They want spiritual truth to relate to everyday life.	• They want Bible study to be practical.
• They can worship God deeply.	• They enjoy service opportunities.

TABLE 2.2
TEACHING IMPLICATIONS OF ADOLESCENT DEVELOPMENT

Because adolescents...	Teachers should...
...are often inconsistent in their moods, attitudes, commitments, and actions,	...be prepared for them to be inconsistent while encouraging them to change.
...are prone to exaggerate the negative aspects of their relationships with their parents,	...be open to listening, but be careful about accepting everything as absolute fact.
...value friends and social relationships so highly,	...work to include social activities in their lessons.
...desire affirmation from adults they admire,	...be very generous in sharing sincere thoughts of appreciation and affirmation.
...enjoy serving others,	...create service-learning activities.
...are technologically savvy,	...take advantage of what their students know to create media presentations for lessons.
...know that something weird is happening inside their bodies,	...help them understand the changes they are experiencing.
...love to eat,	...provide food that is good for them.
...live in a co-ed world,	...teach them to relate appropriately with the opposite sex.
...mature at different rates,	...be aware of individuals who are maturing faster or slower than most of their friends.
...are a mixed bag of raging hormones,	...create safe environments for them to discuss what's really on their minds.
...are becoming deeper thinkers,	...allow deeper discussions.
...know that not every question has an easy answer,	...admit when they are unsure.
...are trying to be more independent,	...create learning opportunities that allow more self-discovery rather than lecture.
...tend to form tight groups of friends,	...challenge them to open up to others more.
...are working to figure out who they are,	...ask a lot of introspective questions during discussion.
...are developing their moral reasoning,	...talk through moral decisions they see youth struggling with.
...are asking more pointed questions about faith,	...allow for deep spiritual exploration.
...are wondering how to make their faith their own,	...ask "What do you believe about that?" and "Why do you believe that?"
...are moving through developmental stages,	...think long-term as they teach to encourage appropriate growth.
...have very different issues at various stages of adolescence,	...create age-graded classes according to developmental levels.
...value having a say in what happens to them,	...use student ideas for topics to study as appropriate.

There is so much more to adolescent development than can be covered in these pages. Current research continues to help us understand more than we have in the past. Implications of this new knowledge will be controversial but should be discussed openly.

The aspects of development discussed in this chapter represent central tendencies for youth in America. Very real differences exist between genders, races, social groups, and so on. To truly have a good working knowledge of adolescent development, I strongly recommend more in-depth study.

FOR DISCUSSION

Think back to your own middle school and high school experience. What do you remember about maturing faster or slower than your peers?

In what ways has the emergence of adolescence in western society been positive or negative for teenagers? For society?

What aspects of adolescent development as discussed in this chapter surprised you most? Of which ideas are you suspicious?

How do you think the teenage experience of guys is different from that of girls? How is the experience of adolescence different for kids from various cultures or subcultures in your area?

What can you recall about your experiences with the assorted identity stages (diffusion, moratorium, foreclosure, negative identity, and achievement)? Which stage best describes you right now?

How does this information challenge (or affirm) the way you teach?

ACTIVITIES

Create a series of lessons to present to parents about what they might expect during their children's adolescent years. Include suggestions for relating to teens.

Design a workshop to teach youth ministry volunteers about adolescent development.

Find the book *What Teens Need to Succeed* discussed in the sidebar on page 39. Write plans for your ministry to have an impact on as many of the 40 assets as possible.

Make a presentation to teenagers about eating disorders, body image, and media messages.

Challenge a group of adolescents to track their sleep for two weeks. Follow up by having them compare the amount of sleep they got to how tired they felt during different times of the day or to how well they performed various tasks (e.g., test taking, sports, work).

ENDNOTES, CHAPTER 2

22. Legislative commission on the economic status of women. Retreived August 1, 2002, from http://www.commissions.leg.state.mn.us/lcesw/fs/marstat.pdf

23. For more on adolescence as a social invention, see Fasik, F. (1994). On the "invention" of adolescence, *Journal of Early Adolescence*, 14, pp. 6-23. And Lapsley, D., Enright, R., & Serlin, R. (1985). Toward a theoretical perspective on the legislation of adolescence. *Journal of Early Adolescence*, 5, pp. 441-466.

24. Steinberg, L. (1999). *Adolescence, Fifth Edition.* New York: McGraw-Hill College, p. 31.

25. Bomar, J., & Sabatelli, R. (1996). Family system dynamics, gender, and psychosocial maturity in late adolescence, *Journal of Adolescent Research* 11, pp. 421-439.

26. Wolfe, S., & Truxillo, C. (1996, March) The relationship between decisional control, responsibility and positive and negative outcomes during early adolescence (Paper presented at the biennial meeting of the Society for Research on Adolescence, Boston).

27. Ibid, pp. 171-181.

28. For a great discussion on this, backed with some pretty firm research, read Rahn, D., & Linhart, T. (2000). *Contageous Faith*, Loveland, CO: Group.

29. Most of this information is taken from the PBS *Frontline* documentary "Inside the Teenage Brain," which first aired January 31, 2002.

30. For more on this, see PBS *Frontline's* video "Inside the Teenage Brain," original airdate January 31, 2002.

31. Smyth, C. (1992). As quoted in the PBS *Frontine* program "Inside the Teenage Brain."

32. Harter, S. (1990) Identity and self development. In Freldman, S. & Elliott, G. (eds.), *At the threshold: The developing adolescent.* Cambridge, MA: Harvard University Press, pp. 352-387.

33. Koenig, L. (1995, March). Change in self-esteem from 8th to 10th grade: Effects of gender and disruptive life events. Paper presented at the biennial meetings of the Society for Research in Child Development, Indianapolis.

34. Erikson's first work on this was a 1959 article, "Identity and the life cycle," in *Psychological Issues,* 1, pp. 1-171. His most complete work regarding adolescents was his 1968 book *Identity: Youth and Crisis* (New York: Norton).

35. Steinberg, L., & Cauffman, E. (1995). The impact of employment on adolescent development. In R. Vasta (Ed.), *Annals of Child Development,* Vol. 11. London: Jessica Kingsley Publishers.

36. "Girls may make less money at summer jobs," Junior Achievement press release, May 21, 2002.

37. Mortimer, J., Finch, M., Ryu, S., Shanahan, M., & Call, K. (1996). The effects of work intensity on adolescent mental health, achievement, and behavioral adjustment: New evidence from a prospective study. *Child Development,* 67, pp. 1243-1261.

38. Steinberg (1999). p. 294.

39. Rice, F. P. (1987). *The Adolescent (5th edition).* Boston: Allyn and Bacon.

40. Fowler, J. W. (1986). Faith and the structure of meaning. In Dykstra C., & Parks, S. (Eds.), *Faith Development and Fowler.* Birmingham, AL: Religious Education Press, p. 15.

41. Muuss, R. E. (1996). *Theories of adolescence.* New York: McGraw-Hill, p. 266.

42. A helpful resource for discussing this in more detail is Shelton, C. M. (1983). *Adolescent Spirituality: Pastoral ministry for high school and college youth.* New York: Crossroad.

CHAPTER 3

WHO ARE THE KIDS *YOU* TEACH?

(Doing a Cultural Exegesis)

"You can observe a lot just by watching."
—YOGI BERRA

*   *   *   *   *

"We must remember that the most relevant ministries are the ones that understand youth for exactly who they are. Being wary of broad, generalizing stereotypes of youth culture, we must take the time to learn about the different groupings and personalities of youth that exist within our own spheres of ministry."[43]

"Choosing to listen or to engage personally in an adolescent's world communicates, 'Who you are matters to me. I care about what you think, how you feel and why you make the choices you do.' "[44]

"Instead of teaching them to see the world as we see it, we must move into their worlds and see through their eyes in order to reveal to them the truth that God's love is real and available."[45]

"The wisdom of God must be translated into a given culture in a particular time and place."[46]

"Society has changed. And if we speak tomorrow as we did yesterday, our words will become just one more sound in a noisy world, addressed to everyone, heard by no one."[47]

"We are visitors in their world, and we will need to learn the correct way to relate."[48]

I once knew a youth minister who was very current on his youth culture knowledge. He could tell you what songs were popular with what types of kids according to *Billboard* or *Rolling Stone*. He knew what movies were big at the box office. He prided himself on being the source of the latest cultural information.

Unfortunately, he related to his youth through those national lenses. He assumed that everything he heard or read in the media applied to his kids as well. While he was a lot of fun to be with and attracted teens in swarms, he rarely got close to individuals, because he didn't know their specific context. Being a cultural guru doesn't help much if those tendencies don't reflect the young people in your ministry.

Case in point: Every spring I teach a class at John Brown University in which we do a careful study of local youth culture. Imagine our shock when the first study we did revealed that 80 percent of the teens in our local public school system reported attending church at least twice a month. (Studies in subsequent years have also shown church attendance by youth in this area to be between 70 percent and 80 percent.) We knew we were in a heavily churched location, but 80 percent is almost twice what typical surveys report nationwide. The ministry implications of this should not be ignored by area youth workers.

We discovered this, and a lot of other helpful information, through a process known as "CULTURAL EXEGESIS." The goal is to find out who a specific group of people is and what is influencing them. I teach my students this process because I believe all youth workers should do this periodically in their ministry contexts. I have had several former students tell me that they used this exercise in the location of their ministry and found it to be very helpful.

DEFINING CULTURAL EXEGESIS

EXEGESIS is simply research and interpretation of something. The term is usually associated with literature. Most of us in the church think of exegesis in terms of interpreting Bible passages. A cultural exegesis, then, is just applying those same principles to a specific group of people in a specific context. Sociologists do cultural exegesis as a daily part of their jobs, but usually they don't call it that. Part of the role of a youth worker is to become a sociologist in this sense.

WHY DOING A CULTURAL EXEGESIS IS ESSENTIAL

In order for you to understand the unique traits, nuances, and influences of the youth you work with, learning to do a cultural exegesis in your ministry context is essential. Too often youth workers take national trends and research from secular media (TV news, magazines, and Web sites) or religious groups (such as Barna Research Group, Search Institute, and the Center for Parent and Youth Understanding) and assume the reported data applies to their teens as well. This is rarely the case.

In chapter 1, I noted a survey from the Barna Research Group that concluded that the number of U.S teens who are evangelical has declined from ten percent in 1995 to only four percent today. Such a trend is certainly disturbing. But it does not mean that exactly four percent of the kids in your youth ministry are evangelicals. In order to find out what your youth believe, you need to ask them.

As another example, if you go to www.billboard.com you will find the Hot 100 singles in the United States. To find out if *Billboard*'s most popular songs are also the number one songs with your teens, you have to ask them.

National data can provide a great backdrop to understand what is happening with adolescent culture on a wider scale. But you need to know what's true of youth in your city and in your ministry. Those who write and publish CURRICULUM don't know your kids or your cultural context, either. In order for you to teach your group most effectively, you need to know how to adapt that curriculum to fit. Doing a cultural exegesis will help you do that better. (We'll talk more about curriculum in chapter 5.)

GETTING STARTED

In order to really find out about your teens, you need to know who and what is influencing them. This requires some digging. Certainly you have observed what music they listen to, movies and TV shows they watch, and friends they hang out with. These observations are a good place to start, but you need more objective data as well.

I have my college students write a survey to help them find out what they want to know. On the next two pages, you'll find an example of what one such survey looked like for a recent class.

YOUTH CULTURE SURVEY

JOHN BROWN UNIVERSITY

Circle one response for each of the following:

1a. Gender: Male

               Female

1b. Class: 9   10   11   12

2. Race: Black

               Hispanic

               Caucasian

               Asian

               Other

Check each item that is true for you:

3. ___ I have a part-time job.
4. ___ I am on an athletic team.
5. ___ I am involved in band, choir, or drama.
6. ___ I am involved with other school clubs or organizations.
7. ___ I hold a leadership position at school or in the community.
8. ___ I have a valid driver's license.
9. ___ I usually attend a church at least twice a month.
10. ___ I watch a lot of TV.
11. ___ I listen to a lot of music.
12. ___ I read a lot of books.
13. ___ I read magazines a lot.
14. ___ I see a lot of movies (rent, own, or in theaters).
15. ___ I play a lot of video games.
16. ___ I hang out with friends a lot.

What are your three favorite TV shows?

17.

18.

19.

What are your three favorite music groups?

20.

21.

22.

What are your three favorite books?

23.

24.

25.

What are your three favorite magazines?

26.

27.

28.

What are your three favorite movies?

29.

30.

31.

At what three stores do you like to shop the most?

32.

33.

34.

What three Web sites do you visit most frequently?

35.

36.

37.

Whose advice do you usually value most for the following situations?
Please rank from 1 (you value their advice most) to 6 (you value their advice least).

EXAMPLE – Buying a car:
_1_ *Close Friends* _3_ *A Teacher* _5_ *Guidance Counselor* _2_ *Parent* _4_ *Some Other Adult* _6_ *Myself*

38) Help with homework:
__ Close Friends __ A Teacher __ Guidance Counselor __ Parent __ Some Other Adult __ Myself

39) Boy-girl problems:
__ Close Friends __ A Teacher __ Guidance Counselor __ Parent __ Some Other Adult __ Myself

40) What to wear:
__ Close Friends __ A Teacher __ Guidance Counselor __ Parent __ Some Other Adult __ Myself

41) Friendship problems:
__ Close Friends __ A Teacher __ Guidance Counselor __ Parent __ Some Other Adult __ Myself

42) Dealing with peer pressure:
__ Close Friends __ A Teacher __ Guidance Counselor __ Parent __ Some Other Adult __ Myself

43) Planning for the future:
__ Close Friends __ A Teacher __ Guidance Counselor __ Parent __ Some Other Adult __ Myself

44) Handling money:
__ Close Friends __ A Teacher __ Guidance Counselor __ Parent __ Some Other Adult __ Myself

45) Handling stress:
__ Close Friends __ A Teacher __ Guidance Counselor __ Parent __ Some Other Adult __ Myself

Please circle the one response for each question that is usually true for you.

46) How often do others look to you for leadership?
Very Often   Sometimes   Rarely   Never

47) How often do you prefer to be in a position of leading others?
Very Often   Sometimes   Rarely   Never

48) How often do your friends wind up doing what you suggest?
Very Often   Sometimes   Rarely   Never

49) How often do you change your mind based on the opinions of others?
Very Often   Sometimes   Rarely   Never

50) How often do you ask others for advice before you make decisions?
Very Often   Sometimes   Rarely   Never

The instrument on the previous pages was intended to determine what social and cultural forces were most influencing the youth in our area. Maybe you noticed that the questions were slanted to find out about their activities and what media they enjoyed most. You can create a survey to find out many different types of information, though. Family relationships, religious activity, substance use, and so on, are all good subjects to research when trying to learn about your community. But you need to keep several factors in mind as you prepare your questionnaire.

What do you really want to know? Putting together something like this is more than just asking a bunch of questions. You have to ask the right questions in the right way. Make sure your questions are specific and direct enough to give you answers that make sense. Asking "Do you pray?" may not help you as much as asking "When do you pray?" and listing several different options. Consider these examples:

> Is Pastor Alan a good teacher?
>
> Do you like music?
>
> Do you listen to your friends' opinions?

What do you learn from these? You get a "yes" or a "no" for each question, but you don't gain any information about why the teens responded as they did. Reformatting and rewording the questions will help you learn a lot more. You could try a wording like this to find out about Pastor Alan's teaching:

> Which of the following does Pastor Alan do well as a teacher?
> (You may circle more than one.)
>
> Explains the Bible clearly   Applies the Bible to my life   Gets my attention
>
> Helps everyone listen   Uses a variety of activities   Leads good discussions

Or try this to find out about music listening habits:

> About how much time do you spend listening to music each week? (Check one.)
>
> ___ 0-2 hours   ___ 3-6 hours   ___ 7-10 hours   ___ More than 10 hours

To learn how much influence friends have on your teens, you could ask them to respond to this:

For each of the following situations, circle the importance you put on your friends' opinions:

Whom you should date	None	Little	Some	A lot	Ultimate
What college to attend	None	Little	Some	A lot	Ultimate
Where to shop	None	Little	Some	A lot	Ultimate
Homework problems	None	Little	Some	A lot	Ultimate
Finding a job	None	Little	Some	A lot	Ultimate
Handling stress	None	Little	Some	A lot	Ultimate

As you can see, the information you would get from the last set of examples is more detailed and helpful than the responses you might get from the first set.

How will you distribute and collect the surveys? We took advantage of a good relationship with our local schools to distribute our survey. The principals at the high school and middle school were very gracious in allowing us access to several classes for this project. We printed out very simple directions for teachers, primarily to clarify our intent, and allowed them to figure out when and how to have their students fill it out.

By partnering with them, we were able to gather some great data, build a working relationship with school administrators, and spend some time in the schools. Doing this in the public schools, though, meant that we had to be sensitive about the nature of the questions we asked. We chose to ask about cultural influences, because the principals and guidance counselors were also interested in that. We did have to sacrifice some specificity in the questions to allow teachers to administer the survey without special instructions and to keep the commitment under ten minutes of class time.

In other settings, it could be done differently. You could simply ask the kids in your ministry to fill out your survey. This would help you find out a lot about

A QUICK WORD ABOUT DOING SURVEYS:

Typically people doing surveys want to be able to generalize the results. This simply means taking the results from those who turned in surveys and applying them to all the youth you are trying to learn about. Ideally you want what is known as a random sample. This means that every person in your target group has an equal chance of being included. When you mail a survey out, you limit it to only those students who open their mail and take the time to fill it out and return it. While those you mailed it to might be truly random, those who returned it would not be. It helps to discuss this with someone who is familiar with research design.

them, but would not help you understand kids in the community who are not part of your ministry.

Mailing them out to students is another option, but then you have increased cost. The percentage of surveys returned is also typically very low. This also raises questions about whether the results can be generalized, since those returning the survey might not be representative of the population.

How many surveys do you need to have filled out? Some fundamental knowledge of research design helps here. You can't just ask the ten kids who show up early to Sunday school to answer some questions, and then extrapolate their responses to the whole community. A good rule of thumb is to get at least 30 good, random surveys for each group or subgroup of students you are researching.

When my classes do this project, our goal is to get responses from 50 students in each grade level. This gives us around 300 usable sets of data and allows us to break down the results by age group and still feel confident that our numbers are representative.

How will you tabulate the data? You could do it yourself by hand, but to have confidence in your results, you need a lot of surveys filled out. That's a heap of information for one person to handle manually.

You could enlist the help of some volunteers, which would be a great way to involve others and bring wider ownership to the project. I am a big fan of this approach, because it gives you more than just help in tabulating numbers. It also offers a variety of ways to think about how to do a cultural exegesis. In addition, if you have plenty of people involved from the start, then they will understand the whole process more thoroughly when you ask them to help interpret the findings later.

Another fairly easy option is to find an automated way to enter and count the results. Most schools have a machine that will read and count responses shaded on a "bubble sheet," which is what I call those sheets used in many standardized tests where you have to use a #2 pencil to fill in the ovals.

The advantage of this is that it makes adding and figuring the results quick and easy. Usually these machines also are able to do item analysis, frequency distributions, and a host of other helpful calculations. The major disadvantage is that, if you want to ask open-ended questions, you will still have to analyze those manually. Another problem is that you need to be pretty thorough in giving options for kids to choose. If you want to find out what TV shows teens are watching, you should list at least twenty for them to choose from (plus leave a blank for them to write in others). This can lead to a very lengthy and cumbersome questionnaire.

The option I use with my classes is to enter information into a spreadsheet program and take advantage of its statistical analysis tools. The popular spreadsheets available on most computers have the ability to sort, count, and average, in addition to calculating several other helpful statistical measures. You don't have to be a computer geek or a stats wiz to do this.

DOING SOME HOMEWORK

When you find out what kids are doing, watching, reading, and listening to, then you're ready to learn more about these influences. Here are a few ideas:

Observe Kids Where They Spend Time

Hopefully you already spend some time where groups of teens are hanging out together. To do this exegesis well, though, you need to make yourself, and whoever's helping you, become an observer for a while. This means taking a note pad with you, sitting in an inconspicuous place, and writing down what you see. Notice how kids interact with each other, the groups that form, how leaders surface, and so on.

Do these observations in a variety of places. I suggest having three or four people go to at least two different places each. Spend at least one hour observing what the kids do in each location. You want to choose places that will give you a variety of perspectives on how kids interact socially. Take thorough notes so you can go back and talk about what you observed with others.

WHERE SHOULD YOU DO THESE OBSERVATIONS?

Mall, school-related football or basketball games (or other sports that attract a large number of kids), school or community dances, movie theaters, store/restaurant parking lots that serve as hangouts, local parks, etc.

Don't rule out observing at school. Tell the principal you are doing a research project about how kids interact socially, and you'd like to watch and make some notes in the cafeteria during lunch or in the hallways while kids are changing classes.

Watch What Kids Watch

Walt Mueller's *Understanding Today's Youth Culture* (Tyndale) is a great resource not only for learning about media influences and impact, but for becoming aware of the messages teens are receiving. Mueller is president of the Center for Parent/Youth Understanding and their Web site (www.cpyu.org) contains a wealth of valuable information, including a weekly youth culture newsletter.

Spend a few hours watching TV shows that are popular with your kids. Make sure to include MTV, VH1, and movies and videos that are popular with most teens. Take note of the themes, messages, attitudes, products, and worldview that they convey.

A disclaimer may be in order here. Many of the movies and shows teens watch are vulgar, explicit, and offensive. Please exercise discretion as you choose what to view for this project. While it is important to be aware of what youth are watching, you don't have to get run over by a truck to know that it hurts, if you know what I mean.

You should also plan to spend time on the Internet visiting Web sites teens frequent. They'll include chat rooms, game sites, sports and entertainment pages, and probably several places you'd rather not be.

Listen To What Kids Listen To

When you get an idea of what songs, groups, and radio stations are influencing your youth, you need to spend plenty of time listening to them. (And only to them—don't listen while doing other things.) As with the other areas, have a notepad in hand, and jot down what themes, ideas, and messages you hear.

It might help to find the lyrics of the most popular songs and read through them. You can get the lyrics for many songs by using an Internet search engine—enter the name of the song in quotation marks then add the word lyrics. The homepages of individual artists or the Web site www.lyrics.com may also be helpful. Look for ways that artists talk about things like relationships, life, disappointment, God, religion, and school. These attitudes both reflect and create reality in many ways.

Read What Kids Read

Kids do read magazines, but there tends to be a big difference in the reading habits of guys and girls. Guys typically look at magazines as opposed to reading them. Anything sports oriented or that has video game tips is usually geared towards them. Girls read magazines at a much greater rate and tend to like the fashion or celebrity genres more.

Your survey should ask adolescents what magazines they read frequently. Once you have determined a top-ten list for the group you're exegeting, grab your note pad and spend a few hours at your local bookstore or news-stand looking through the most popular ones.

Notice the ads, articles, and pictures. Ask yourself about the editorial philosophy of the magazine. What are they saying to and selling youth? Pay special attention to the images that magazines use. Look at the models in the pictures. All of this sends messages to readers.

Research the Research on Adolescent Culture

Find Web sites, books, and magazine or journal articles regarding today's youth culture. Anything done more than two years ago is not recent enough. This comparison data will help you determine how the teens in your area are similar or dissimilar to national norms. A few good sources of info include the Youth Specialties Web site at www.youthspecialties.com (which includes *Youthworker* magazine) and the *Group* magazine Web site at www.groupmag.com. Other valuable sites include: www.antithesis.com, www.christiancounterculture.com, www.youthoutlook.org, and www.cpyu.org.

To find specific information about the most popular TV shows, radio stations, or movies, you will likely need to go to a local public library and find trade journals for the different media. *Billboard* covers the music industry, for example. Nielsen Media Research, the TV ratings company, used to make their latest ratings information available on their Web page (www.nielsenmedia.com), but no more. For a research fee, though, they will tell you what shows were most popular with teens in Florida on Tuesday afternoons last October.

SOME OF THE MOST POPULAR MAGAZINES WITH TEENAGERS ARE

16	Sport
Mad	Sports Illustrated
People	Thrasher
Metal Edge	Cracked
Teen Beat	Glamour
ESPN The Magazine	
Play Station Magazine	
Teen People	Rolling Stone
Twist	Heavy Metal
Seventeen	Vibe
Spice	Sidewalk Surfer
Jump	Jane
Cosmopolitan	Teen
Self	Bile
YM	Us
In Line	Circus
You	Spin

(Also various comic books)

ANALYZING WHAT YOU'VE FOUND

This is where you will really benefit from having some critically thinking volunteers help you look at everything you've learned. Your goal is to create a profile of the teenagers your ministry desires to impact. Then use that information to create the ministry opportunities and teaching-learning settings that will make the most difference. The more good brains you have to help with this, the better. Below are some steps to help you with the process.

Step 1: List general descriptions of the youth. Pay attention to details such as where they go to school, what extracurriculars are most important, leadership skills, how they spend their time, and who their key relationships are with, in addition to the media influences discussed above.

WHO SHOULD YOU ASK TO HELP?

Youth sponsors
A parent or two
A couple of deacons or elders
A couple of recent ministry graduates
Lay people who teach in the local schools

  Yes, you can get too many, but some will drop out along the way. You are better off starting with more than you need, so that those who don't really want to be helpful can weed themselves out as you proceed.

Sample Profile:[49] The middle schoolers at Southside Public tend to be very active in their local churches. About 35 percent live with single parents and another 20 percent live with a stepparent. Most report listening to music ten or more hours per week. Creed is the most popular group and rock or pop is their favorite type of music with a significant percentage liking rap or hip-hop. Their favorite TV shows are *Friends* and *SpongeBob SquarePants*. They prefer spending time with their friends, but still primarily trust their parents when it comes to important decisions. They like action movies (the more blood and gore the better) over comedies. Few see themselves as leaders, although over 75 percent are involved in extracurricular activities.

Step 2: Synthesize the information from your media observations. What dominant messages are your kids getting? What is their preferred mode of entertainment?

Sample Analysis: The students at Southside get a lot of mixed messages from the media they prefer. They like TV shows aimed at young adults as well as those aimed at children. The messages they get range from "Share your toys" to "Share your boys." They hear a lot of profanity and sexual discussions. The images they see on TV and in magazines promote the idea that to be cool you have to be perfect, which means no fat and no blemishes. Guys must be strong and athletic, but sensitive. Girls must be beautiful, smart, and independent. Even though most go to church regularly, few have a strong idea of what Scripture says or how and why it should make a difference in their lives.

Step 3: Compare the information from your local study to the national data on youth culture. Look at areas of similarity and difference. How do things like musical preferences, favorite movies, time with family, attitudes toward school, and alcohol use, stack up against the rest of the nation?

Sample Comparison:[50]

	Nationally	**Locally**
TV Shows	*Friends* and *CSI*	*Friends* and *SpongeBob*
Music Groups	Creed and Linkin Park	Creed and Aerosmith
Sex	67% have lost their virginity	48%
Alcohol	45% drink monthly	65%
Smoking	53% smoke daily	58%
Church	47% attend monthly	85%
College	85% plan to attend	63%
Bible	12% can name all 10 commandments	14%
Leadership	47% see themselves as leaders	31%

Step 4: Create a list of implications for ministry and teaching based on your conclusions. It should include all of the factors that shape who your kids are and will be a tool for helping you think about how to design your ministry. It might look something like this:

BECAUSE OUR TEENS. . .	WE NEED TO. . .
Are heavily churched. . .	Emphasize Christian growth
Listen to a lot of music. . .	Use a variety of music as we teach
Trust their parents but spend more time with friends. . .	Create activities for youth and parents to do together
Are heavily involved in sports. . .	Make sure our sponsors get to games
Are pressured to look "perfect". . .	Emphasize who they are in Christ
Receive negative media messages about Christianity. . .	Teach them to be discerning and to know God's WORD well
Do not see themselves as leaders. . .	Concentrate more purposefully on leadership development

Many more items could be listed, depending on what your exegesis reveals, but this gives you a general idea of how to begin.

APPLYING THE CONCLUSIONS TO YOUR TEACHING

As my students at John Brown University have done this project over the past few years, some trends have emerged that should influence the way youth workers in our area do ministry. For example, the fact that 80 percent of the students in public middle-high and high-schools report that they attend church at least twice a month should shape our teaching approach and ministry activities. We also have a couple of Christian schools in the area, as well as a high number of home-schooled youth, most of whom also go to church regularly.

Spending a lot of time teaching churched teens to do street evangelism does not make sense in our context. Neither does explaining the basic concepts of the gospel on a regular basis. These highly churched adolescents need to be discipled deeply and challenged with the meat of God's Word.

Another conclusion from our study is that the TV shows, music, and movies most of the youth in this area watch are not as violent and sexual as the national norms. Our assumption is that this is a result of living in a highly churched community. This would seem to be good news. We have also determined, though, that the levels of alcohol, marijuana, and methamphetamine abuse here are just as high, if not higher, than in other parts of the country.

There are a couple of good resources you could use to do some research with your own group as well. Search Institute has a few survey tools designed for use with church youth groups, but they could be adapted for use in other settings. I have used one of these with a youth group and found I got good, useful data.

Another good resource is Mike Nappa's book *What I Wish My Youth Leader Knew About Youth Ministry* (Standard, 1999). It shares the results of an extensive questionnaire he asked 800 students to fill out. (He received just over 400 in return). The questions are the best thing about the book. A former student told me he took it in the van with him on a long trip and asked the kids to respond to the questions as they drove. I thought that was a great way to use a tool like this.

This is another great way to see in real-world ways just how multifaceted your youth are. Understanding more about the many influences that shape their lives should motivate you even more to teach holistically.

However you do it, learning more about who your adolescents are and the unique culture in which you minister will reap benefits for you in the long run. It can be a lot of work—but doing youth ministry and teaching teens is a lot of work. As another of my students reluctantly confessed, "At first, I hated this, but it does serve its purpose well."

OVERWHELMED?

"Sounds great," you're thinking, "but there's no way I'd ever have time to do all this." Here's a radical thought: Stop all your typical ministry activities for a month and get all your volunteers and kids to do a massive cultural exegesis instead. The benefits you'll gain from those insights will wind up being a lot more important than what you had on your program calendar anyway.

For Discussion

When you were in high school, how was the culture in your area similar to or different from national norms at that time?

In what ways do you think the local adolescent culture where you minister now is unique?

What are some specific questions you would like to ask the youth in your area to learn more about them?

Even if doing a cultural exegesis sounds good in theory, what potential problems do you see with it in practice?

What are some ways that doing a cultural exegesis might change the way you approach youth ministry in your context?

ACTIVITIES

Talk with a principal or guidance counselor at a local school to see if there is an aspect of adolescent culture they would like to know more about. Use their ideas to shape what you want to do, and work together with them on this project.

Interview some teens who are not part of your ministry. Ask them how they view their culture. Compare that to how your youth respond to the same questions. Analyze how similar or different their opinions are.

Write out some aspects of local youth culture you would like to know more about. Work with a group to write a survey instrument based on the list. You should have someone who is familiar with research (a teacher or professor with a research degree would work) look it over and help you make it better.

ENDNOTES, CHAPTER 3

43. Atkinson, H. (2001). *Teaching Youth with Confidence*. Wheaton, IL: Evangelical Training Association, p. 51.
44. Dunn, R. R. (2001). *Shaping the Spiritual Life of Students*. Downers Grove, IL: InterVarsity Press, p. 16. Emphasis added.
45. Fields, D. (2002). Relational Basics, *Youthworker*. Nashville, TN: CCM Communications, XVIII, 4, p. 21. Emphasis added.
46. Borgman, D. (1997). *When Kumbaya is Not Enough*. Peabody, MA: Hendrickson, p. 19.
47. Henderson, D. W. (1998). *Culture Shift*. Grand Rapids, MI: Baker, p. 22.
48. Ward, P. (1999). *God at the Mall*. Peabody, MA: Hendrickson, p. 58.
49. The data used in these examples is for illustrative purposes, and does not represent actual findings.
50. These numbers are used as an example only and should not be taken as actual facts.

CHAPTER 4

HOW DO KIDS LEARN?

(An Introduction to Learning Styles)

"I've got to rethink my teaching. I'm missing kids, even though they're in their seats every Sunday."

—AN ANONYMOUS SUNDAY SCHOOL TEACHER[51]

*   *   *   *   *

Eddie was always giving me headaches when I was teaching Sunday school. He was constantly causing problems by talking out of turn, throwing paper across the room, and making snide comments. While most of the other kids were attentive and involved, Eddie was distant and bored.

Once at a lock-in, I accidentally discovered the key to teaching Eddie. It seems that during that day in science class, the teacher had demonstrated the flammable properties of aerosols. Eddie was impressed with the experiments they did in class, and brought one of his own to the lock-in that night.

With a lighter and a can of his mom's hairspray, Eddie put on a private display of his newfound knowledge in a corner of the church basement. I found out only because another one of the youth who saw it became frightened Eddie would burn the church down.

After calling Eddie's mom to come get her hairspray and have a stern discussion with her son and me, I was thinking about why Eddie was so enthralled with his makeshift flamethrower. It hit me that he didn't learn the way I was teaching. He needed challenging and fascinating hands-on activities. I typically relied on my trusty lecture-and-discussion method. So I decided to try an experiment of my own for a month.

When I was done preparing my Sunday school or youth group lessons, I reread them through Eddie's eyes. "What will Eddie learn from this lesson?" I asked myself. I created specific ways to engage him in each topic. My lessons that month included visiting the cemetery by the church to find out about the great cloud of witnesses who have gone before, washing the windshields of the cars in the parking lot to learn about service, and having him help me create and teach a lesson.

At the end of the month, I concluded that Eddie not only was much less disruptive but actually seemed to enjoy most of the lessons. An unexpected bonus was that some of the other teens mentioned to me how much they were getting out of my new and more active approach. Apparently I had stumbled onto something that I was probably told in college: Different people learn in different ways.

Since that epiphany with Eddie, I have discovered a lot more about LEARNING STYLES. A rudimentary understanding of the principles involved and an ability to begin to discern learning styles (sometimes also called learning preferences) will help you become a much more effective teacher with a wider variety of adolescents.

OUR SENSES AND LEARNING

God has created us with five basic senses—sight, hearing, touch, taste, and smell. It is through these five senses that we experience everything we encounter. These multisensual encounters are how we learn.

From the first days after her birth, the people a baby sees most are the ones she learns to call parents. She hears their voices and looks in that direction to find them. She associates certain smells and tastes with her parents. Even physical touch is an avenue for learning as the infant explores her feet and face and the world around her.

For some reason, the typical educational system, and church education as a result, has come to depend primarily on one sense—hearing—as the primary mode of learning. While most educators now recognize that few people actually learn well by listening to lecture after lecture, it is still the predominant method for those who teach adolescents in nearly every setting.

There's a simple reason why using multiple senses enhances learning. Something unique happens to the brain when the body performs an action. A change occurs that dramatically increases the probability of remembering that action and the information surrounding it.[52] The fact is that the more senses you involve in something, the more you will remember. That is why you can recall with vivid detail events like that time you broke your arm, family Thanksgiving dinners, your first kiss, or learning how to drive. These moments intensely involved all or most of your senses.

In our discussion of learning styles we need to keep in mind that these five senses determine how we experience all of life. Because God made each person unique, though, the ways our brains process what we experience vary greatly from person to person. It is these different ways of processing that affect how people learn.

A VARIETY OF THEORIES

There may be as many different ways of thinking about learning styles as there are researchers studying them. For the sake of our discussion, I will focus on four of the most popular and widely accepted theories.

The Sensory Model
(Visual Auditory Kinesthetic Tactile)

Possibly the most popular learning theory—and certainly the easiest to understand—involves three of the five senses discussed above. This idea postulates that people learn primarily in one of four ways.

Students who prefer to read or need to see something in order to learn are called VISUAL LEARNERS. These are the people in society who actually use the owner's manuals that come with video cameras and computers. In order to really understand a concept, these students need to see a written explanation or a graphic aid. The youth who ask you to write something on the board or to see something tangible most likely fit this style.

CAUTION!
There is a tendency to try to absolutely categorize and label yourself and everyone you know when reading about learning styles. DO NOT do this!! These are intended to be helpful tools, not absolute diagnoses.

Also, remember that everyone has a combination of learning styles that may vary from day to day or from event to event.

AUDITORY LEARNERS are those who prefer to hear information in order to process it best. These are the ones who love a good lecture or who put lists and ideas to music. Sometimes they can be seen talking to themselves as they work. They also tend to be the students who help class discussions along by asking great questions so they can hear more. Most formal education today tends to assume every student is an auditory learner.

People who neither read the directions nor ask someone for help tend to be the KINESTHETIC LEARNERS. They don't want the instructions for assembling the bicycle, they don't need help learning how to program a Web page, and they figure out the secret strategies in video games all by themselves. These kids need to engage themselves in the learning process through action.

Often lumped together with the kinesthetic learners are the TACTILE LEARN-ERS, who need to touch something physically to engage their brains. They can be annoying because they often tap a pencil on their desk or drum their fingers, which is especially distracting to auditory learners who are acutely in tune with sounds. I have three children, and the middle one, Caley, is especially tactile. She will often sit close to me and stroke my head or arm. Her favorite clothes are those with unusual textures. ("They're feely," she says.)

As mentioned above, most educational methods tend to be auditory. Sometimes visual aids are sprinkled in to add variety. But research indicates that only 20 to 30 percent of school-age children appear to be auditory learners, that 40 percent are visual, and that the remaining 30 to 40 percent are tactile/kines-thetic, visual/tactile, or some other combination.[53] One obvious caution this brings to mind is that by teaching through lecture, we touch the dominant learning method of only about one-fourth of our students.

I have a series of statements I ask students to respond to in order to help them evaluate which learning style may be dominant for them. Below is the tool I use. To complete it, just check the statements that are typically true for you.

ASSESSING YOUR LEARNING STYLE: VISUAL-AUDITORY-TACTILE/KINESTHETIC

__People say you have terrible handwriting.

__You don't like silent films, pantomimes, or charades.

__You would rather perform (or listen to) music than do (or view) art.

__You sometimes leave out words when writing or get words or letters backwards.

__You can spell aloud better than when you have to write it down.

__You remember things that you talked about in class much better than things you have read.

__You dislike copying materials from the blackboard or bulletin board.

__You like jokes or riddles better than cartoons or crossword puzzles.

__You like games with lots of action or noises better than checkers or most other board games.

__You understand better when you read aloud.

__Sometimes you make math mistakes because you don't notice the sign or read the numbers or directions wrong.

__It seems like you are the last one to notice something new (e.g., that the classroom was painted or that there is a new bulletin board display.)

__Map activities are just not your thing.

__You must struggle to keep neat notes and records.

__You must use your fingers as a pointer when you read.

__You hum frequently or whistle to yourself when you are working.

__Sometimes your eyes just bother you, but your eye test was normal, or you have glasses that your eye doctor says are right for you.

__You hate to read from the computer, especially when the backgrounds are busy.

__Matching test questions are a problem to sort out (over and above not knowing some of the answers).

__When you read you sometimes mix up words that look similar (pill-pull, bale-hale).

__It seems like you always have to ask somebody to repeat what s/he just said.

__Sometimes you find yourself tuned out or staring out the window when you were trying to pay attention.

__Often you know what you want to say, but you just can't think of the words. Sometimes you may even be accused of talking with your hands or calling something a "thingamajig."

__You have been in speech therapy some time previously (or currently).

__You may have trouble understanding a person talking to you when you are unable to watch the person's face while s/he is speaking.

__You would rather receive directions in a demonstration format than in spoken form.

__When you watch TV or listen to the radio, someone is always asking you to turn it down.

__Your family says that you say "Huh?" too much.

__You would rather demonstrate how to do something than make a speech.

__Spoken words that sound similar give you trouble. Sometimes you can't tell them apart.

__You have trouble remembering things unless you write them down.

__You like board games such as checkers better than listening games.

__Sometimes you make mistakes when speaking (like saying, "He got expended from school").

__You like artwork better than music.

__You have to go over most of the alphabet in order to remember whether M comes before R.

__You like it better when someone shows you what to do rather than just telling you.

__You usually answer questions with yes or no rather than with complete sentences.

__You can do a lot of things that are hard to explain with words.

__Often you forget to give verbally received messages (such as telephone messages) to people unless you write them down.

__You are always doodling or drawing little pictures on the edges of your papers.

Total the ones you marked in the left column and the ones you marked in the right column. If the left totals much more than the right, you are likely an auditory learner. If the right totals much more than the left, you are likely visual. If you checked a lot on both left and right, then you may be more kinesthetic or tactile. If you did not mark many items at all, then this theory of learning styles may not be very helpful for you—but one or more of the following models may be.

Teaching Implication: One value of this theory is that it helps those of us who teach keep in mind that we can't just talk all the time. Students need visual aids and hands-on engagement as well. By having the youth in your group occasionally take an inventory similar to the one above, you can get a sense of the dominant learning style of the group compared to your dominant teaching style. If they are not matched closely, then it's you who needs to change, not them.

Bi-Polar Models

Not to be confused with the psychological term, anything bi-polar simply has two extremes. Typically these poles are connected by a continuum. For the sake of our discussion in this section, it will be helpful to think of BI-POLAR MODELS of learning theory as consisting of a series of opposing terms, each being connected by a continuum. Very few people will fit any one of these poles absolutely. Most folk fit on varying places on the different continua depending on a variety of circumstances.

Convergent–Divergent

This learning theory concerns how your brain processes new information. When a teenager receives new information, she must decide what to do with it. A CONVERGENT thinker will likely find a way to connect it to information she already knows, so she can determine how it might help answer existing questions. The new information converges (comes together) with specific old information.

The DIVERGENT thinker, on the other hand, tends to look for a variety of ways to use the new information. He may link it to an urgent question, but he would also think about new ways to understand it. In this way, he is diverging (branching off) from the specific given application of the information.

For example, let's say you are teaching a lesson that examines the role of Jesus as priest. You will likely discuss what specific aspects of our relationship with Jesus reflect his priesthood. A convergent processor would probably think about ways she could allow Jesus to be a priest to her in regard to specific issues she is currently facing. The divergent thinker might wonder what other implications the priesthood of Jesus might have, not just for him, but for his friends, his church, and the world.

This particular bi-polar set also appears in other learning theories, typically combined with other bi-polar pairings, to create a quadrant theory. Some teachers find these quadrants more helpful; others find them confusing.

Teaching Implication: Your youth will benefit by learning from each others' strengths. As part of your discussion time, ask students what they are doing mentally with information they learn. You will quickly be able to discern who your convergers and divergers are. Use their thoughts and comments to enhance your teaching.

Assimilate–Accommodate

Another way of thinking about how students deal with new information is the assimilate-accommodate set. When students blend new ideas into their existing ideas, this is ASSIMILATION. When students make room for the new information, but do not necessarily combine or blend it with their own, this is ACCOMMODATION.

Think about paint. If you start with a big spot of blue paint and add some yellow paint to it, the blue will move out of the way to accommodate the yellow. Not until the two are stirred will they blend. This assimilation creates green. Accommodation makes room for something new. Assimilation combines new and old.

Teaching Implication: It is very tempting to believe assimilation is always better than accommodation. Don't confuse intellectual assimilation with emotional ownership. We can't assume that real learning has happened just because a student can accurately restate what was taught. Learning results in changed lives, not just knowing more info.

CAUTION!

These bi-polar styles should not be used to infer qualitative value. In other words, one is not better than another, they are just different.

I once had a student do a presentation on how to "fix" introverts so they could be extroverts as God intended. He missed the point.

Global–Analytic

The difference between big picture implications and a specific application may be the best way to understand the global-analytic pairing. A GLOBAL-thinking teen will want to know what an idea can become and will deal with it in a broader context. A more ANALYTIC teen will want to think through specific implications logically and purposefully.

I have always found it humorous to make global thinkers and analytic thinkers work together on projects. The globals tend to want to make sure that the fun or interesting stuff gets done. Their attitude is "Hey, at least we got through it." The analytics are always asking clarifying questions to make sure they understand every little detail. Their attitude usually is "Let's make sure we're doing it absolutely correctly and not forgetting anything."

Teaching Implication: The globals need to be pushed to work on paying attention to details while the analytics need to be pushed to lighten up. Again, using their individual strengths in a teaching situation will help everyone learn more and think better.

Extroverted–Introverted

I know these terms are usually employed as personality descriptors, but they have implications for learning styles as well. If, for example, you rely heavily on discussion and student interaction when you teach, you have certainly noticed that the same few students always answer questions and are enthusiastic about discussion. These are your extreme EXTROVERTS. There are other students who usually pay pretty good attention and will answer questions occasionally. These are your borderline extroverts.

Then you'll have students who will rarely say anything. They just sit there while everyone else is having all the fun. Even when you call on them, they say little. These students are your extreme INTROVERTS. They are also okay—they do not need fixing, laying on of hands, or an extra quart of Mountain Dew.

I have found that most youth workers tend to be extroverts rather than introverts. We also tend to have a harder time dealing with and teaching introverts (note my caution above). We need to get over that.

Teaching Implication: Because introverts tend to be process thinkers, they often will have insights and questions extroverts don't. Be sure to ask the quiet kids for their thoughts once in a while, but give them time to process before you do. You may even want to ask the group to write down thoughts before your discussion, primarily to solicit input from your introverts. They are often among the brightest students. You should also sprinkle in some quiet time for reflection when you teach. Introverts often love this stuff, while extroverts hate it. Silence is threatening to extroverts (though they can't explain why), and it can be refreshing to introverts.

Concrete–Abstract

Sometimes we teachers get frustrated when students don't get a concept we are trying to convey. We explain as clearly as possible. We use clever analogies and illustrations. We even employ creative visual aids. Some students just never get it.

Some students never will get it—at least not anytime soon, because they think concretely and not abstractly. CONCRETE thinkers see the practical and tangible connections between ideas. They don't like to deal with the whys and hows.

Age, maturity, practice, or other factors will often lead people to become more abstract in their thinking. That is, they can understand the concepts behind ideas. Concrete thinkers need something tangible and real to help them learn. ABSTRACT thinkers enjoy operating in the realm of the intangible.

This is one of the things that makes teaching groups that include both 12-year-olds and 17-year-olds so difficult. Because of very real maturity differences, older teens tend to think more abstractly than younger ones. Creating lessons that touch the life situations and learning styles of students who are five to seven years apart in age is nearly impossible.

Teaching Implication: When your class includes a variety of concrete and abstract thinkers, make sure your lesson plans include methods that will touch each of them. You also have to consider the types of topics you teach. Make sure the topics, not just the methods, are appropriate.

Random–Sequential

Here's another one of the bi-polar pairings that can be like mixing oil and water when grouping students. Some students are RANDOM thinkers while others are more SEQUENTIAL. The difference is seen in how youth deal with a series of new information. Random thinkers can take an idea as it comes and glean from it no matter what it is—or isn't—related to. Sequential thinkers greatly prefer learning to be logical and orderly. They need to learn the history of Israel chronologically.

They need a step-by-step guide to discipleship. Disorganization is very distracting and problematic to them.

We often try to discourage random thinkers from learning randomly. It seems haphazard to sequentials. We also try to get sequentials to deal with disorder better. I am not sure this is a good idea. Instead, we should allow these students to thrive in environments that encourage both learning styles as much as possible.

Teaching Implication: The next time a student says, "This doesn't make any sense," think about how you are presenting the information. Maybe you are teaching randomly, and the student is a sequential. I observe this a lot in youth ministry. We think we're connecting ideas well, but that is very relative for a random thinker. This is a good way to utilize your volunteers. Hopefully at least one of them is a sequential. If not, go find an accountant or a chemist to sit in your class and give you feedback.

Intuitive–Reflective

Do you have students who raise their hands as soon as you've asked a question, even a difficult one? Those students who do (and actually have a good response!) are INTUITIVE thinkers. That is, they seem to process information quickly without taking a long time to reason it out. Those students who reach the same correct conclusion but take longer are more REFLECTIVE thinkers. They need to process and ponder for a longer period to settle on something.

There is not a difference in intelligence between these two groups. They just have different mental clocks as they deal with information. American society tends to put a higher value on intuitive thinkers, and that's unfortunate. It's a reflection of our microwave, headline news, instant-everything culture. We make kids think they need to come up with the right answer fast. Why? There's really no need for it.

Seemingly every year I have a student who becomes Mr. Reliable for getting good responses during discussion. While the rest of the group is floundering, trying to outtalk everyone else in an effort to come up with an answer, Mr. Reliable is sitting quietly, taking it all in. When I notice his facial expression change to one of resolve, I'll ask what he's come up with. Inevitably his comments are deep, insightful, and on the money. After a chorus of oohs and ahhs, it becomes clear that his peers are impressed. He's not slow, he's reflective.

Teaching Implication: Allow time on occasion to think. Don't be afraid to let silence become an important part of your teaching bag of tricks. Be on the lookout for those students whose brains are churning while everyone else's lips are flapping.

Competitive-Collaborative[54]

Scripture baseball, Bible quiz teams, attendance contests, and camp tournaments. Youth ministries tend to reward those who can memorize the most, show up every week, have the most friends, excel in athletics, and sell the most. What does any of that have to do with growing as a disciple of Christ?

We tend to act as though every young person is a COMPETITIVE learner and is motivated, or ought to be, by the thrill of whipping all comers at whatever the current contest is. A great many teens do like that, but a lot don't. Many are threatened by the thought of losing all the time. And make no mistake about it, whenever there is a competition of any type, one person or team wins, and everybody else loses.

I have known too many youth pastors whose ministry was centered on a series of contests. Kids who are naturally competitive love that kind of stuff. Most of the others go elsewhere or, worse, stop attending youth activities all together.

COLLABORATIVE learners want to work together with other students in a way that is fun and educational, but does not involve winning or losing. Competition is often very upsetting to collaboratives when it's done in a situation that is not naturally competitive (e.g., school, family, or church).

Without going into a long discussion of the pros and cons of competition, suffice it to say that a great many kids hate it when there are winners and losers. They thrive in environments where they can work together with a group toward a common goal without keeping score or awarding prizes.

Teaching Implication: Be aware of how often you have competitions of some type as part of your teaching. Instead of always getting into teams to see who can do an activity the fastest or best, have the whole class work as a team and see how each student can help everyone else. You should also help the collaborative types understand that contests can be helpful and do have a healthy place in a person's life.

Avoidant-Participative

By the time you've read this far, you may be thinking that some of these look similar. They do, but there are important nuances you need to understand. This pair considers how a person prefers to experience learning—alone or with others. This might seem the same as extrovert-introvert, for example, but it has its differences.

Teens who are AVOIDANT learners prefer to process information without the pressure of others. It's not that they want to be in a room by themselves, but they like to struggle with ideas in their head rather than through a group activity. A PAR-TICIPATIVE student would rather be part of a shared activity.

Avoidants can be extroverts, and participators can be introverts. I am very much an extrovert, but I tend to like to learn individually. Group activities are often distracting for me. I find myself interacting and not really learning what I should. I also know introverts who are participators. They like to be part of a group working on something, but they do it as a silent member typically. They learn by listening to and watching the rest of the group work.

Teaching Implication: Don't make kids participate in every activity. Often they have a very good cognitive reason, even if they can't articulate it. (I've never had a student say, "Can I just sit here and watch? I'm an avoidant learner.")

Dependent–Independent

This is another pair that seems like it could be lumped somewhere else but has its unique contribution to the understanding of learning styles. If you prefer some structure and the guidance of a teacher to learn, then you are a DEPENDENT learner. If you enjoy a casual environment where you can work at your own pace with little guidance, then you are an INDEPENDENT learner.

My science classes growing up were all set up as independent learning environments. We had a series of workbooks, stations with activities, and places to listen to taped lectures. Everyone was expected to work through a certain number of chapters to get specific grades. I zipped through as rapidly as possible, because I thrive in that type of environment (well, except for physics). Others worked much more deliberately. Still others hated that set-up and relied heavily on teacher assistance.

You might try to guess which students were most intelligent by how well they did in these science classes, but you'd be wrong a lot. The key in these classes seemed to be the teachers' understanding of different types of students. The best teachers knew which students needed help and which didn't.

Teaching Implication: Know your students well. You undoubtedly have teenagers who could benefit from some independent study. You have others who need more time with you to digest the same information. This is another important reason for having a strong team of great volunteers.

The 4MAT® System

Another system educational researchers use to understand learning preferences is known as the 4MAT® system.[55] This system identifies learning strengths by using a simple grid that is created by a pair of axes similar (but not identical) to those used in the bi-polar theories. By plotting scores on each of the axes, learning strengths are identified by plotting points on each of these axes.

The vertical axis plots scores on a continuum of concrete experience vs. abstract conceptualization. The horizontal axis uses a continuum of active experimentation vs. reflective observation. This creates four quadrants as listed here:

Concrete–Reflective = IMAGINATIVE LEARNERS
Abstract–Reflective = ANALYTIC LEARNERS
Abstract–Active = COMMON SENSE LEARNERS
Concrete–Active = DYNAMIC LEARNERS

The 4MAT® Model

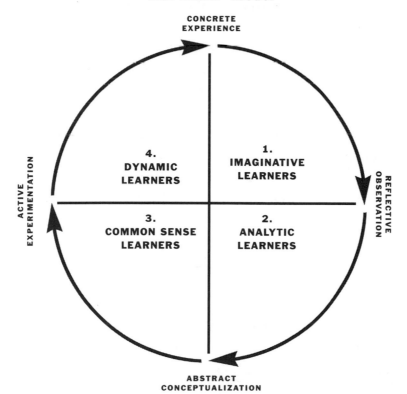

The IMAGINATIVE LEARNER (quadrant 1) tends to look for the meaning in the material and asks the question, "Why do I need to know this?" He's the youth who sits in the back with his arms crossed and wants you to convince him you won't waste his time.

I love food metaphors, and a good friend and mentor of mine created a very helpful one to better understand the differences between these quadrants.[56] According to him, when you go out to eat, the last one to make up his mind is probably the Imaginative Learner. He is trying to figure out what to choose long after everyone else has ordered. He's looking for a good reason to order something specific. The catch of the day or the lunch special rarely does it for him.

The ANALYTIC LEARNER (quadrant 2) needs to gather all pertinent information as she learns. "What do I need to know?" is her guiding question. She'll tire you out with background questions and seemingly useless information, but it's important to her.

"About that salmon, how is that cooked? Is it grilled over an open flame? Will it be cooked in olive oil? Is it extra virgin olive oil? Okay, I'll have the lasagna." Sound familiar? She's the analytic.

The third quadrant is the COMMON SENSE LEARNER. She is the no nonsense type who wants to cut right to the important part of the lesson. Get to the point and move on. No sense asking a lot of background questions. "How does this work in real life?" is what she wants to know.

When it comes to dining out, she knows what she'll order as soon as the restaurant is chosen. She might glance at the menu out of courtesy or to kill time, but not to choose what to eat. Experience is her greatest teacher, so there's no sense trying the new grilled shrimp when the eggplant parmesan has always tasted good before.

The DYNAMIC LEARNER of quadrant 4 is the creative, think-outside-the-box youth who wants to know, "What else can I do with this information?" For him, the basics are just not enough. He wants to go to another level, even if it doesn't make sense. He'll take the risk and evaluate how smart it was later.

He's the guy who eats all the nacho chips before it's time to order. He'll be looking around at the decorations or talking to someone and totally forget that he has to order at some point. When it's his turn, he'll just have what someone else is having or whatever the special is. Maybe he'll choose whatever is pictured on the front of the menu. It doesn't matter, because there's so much stuff to take in. Besides, it's all just food anyway.

Many who teach find this theory helpful for lesson-planning. The idea is that the opening activity should reach Quadrant 1 Imaginative learners, who ask why they should pay attention. The next part of the lesson should address the Quadrant 2 Analytics' question about what content they need to know. The application portion comes next, which fits the Quadrant 3 Common Sense learner. And the lesson ends with a focus on the Dynamic learner of Quadrant 4 and the challenge to actually do something with the lesson.

Teaching Implication: There's a lot to this theory—whole books have been written on it. To me the value is in how it pushes teachers to use a variety of teaching approaches during every lesson. There are many resources available to aid in creating lessons and curriculum for educators who are sold on this theory.

Multiple Intelligences

Nearly all of us have had the experience of sitting in a class and feeling absolutely clueless. Maybe for you it was history or math or English or P.E. or art. It seemed as though the whole world got it but you. "I guess I'm just stupid," you thought to yourself. Or worse, maybe someone you trusted said it to you.

Dr. Howard Gardner of Harvard University created a theory of learning called MULTIPLE INTELLIGENCES that might help you understand why you didn't do well in certain subjects.[57] His research indicated that every person has a natural aptitude in at least one of seven areas (an eighth area has since been added). Gardner believes that intelligence is shaped differently for each of us, and that we should strive to find the area of study that best suits our natural tendency.

These aptitudes are created through a complex mix of nature (the genetic codes we inherited from our parents) and nurture (the influence of the culture in which we are raised). This theory has been widely studied and embraced by all manner of experts in fields from cognitive psychology to education. I believe Gardner's work has many merits, especially when understood to be one helpful ingredient among others as we seek to know more about how adolescents learn.

On a practical level Gardner's theory reminds us that nobody is stupid. We all have certain areas that we naturally understand and gravitate toward. The following is a brief description of the eight intelligences identified by Gardner:

LINGUISTIC INTELLIGENCE. People who function well in the world of words have linguistic intelligence. They can think and communicate well using verbal or written language. The ability to use and understand complex messages is typical for linguistics. They may also have a natural ability to learn a foreign language more easily. Interests of people with this intelligence include writing, public speaking, translating, journalism, and broadcasting.

LOGICAL-MATHEMATICAL INTELLIGENCE. Those who are able to unravel complex mathematical problems or wrestle with difficult hypotheses may have logical-mathematical intelligence. They are sequential thinkers who thrive in problem-solving of all types. These folks tend to be scientists, accountants, engineers, and detectives.

SPATIAL INTELLIGENCE. Thinking three-dimensionally is the unique ability of individuals with spatial intelligence. These folk can think in images and visualize the internal and external components of an object. Sailing, sculpting, and architecture are some of the occupations that depend on spatial intelligence.

MUSICAL INTELLIGENCE. A natural understanding of rhythm, tone, pitch, melody, and other aspects of music are inherent to those with musical intelligence. The ability to play an instrument does not necessarily include or exclude someone from having this ability. Musicians, singers, conductors, and composers all have this intelligence.

"YOU MEAN I'M NOT STUPID AFTER ALL?"

After reading this chapter, one of my students wrote, "Made me feel less stupid to read this. Thanks." This is all too typical and shows how important it is for us to help adolescents learn how to learn. Again, impacting the whole person requires that we teach holistically. As we do that, more youth will be touched in the ways they learn best.

BODILY-KINESTHETIC INTELLIGENCE. The ability to expertly control all or part of your body is a strength of those with bodily-kinesthetic intelligence. From large movements to fine manipulations, people in this group often amaze the rest of us with their physical abilities. Athletes, surgeons, dancers, circus performers, and artisans typically have this intelligence.

INTERPERSONAL INTELLIGENCE. If friends and acquaintances say you are a people person, you might have strong interpersonal intelligence. This includes a natural ability to relate with and understand a variety of individuals, but it is not the same as extroversion. Extroverts love being around people, but they are not all good at relating to or understanding others. People who are great actors, teachers, and politicians typically have interpersonal intelligence.

INTRAPERSONAL INTELLIGENCE. Some people just seem to know themselves really well. They have an accurate picture of who they are, with all their strengths and weaknesses. These folks have high intrapersonal intelligence. It is hard to say what occupations or hobbies are most attractive to this group, but some researchers have suggested psychologists, theologians, and philosophers might typically be strong in this area.

NATURIST INTELLIGENCE. This is more than just enjoying the outdoors. People with naturist intelligence seem to have a natural ability to see groupings in plants, animals, or rocks, for example. They can discern nuances in nature, even distinct sounds, that most others cannot. Biologists, farmers, and rangers might be good occupations for naturists.

One of the difficulties with multiple intelligence theory is that it is so complex that teachers often do not know what to do with it. Some researchers have dedicated their careers to studying and understanding this theory. You will not totally grasp it in these few pages. But you might be able to see yourself in one or more of these. And you can probably think of others you know who fit into some of these intelligences.

This might also help you understand why you could ace biology and struggle through literature in school. People who are excellent in science are supposedly the smartest students, right? Not according to Gardner. It might be a relief to know that you're not stupid after all. Your main intelligence is just in a different area.

Teaching Implication: While it is not practical to try to figure out the different intelligence strengths of all the teens you work with, you should at least be aware of these eight areas. You may have a kid who really struggles in your Bible study because reading Scripture and discussing it are not very compatible with his intelligence strength. In that case, learning more about appropriate teaching strategies would help.

INFORMATION OVERLOAD

So which of these theories is best? Which should you buy into or adopt as your own? Probably none of them—and all of them. I find some of these theories more helpful or easier to grasp than others, but I find value in each of them. As you teach more and wrestle with these theories, you will notice that being aware of them does help you teach better, especially with adolescents who are very different from you.

Do not try to become an expert in all of the theories. That will not necessarily help you teach better. If you think about all the possible combinations of learning styles you could have in one student, there are 131,072 variations. Multiply that by the number of students in the group you're teaching. That's more than a little intimidating. Instead think more about how you teach and do some monitoring of how teens learn. Your powers of observation and your listening skills will be your best allies as you try to teach all of your students in ways they can best learn.

A good way to begin to pay more attention to this is to look back on the previous month's lessons that you taught. What types of activities did you do? How much did you lecture? How much creativity or variety did you use? How were the tactile, or the divergent, or the reflective, or the analytic learners challenged? These types of personal evaluation questions should help you be more aware and more holistic.

FOR DISCUSSION

Does the whole idea of learning styles (or learning preferences) make much sense to you? If so, how can teachers benefit from learning about them? What are the dangers?

What classes did you struggle with in school that you now realize may have been a learning-style issue, not one of general intelligence?

How might this chapter be helpful when you have a student with a learning disability in your group?

Now that you have learned something about learning styles, how do you think you should approach subjects that do not naturally fit with you?

ACTIVITIES

Using the list below of the learning theories discussed in this chapter, put a mark on each line between the terms where you believe you fit best. You do not need to mark on each line.

VISUAL

More ←--→ Less

AUDITORY

More ←--→ Less

KINESTHETIC

More ←--→ Less

TACTILE

More ←--→ Less

Convergent ←--→ Divergent

Assimilate ←--→ Accommodate

Global ←--→ Analytic

Extroverted ←--→ Introverted

Concrete ←--→ Abstract

Random ←--→ Sequential

Intuitive ←--→ Reflective

Competitive ←--→ Collaborative

Avoidant ←--→ Participative

Dependent ←--→ Independent

Now try the 4MAT® grid. Start by plotting a dot on each axis. Then draw a horizontal line and a vertical line to find where they meet. That intersection indicates which style is yours. The farther from the center your intersection is, the stronger that style may be for you.

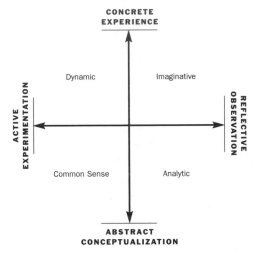

To determine which of the multiple intelligences you may have, go to an Internet site to find an inventory designed for this purpose.

As you look at the combination of learning styles that may illustrate your preferences, write a description of how you may learn best (and worst). What are the implications of this for you as a student? As a teacher of youth?

Search the Internet using "learning styles" as your search phrase. Look for different tests that you can use to determine learning styles for yourself or your youth.

Create your own chart or tool to help you understand the variety of learning-style theories. This will help you use your unique strengths and intelligences to grasp key concepts.

Design a one-hour workshop for ministry volunteers and parents to help them understand how knowing their teenagers' learning styles might help them better relate to their kids.

ENDNOTES, CHAPTER 4

51. LeFever, M. D. (1995). *Learning Styles: Reaching Everyone God Gave You to Teach.* Colorado Spring's: CO: David C. Cook Publishing Co., p. 6.

52. Engelkamp, J. (2001, Spring). *The American Journal of Psychology,* Urbana IL:, pp. 144-150.

53. Dunn, R., & Dunn, K. (1979). Learning styles/teaching styles: Should they...can they...be matched? *Educational Leadership,* 36, pp. 238-244.

54. This model, as well as the next two discussed, are taken from Grasha, A. (1996) *Teaching with Style.* Pittsburg, PA: Alliance Press.

55. Dr. Bernice McCarthy developed the 4MAT® system in her book *The 4MAT System: Teaching to Learning Styles with Right/Left Mode Techniques* (Excel, Inc., 1987). Marlene LeFever of Cook Communications was the first to modify 4MAT® to Christian education. (See note 51 above). Much of the material in this section was adapted from her work.

56. My thanks to Dr. Myron Williams, former Dean of Cincinnati Bible College, for letting me steal his creative analogy here.

57. Gardner, H. (1993). *Frames of Mind: The Theory of Multiple Intelligences* (10th Anniversary Edition). New York: Basic Books. To learn more about specific education strategies associated with Gardner's theory, I highly recommend *Teaching & Learning Through Multiple Intelligences,* by Campbell, Campbell, & Dickinson (1996). Needham Heights, MA: Allyn & Bacon.

CHAPTER 5

WHAT SHOULD YOU USE TO TEACH?

(Navigating the Curriculum Maze)

"These sessions aren't just hot. They're flexible. They're active enough for youth group meetings and retreats, biblical enough for Sunday school...In other words, you can use them any time you want to get kids talking about—and applying biblical principles to— their favorite subjects...And next time you have to talk about Sibbecai the Hushathite, they may even listen."

—FROM THE INTRODUCTION TO A POPULAR COMMERCIAL LESSON SERIES[59]

* * * * *

What are three of the most important lessons you have learned in your lifetime? Did you learn them in a formal class setting? Who planned to teach them to you? Were these lessons part of a CURRICULUM? The way you respond to these questions reflects your understanding of what curriculum is. The lessons you have learned and the way you perceived yourself as learning them shapes your understanding of curriculum.

CURRICULUM DEFINED

As we begin this discussion of curriculum, we need to focus on some foundational issues first. Task one is defining curriculum. Start by thinking about the following situations. Which are part of a curriculum and which are not?

- You stub your toe on a chair.
- You must take a part-time job to pay bills.
- You oversleep for a class, arrive ten minutes late, and are counted absent.
- You figure out that what you eat for lunch makes a difference in how awake

you are an hour later.

- You learn how to cheat in a class with an unfair professor.
- You become a good memorizer of facts to pass tests but do not really understand what you have memorized.
- You learn how to tell someone what they want to hear even if it's not the truth.

Again, your responses to those situations will depend on how you define curriculum. Many educators in both Christian and secular settings have suggested definitions. Among the most popular are these:[60]

Curriculum is…

…the content made available to students.[61]

…the planned and guided learning experiences of students.[62]

…the actual experiences of students.[63]

…generally, both the materials and the experiences of learning.

…specifically, the written courses for study used in education.[64]

…the organization of learning activities guided by the teacher with the intent of changing behavior.[65]

…the content made available to the students and their actual learning experiences guided by the teacher.

…anything purposeful and planned that affects what a person does.

…an educational plan.

…all of life's experiences, both planned and unplanned.

Each of these has its strengths and weaknesses. Rather than settling on one as the perfect definition, I suggest thinking about curriculum on different levels. Teaching and learning happens in a variety of settings, and our definition of curriculum should reflect that.

LEVEL 1: UNIVERSAL CURRICULUM

UNIVERSAL CURRICULUM involves lessons anyone can learn at any given time. It may be best described by the last definition from the list above, "All of life's experiences, both planned and unplanned." This level accounts for what you learn when you are out for a jog, on vacation, fixing supper, or doing any number of other activities as part of your daily life.

My guess is that, of the three most important lessons you listed above, at least two of them are from this level of curriculum. That is because most of what we learn does not neatly fit into a formal educational plan. Few of us take classes in learning how to speak, being tactful, sharing our toys, loving our neighbor, or forgiving transgressors, but these are lessons we learn from the proverbial School of Hard Knocks.

I loved to ride my bicycle when I was a kid. I grew up in a mobile-home community with lots of other kids who loved to ride as well. My bike was the coolest ever. It was an emerald green Huffy muscle bike with an extra wide Cheater Slick rear tire, flashy green banana seat, and a three-foot-high sissy bar. It was the fastest, meanest two-wheeler ever made. I was good enough on it to do wheelies and several other tricks. Once I was trying to learn how to do a wheelie on my front tire but just couldn't get it started the way I wanted. In the middle of the main street going into the mobile-home park was a sink hole that had been repaired. When the landlord had fixed the hole, he'd overfilled it with cement, so that it created a kind of speed bump.

I decide to ride up to the bump so that I would hit it with my front tire and use my front brakes and the edge of the cement patch to make the rear of the bike go up. My first attempt failed, so I thought I needed more speed. I started my second run, hit the front brakes just as I hit the edge of the bump, and promptly propelled myself, forehead first, onto the cement in front of me. I have never bled so much in my life. In the weeks it took me to heal, I decided that the combination of forward speed, quick-gripping front brakes, and a cement bump would not be part of my future plans again.

Lesson learned, but where did that curriculum come from? Who planned it? Who assessed my learning? Theological arguments aside, it was just something I learned from a stupid decision I made as a ten-year-old boy. This is Level 1, Universal Curriculum.

LEVEL 2: PROGRAM CURRICULUM

When you enrolled in high-school or college classes, you were following what I call PROGRAM CURRICULUM. This is the overall plan that moves learners from the beginning to the end of a specific aspect of education. In order to complete a college degree, students have to complete the core (sometimes called liberal arts) curriculum as well as specific classes for their major and minor. The set of classes required to achieve one's degree is Program Curriculum.

As a college professor, I meet with a lot of students for academic advising, usually at least twice a year, to discuss what classes they need in order to graduate. That Program Curriculum is created by groups of administrators and faculty who devise a methodical plan to educate students for each major. There are specific groups and sequences of courses designed to be developmentally appropriate and to move a student from learning basic knowledge to doing advanced problem-solving and critical thinking.

In the typical church setting, this could be a litany of topics to study and experiences to have before high-school graduation. Few youth ministries have thought about what they teach and why they teach it to the point of having a Program Curriculum as part of their plan. The section on creating a SCOPE AND SEQUENCE CHART, which appears later in this chapter, will help you learn more about why this is important and how to begin creating one.

Level 3: Lesson Curriculum

This is what most people think of when considering a definition of curriculum. Most of the definitions earlier in this chapter approach it at this level as well. LESSON CURRICULUM is the plan for how a teacher will present a lesson to students. It involves the specifics of content, METHODOLOGY, goals, assessment, and experiences that are part of formal learning.

Lesson Curriculum involves the exact ways a teacher plans to teach. This is what we think we will do whenever we step into a Sunday school class, youth group meeting, discipleship group, or Bible study. These lesson plans can be vague or detailed, written down or committed to memory, purchased from a commercial publisher or created from scratch.

Lesson Curriculum is not limited to each lesson, though. It is also the plan you make for a series of lessons. When you plan a four-week series on friendship, six lessons on tithing, or an indefinite series about the life of Christ, that is Lesson Curriculum as well. A series of Lesson Curricula with an intentional direction constitutes Program Curriculum. You cannot have an effective Program Curriculum without well thought out Lesson Curriculum.

While the idea of Universal Curriculum really is random and unplanned for the most part, both Program and Lesson Curriculum have specific and exact aspects. That leads to a variety of theories about the nature of curriculum and how it should be used.

CURRICULUM THEORIES

One of the most important factors to consider after you have a working definition of curriculum is to understand various ways that curriculum is designed. Educators from many disciplines have suggested ideas of what curriculum should do in different settings. The purpose, role, and interaction of material, teacher, student, and other factors in teaching combine to form an individual's ideology of curriculum, or CURRICULUR IDEOLOGY. This can be helpful to know because your ideology determines how you live, and your curricular ideology determines or describes how you believe you should teach. Table 5.1 shows what some of those ideologies are and the meanings they put into curriculum.

Table 5.1

CURRICULAR IDEOLOGIES[66]

	Preservation	Romantic	Humanistic	Transcendental
Priority	Passing on cultural ideals from one generation to the next	Allowing students to grow individually with a minimum of influence	Helping students learn in ways that are appropriate to their personal maturity	Meditate on a focal point for the purpose of becoming one with that object
Philosophy of Education	Mechanistic/ Controlling	Existential	Dialectic/ Developmental	Mystical/ Developmental
Epistemology	Objective	Subjective	Pragmatic	Mystical
Psychology	Behavioristic	Humanistic	Developmental	Mystical
Aims	Transmission	Growth	Maturity	Centering
Learning Domain	Cognitive	Affective	Application	Spiritual
Instruction	Presentation	Undefined	Guiding/Coaching	Co-traveling
Focus	Controlling	Liberating	Equipping	Transcending

While it is certainly possible to find educational researchers who discuss curricular ideologies in anywhere from three to twelve different categories, I believe that the four listed in this table represent a good way to begin to understand vital differences between them. They represent four divergent approaches to how people reflect their worldview through their use of curriculum. As I explain the aspects and implications of each one, try to recognize both the ideology you experienced at your home church and school, as well as the one you are using now.

The PRESERVATION ideology is dominated by the pressing need to pass on cultural ideals from one generation to the next. "Keep the culture alive!" could be its motto. In this philosophy of education, the teacher has absolute control over content, methodology, and outcomes. Those who operate with this mindset believe their biggest challenge is to make sure students come to think the same way they think. They tend to see teaching as a mechanical science in which, if they follow the right directions, students will turn out exactly as they desire.

This philosophy leads to a very objective EPISTEMOLOGY, because it focuses on passing on facts. Facts are easy to know and identify without having to deal with uncertainty and relativism. When students are taught the correct information, then they will behave the way the culture expects them to. Emotions are not a priority, because learning is cognitive. Facts should cause intellectual growth, regardless of how students feel.

Pedagogically, the predominant teaching method is lecture. This is the fastest, most efficient way for teachers to communicate information to students. Any other learning activity would be controlled by the teacher to make sure the students do not lead themselves astray. Any questions raised would be answered and resolved before the class is dismissed.

It is easy to look back on the history of the church and see that Preservation ideology has been predominant for most of the past 2,000 years. Memory, recitation, and replication were the preferred teaching strategies dating back to ancient Israel, Greece, and Rome. Today's Christian education still relies on this cultural transmission mode of education to a large degree. That has both positive and negative outcomes.

On the positive side, Scripture is full of information that is important to know, memorize, and pass on. The Christian faith is certainly a cultural lifestyle that we want to impart from generation to generation. And there is certainly much to be said for teachers maintaining strong command over their classrooms. It is not unusual to walk down a church hallway during Sunday school and notice that a number of teachers are spending more time on crowd control than on teaching.

The problems with this ideology should be self-evident in many ways. God in no way wants teachers to control the minds of their students. He does command us to teach, but that teaching is a two-way dialog that values more than just committing facts to memory. It means challenging students to use the information they learn to think critically, solve problems biblically, and incorporate their faith holistically.

We too often lose sight of the fact that our primary aim as Christian teachers is to make disciples of Jesus Christ, not to ensure the future of any one local church or denomination.

The ROMANTIC ideology stands in stark contrast to the Preservation ideology. The Romantic ideology simply allows students to grow individually with a minimum of influence from a teacher or guide. It sees education as EXISTENTIAL, meaning that learning happens because we exist and have experiences. To be alive is to learn, and to learn is to be alive.

THEY BLEND WELL

Very few people operate under only one of these ideologies all the time. Most teachers use a blend of all four, with some being more or less dominant depending on the subject, setting, and purpose of the teaching.

This paradigm believes educational goals and outcomes should focus on people rather than society. There is a desire for growth in a variety of ways, but such growth should not be forced by a teacher. It should come naturally, whenever each person decides he is ready.

Knowledge in this philosophy is mainly subjective and relative. Each student constructs meaning for herself in any given situation. While some facts may be necessary for aspects of growth, learning is deepest in the AFFECTIVE, or emotional, domain. Students should feel good about learning and should not be threatened by others who are learning faster or who may want them to learn differently.

Teachers are mainly encouragers who have no personal agenda, but who desire to help students become liberated from whatever is holding them back. There are no real lesson plans or organized learning activities. Instead there may be a series of learning stations that students are free to roam among whenever and in whatever order they desire.

I have seen schools and ministries operate under such a system. I once toured a Montessori elementary school that had adopted this system. The students basically just roamed around from room to room and station to station all day, doing a variety of activities, some alone and some with other students. Teachers were supervising, but would only interact to give words of encouragement or to respond to a question. As odd as it may have seemed, the school claimed their students went on to secondary schools and became top scholars.

Romantic influenced teaching does a good job of emphasizing personal growth and of minimizing inappropriate agendas some teachers may have. This ideology may also work well for teachers who may feel inadequate to truly teach. Curriculum dominated by student activities with a minimum of teacher involvement reflects this influence. There is a concern, though, about ceding teacher control and substituting a degree of pedagogical anarchy in its place. This concern has some legitimacy. Knowing that we teach because we have something to offer teens, we also need to remember that God has given us authority to teach. That means our role as a guide is important. Too much student choice or control is not good.

A third ideology, HUMANISTIC, seeks to help students learn in ways that are appropriate to their personal maturity. The word *humanistic* here does not refer to "secular humanism," that phrase from the depths of Hades that causes preachers to call down fire and brimstone, Christian mothers to pull their children in off the streets, and youth workers to pray a hedge of thorns around their teenagers. The terms *humanistic* and *humanism* simply mean there is an emphasis on the personal value of the individual. This means both the teacher and the student are valuable in the educational process. The teacher needs to be a skilled guide or coach who both knows subject matter very well and knows students very well. Pedagogy is dialogical, with teacher and learner each participating.

As the student matures in different ways, the observant teacher challenges her in ways that match her developmental stage and challenge her to continue to grow. This allows learning to be practical and useful. By having a PRAGMATIC view of education, learning becomes multifaceted. There is a reason to learn facts, because those facts have real-life application. When students understand this connection and see the impact of what happens in class on their lives, they are more motivated to learn. As teachers become more aware of this process, they tend to enjoy teaching more and put greater effort into preparation.

The reward for educators in this philosophy comes when they see the fruit of their coaching realized in mature students. Then teachers feel good about students being equipped to tackle life's situations because the students have both knowledge and the skills to apply it. Probably more than any other ideology, this one requires teachers to work hard at knowing human development, at preparing to teach well, and at considering the impact of their teaching outside the classroom.

While the advantages of this paradigm may be obvious, there are some cautions as well. Any time there is an emphasis on pragmatism, learning for the sake of learning can be sacrificed. There is information worth knowing simply because it's good information, even if it doesn't particularly motivate you or if you never do anything with it. For many, this is the case with history, for example. It is good to know about World War II, its causes, combatants, and results. However, there's little practical that most of us will ever be able to do with that knowledge.

There is also a tendency to confuse Humanistic ideology with Romantic. A key difference is the degree of intentional emphasis that humanistic ideology places on being developmentally focused. Some who claim to identify with this theory, which is also sometimes called Progressive, really have few goals for their teaching and have little idea of how their students are maturing.

The fourth of these philosophies is called TRANSCENDENTAL. Meditation is the most important aspect of this ideology. The primary goal is to become one with whatever the object of the meditation is. How this process occurs varies according to each person, his maturity, and what is being meditated on. This is at best a MYSTICAL practice with an undefined role of the teacher.

In popular movies and television shows, the teacher is often portrayed as a mentor. Yet the teacher in transcendentalism is really a co-traveler, a fellow pilgrim en route to an elusive destination. The teacher offers insights that may or may not help the learner, but simply reflect her own experiences and reality. Learning is ultimately spiritual, and knowledge or practical application is really unimportant. It is the process of shutting out all distractions, emptying the self, and focusing on the object that makes the difference.

The object of meditation may be just about anything. While Eastern religions, most notably Buddhism, come to mind when discussions turn to transcendentalism, today's focus on spiritual disciplines also has many characteristics of this philosophy. By meditating on God, by practicing silence, solitude, and service, and by seeking to empty the self on a human level, Christians are really practicing transcendentalism.

It is important not to dismiss this ideology simply because of its identification with mysticism and Eastern religions. There certainly is value in meditation as an educational tool. Time spent concentrating on the Lord can help Christians focus on him. In fact Psalm 145:5 says, "They will speak of the glorious splendor of your majesty, and I will meditate on your wonderful works." That at least indicates meditation is not foreign to biblical principles. I have noticed an attempt to recapture the biblical idea of meditation, and teens seem to identify with it. There is a danger in taking it too far, though. Some ministries appear to be guilty of that, for example, in worship that is focused on individual experience rather than corporate praise.

Regardless of which ideology suits your own ministry goals best, the reality is that you will use each of these at different times. The bigger challenge is to determine which curricular paradigm your ministry operates under now. Ask the following questions:

- What is the priority of your teaching?
- What is the nature of education?
- How do people learn?
- What is the most important outcome of teaching?
- What is the role of the teacher?

Your answers to these questions may represent your ideal, so you also need to look at the actual educational practices of your teaching ministry. Do those practices reflect what you want them to? If not, what needs to change? If so, how can you emphasize those strengths?

COMMUNICATED CURRICULUM

Regardless of which ideology you adopt, what you teach also is communicated with various levels of purposefulness. Everything you teach and don't teach sends messages to students, so it is important to be aware of some of the possibilities.

Everything that we plainly tell students, either orally or in writing, is known as EXPLICIT CURRICULUM. In college, professors hand out a syllabus for each class. These documents usually explain the course goals, rules, expectations, and assignments. In addition, the professor may give more detail or discuss things not found on the syllabus. All of this information is part of the professor's explicit curriculum. It is what he tells you that he expects you to learn or do.

In my syllabi, I express my attendance and punctuality expectations, for example. I do not allow students to be tardy (those who come in after I shut the classroom door are counted absent for the day), nor do I accept late papers. There are penalties for students who violate those policies. I always explain that I have these policies because I want to discourage young people going into ministry from developing bad habits. I am tired of hearing jokes about youth workers being late, running on their own clock without regard for others, and doing poor work. By having these standards in my youth ministry classes, I hope to instill in my students a professional and courteous work ethic that they will take with them to their ministries. These expectations, their penalties, and their rationale are all part of my explicit curriculum, because I share this information directly with my students.

Similar to explicit, but with a couple of key nuances, is OVERT CURRICULUM. Anything that is overt is obvious. Overt and explicit curriculum differ in that explicit curriculum is communicated openly, while overt curriculum may be obvious without being communicated. Every explicit curriculum is overt, but not every overt curriculum is explicit. A good example of this might be the purpose some churches have for teaching certain topics.

If you are a youth leader at a Southern Baptist congregation, then you will likely teach what it means to be Southern Baptist. Without using materials titled "How to be Southern Baptist," you could still make your goal obvious without ever stating it. Your students might say, "You sure want us to be good Southern Baptists, don't you?" without you ever saying to them, "I'm going to teach you to be a good Southern Baptist." The topics you teach, the questions you ask, the points you emphasize, and the applications you make all send messages. This is what it means to be overt without being explicit.

A third type of curriculum is IMPLICIT CURRICULUM. This is not the opposite of explicit curriculum but a complement to it. Implicit curriculum is what students learn from what you teach that you do not intend for them to learn. Throughout my ministry I have valued group discussions as a teaching method. I believe it can be a great way to get students to think deeply about a topic and share their thoughts and questions with their peers. I make this strategy overt and explicit in class by telling them why we discuss so much.

I have noticed that adolescents in my classes will begin to think more carefully about what they say, which is evidence of growth in their thinking and communication abilities. I have never claimed that one of my teaching goals in a specific class is to improve the students' communication skills, but it has happened a lot. They learn how to be clear, concise, and thoughtful during discussion. The fact that students get that from my classes is an aspect of implicit curriculum, because I do not plan for that to happen (at least I didn't used to).

Yet another consideration is called RECEIVED CURRICULUM and refers to what students actually take from a given setting. This involves what happens in the communication process when a student hears a message and filters it through her own set of experiences and biases. Received curriculum may be the most important consideration in this discussion, because what students actually learn is more important than what we teach, anyway.

Being aware of received curriculum helps you understand why a group of youth can read the same book, watch the same movie, or go to the same camp, but come away with very different interpretations and conclusions. In teaching, it may be impossible to anticipate the vast number of ways adolescents will receive your lessons, but trying to anticipate the factors that influence how they hear what you say will help you formulate your message more carefully.

While implicit curriculum is not the opposite of explicit, HIDDEN CURRICULUM is the opposite of overt. Another of my very popular tactics with my youth ministry students is that I always schedule the Foundations and Practices of Youth Ministry class at 8 a.m. on Monday, Wednesday, and Friday each fall semester. I do that because most college students have a bad habit of staying up way too late. By scheduling a very interactive class that requires mental acuity so early in the morning, most students discover they have to go to bed earlier the night before. That is an example of hidden curriculum. It is simply what you hope students learn without your ever telling them.

Often the idea of hidden curriculum is perceived to be negative, yet it is much more common in ministry settings than Christians like to admit. Everything from who gets appointed to committees to what the pastor preaches about can carry hidden messages. They do not all have to be negative, though. I like to use hidden curriculum in a variety of settings. I often find that what students learn through hidden curriculum is more powerful and permanent than if I had tried to teach the same lessons in class.

The final way curriculum is communicated is a bit more elusive and hard to determine. The NULL CURRICULUM is what students learn that is not taught and is not meant to be learned. Some examples should help. Think about the make-up of your youth ministry. What could a first-time visitor assume by simply looking at your group? If all of the young people are white, a visitor might conclude that no Hispanics are welcome. That is not something that you intend or want an adolescent to think, but it likely happens more than you know.

What you don't teach fits the null curriculum as well. If you never address the topic of finances, for example, kids might assume that money management and Christian faith have nothing to do with each other. A more common example might concern your teaching style. If you always lecture, then youth could learn that what they have to say or ask is not important. On the other hand, if you never lecture or explain a topic, then they may think you don't know much about the subject you teach. That is the danger of the null curriculum: Since you rarely stop to evaluate what you are not teaching or doing, you may not be fully aware of what students might be teaching themselves, and whether these lessons are correct or not.

Remember the list of scenarios from earlier in this chapter? I asked which were part of curriculum and which were not. Here's the list again:

- You stub your toe on a chair.
- You must take a part-time job to pay bills.
- You oversleep for a class, arrive ten minutes late, and are counted absent.
- You figure out that what you eat for lunch makes a difference in how awake you are an hour later.
- You learn how to cheat in a class with an unfair professor.
- You become a good memorizer of facts to pass tests but do not really understand what you have memorized.
- You learn how to tell someone what they want to hear even if it's not the truth.

Try to determine which might be explicit, overt, received, implicit, hidden, or null curriculum. Try to create your own situations for each.

COMMERCIAL CURRICULUM

One of the very few financially profitable aspects of youth ministry is the publishing and selling of COMMERCIAL CURRICULUM. Most youth workers are happy to browse a catalog or a Christian bookstore to find a series of lessons on some relevant topic. Fortunately, or so it may seem, these lessons come with ready-to-use activities. Most even tell you word-for-word what to say or ask.

For all the good that commercial curriculum has done for Christian education in the past generation or so, there are many issues involved that few people think about. It is easy to assume that if someone published it, it must be good (or safe, or theologically sound, etc.) As in all other aspects of life, you need to know what the purpose of printed curriculum is, how to tell the good from the bad, and how to use what you purchase.

In the early 1980s there was a remarkable boom in sales of Christian curriculum for youth ministry. Both denominational and independent publishers tried to jump on this moneymaking bandwagon. As publishers became more and more market savvy, the desire for sales and profit too often led to a compromise in sound educational philosophy. This resulted in the dumbing down of curriculum.

What happened is that as churches began to grow rapidly, they needed more volunteers to teach. Rather than take the time to help these new teachers learn about teaching, churches looked for easy-to-use materials with ready-made lessons. The promise of quick preparation and "If you can read, you can lead" lesson design became a cash cow for publishers, especially if the material was packaged in a slick and flashy cover. It looked attractive, told the teacher what to say and do and when to do it, used the Bible, and referred to Jesus enough, so it sold very well.

The result was a decade or more of poor teaching by underprepared teachers relying on canned lessons written by authors who didn't know their students and published by companies who were too focused on the bottom line. There was (and is) plenty of blame to go around. In the 1990s publishers began working harder at producing creative materials that helped the teacher understand the teaching-learning process, the subject matter, the students, and how to best use the curriculum. Unfortunately, too many teachers skip all that helpful introductory information and go right to the first page of the first lesson (sometimes as they drive to church to teach it!)

To their credit, most publishers strive to produce curriculum that not only will sell well, but that will help teachers teach better. While many are still pushing the quick-prep selling point, the best publishers explain how they expect teachers to use their lessons. Here are a few excerpts from recent material:

- "These [lessons] are user-friendly and very flexible. They can be used in a youth group meeting, a Sunday school class, or a Bible study group. You can adapt them to either large or small groups. And, they can be covered in only 20 minutes as well as more intensively in two hours." (This is followed by more than a dozen tips and ideas for teachers to think through before they begin to teach.)[67]

- "Each of these sections contains more than one option for you to use, depending on your needs and the needs of your students…Typically, one idea is more active than the other. Feel free to select the [option] that's most appropriate for your group."[68]

- "These sessions are guidelines for you—ideas, suggestions, and possibilities…Of course, you can manage this best when you plan and prepare in advance."[69]

- "You don't have to complete the entire meeting each week…Do what parts fit you and your group…Don't tie yourself to the curriculum."[70]

- "You can adjust the speed to fit your group. To cover more…just pick the points you want to emphasize and drop the activities…you don't need."[71]

This sampling indicates that publishers and authors are aware that teachers need more information on how to use what they provide. My conversations with some people involved in creating youth ministry curriculum have often turned to this issue. Here are a few important items that curriculum writers and publishers want teachers to keep in mind about published curriculum:

- Publishers intend for teachers to adapt the material for their own classes, not to teach it word-for-word as printed.

- The ideas, activities, and questions are helpful guidelines, not mandatory requirements.

- There is no "Curriculum Police" secretly checking to make sure you use materials correctly.

- The authors and publishers do not know you, your students, or the culture and context in which you minister.

- Teaching students is more important than covering all the material in a given lesson.
- It is okay, even preferable, to use a few different published curricula and create your own lesson from the best ideas of each.
- Glancing through the lesson once just before class begins is inadequate preparation.

Even when you understand what printed curriculum is and how publishers intend for teachers to use it, there is still the matter of determining which material is good and which is not.

CHOOSING CURRICULUM

Anyone who has ever spent time browsing catalogs, Christian bookstores, or online vendors to find the right curriculum understands that deciding which is best can be a real challenge. In reality, you are probably better off gathering a few different resources and creating your own lesson (more on that in chapter 6). However, if you need to use only one source, you should know how to evaluate your options.

Each youth worker and each ministry is different, so one size definitely does not fit all as far as curriculum is concerned. Here are a few helpful questions to consider, though. You can decide how to weigh each one for your individual situation:

How Bible-based is the material? I am amazed by how much curriculum claims to be Bible-based, but really only uses one Scripture to support an idea, and then it's only used briefly in the lessons. If this is important to you, skim over several lessons and get a feel for how the publisher uses Scripture. Look for supporting passages and if they are used in context. Notice how Scripture is woven throughout the lesson. This is more than simply asking, "How much Scripture is used?" It's also, "In what way is Scripture used?"

How Christ-centered is the material? If you feel strongly that you need to help students understand the centrality of Christ in the faith and in their lives, then using Christ-centered curriculum should be important to you. Even when studying a passage from the Old Testament, lessons should help students understand how that Scripture anticipates Christ in some way. When teaching on hot topics, Jesus should always be central to helping students learn how to think about them.

How good are the teacher's materials? Publishers vary greatly on the type and quality of teacher helps they include with curriculum. Sometimes there is a separate teacher's guide with the material. Others have a few pages at the beginning of the book devoted to teachers. Some curriculum has nothing at all to help teachers. You might look for the following:

- A section explaining how to use the material.
- An explanation of the topic and why it might be important to your students.
- Clear lesson goals that help you know where each lesson is headed and what outcomes to expect.
- A variety of teaching options for each part of the lesson so you are not stuck with ideas that don't fit your group.
- Lessons that are adaptable to a variety of contexts so that you have flexibility.
- Well-organized materials so that the lesson flows smoothly and teachers do not have to guess how an activity fits in with the rest of the lesson.
- A variety of methods used to hold student attention, not just for each lesson, but from week to week as well.
- Attractive presentations (though this should not be the most important factor).
- Effective use of visual aids such as video, music, skits, posters, and so on, to enhance learning.
- Creative teaching ideas rather than the same old recycled lessons over and over.
- A balance between ease of use and the need to prepare well.

How good are the student materials? The impressions students get of the material teachers give them go a long way toward determining their impression of whether the curriculum is worthy of their attention or not. With that in mind, here are some items to look for:

- Attractiveness to the age group. The design and graphics need to be contemporary and appropriate so kids give it a chance. I have seen groups laugh at good curriculum in the first lesson because they thought it looked stupid.
- A variety of activities that teens will enjoy and learn from.

- Memory verses for those who value that aspect of a lesson.
- Challenging lessons to promote growth and thinking skills. Lessons that are too hard or too simple are killers to youth.
- Lesson goals that promote Christian values rather than simply giving information.
- Life applications that are real and practical to adolescents.
- Contemporary activities and questions, in addition to a current visual presentation. (My students suggested I warn against the "cheesiness" factor.)
- An emphasis on encouraging Christian growth. This may seem like a given, but a lot of curriculum has other aims.
- Age-appropriate activities that make learning fun and personal.
- A good balance of information and application that leads students through a pattern of learning something new and applying it to their lives.
- Fun. No matter what else is true about the curriculum, if it is dull, students won't learn. Like it or not, it's true.

What is the theological bent? If you need material that teaches denomination-al dogma, then you should take that into consideration. Others want lessons that are more generic theologically or that teach a variety of opinions.

What is your overall impression? Even if you are a "detail person" who enjoys analyzing every aspect of curriculum, you still need to gain a general idea of how good it is overall. This is important for you to have confidence in the cur riculum.

Below I have included an evaluation sheet I created several years ago. I have used it in my own ministry to evaluate curriculum, as well as with my volunteer teams and college students. It can be valuable in helping people consider the variety of factors that affect the quality of curriculum. It can also help overcome objections to changing curriculum when there is a fairly objective and detailed tool to use in evaluating the materials. Hopefully you will see some parts of it that you can combine with your own ideas to create a tool that is uniquely helpful to you in your ministry.

CURRICULUM EVALUATION SHEET

Publisher _____   Topic _____

Rate each item on a scale of 1 to 7. "N/A" means it does not apply

Category	Rating							
	Horrible					Perfect		
A) Is it Bible-based?	1	2	3	4	5	6	7	N/A
B) Is it Christ-centered?	1	2	3	4	5	6	7	N/A
C) Teacher's Materials								
1) Explanation of topic	1	2	3	4	5	6	7	N/A
2) Clear lesson goals	1	2	3	4	5	6	7	N/A
3) Gives teaching options	1	2	3	4	5	6	7	N/A
4) Adapts to a variety of contexts	1	2	3	4	5	6	7	N/A
5) Well-organized	1	2	3	4	5	6	7	N/A
6) Uses a variety of methods	1	2	3	4	5	6	7	N/A
7) Attractive	1	2	3	4	5	6	7	N/A
8) Uses visual aids	1	2	3	4	5	6	7	N/A
9) Creativity in teaching ideas	1	2	3	4	5	6	7	N/A
10) Ease of use	1	2	3	4	5	6	7	N/A
D) Student Materials								
1) Attractive to the age group	1	2	3	4	5	6	7	N/A
2) Variety of activities	1	2	3	4	5	6	7	N/A
3) Memory verse	1	2	3	4	5	6	7	N/A
4) Challenging	1	2	3	4	5	6	7	N/A
5) Promotes Christian values	1	2	3	4	5	6	7	N/A
6) Life application	1	2	3	4	5	6	7	N/A
7) Contemporary	1	2	3	4	5	6	7	N/A
8) Encourages Christian growth	1	2	3	4	5	6	7	N/A
9) Age-appropriate activities	1	2	3	4	5	6	7	N/A
10) Balance of content and experience	1	2	3	4	5	6	7	N/A
11) Fun	1	2	3	4	5	6	7	N/A
E) Theological Bent	1	2	3	4	5	6	7	N/A
F) Overall Impression	1	2	3	4	5	6	7	N/A

SCOPE AND SEQUENCE

Another important aspect to consider in the evaluation process is how well the material helps you plan for the future. I encourage the use of a SCOPE AND SEQUENCE CHART to do that. A Scope and Sequence Chart is a visual aid that lists the age groups and subjects youth will study over a certain period of time. These charts typically cover from one to three years, but can go farther into the future than that.

The key advantages of a Scope and Sequence Chart are manifold:

· It helps you to be intentional about what you teach each age group from week to week and month to month.

· It keeps you from teaching randomly each week.

· It forces you to think holistically and developmentally so that you are moving your students to intentional maturity in Christ.

· It keeps you from needlessly repeating your favorite five topics over and over again.

· It really impresses parents and others who evaluate your ministry.

Most publishers use a Scope and Sequence Chart to help them plan for the future. Some make these available, so that those who use the curriculum can know what is forthcoming. If you visit the Web site of Cook Communications (www.cookcommunications.com) and go to the David C. Cook page, you will find a link to their chart.[72] It shows, at a glance, the age groups they publish for (toddler through adult) and what topics they will address each quarter for three years.

Cook uses what is known as a unified curriculum structure. That means they have the same basic lesson or Scripture for each age group on any given Sunday. Each age level has a focus and activities that are developmentally appropriate based on that topic or passage. One advantage of this approach is, ideally, that the family can talk about the same basic idea after Sunday school. This is a wonderful aid that helps churches plan their teaching ministries much better. Cook is not alone in using this philosophy, or in making their chart public, so check the Web site or ask a sales rep from the publisher you use to see if they have a Scope and Sequence Chart you can review.

Rather than relying on some commercial publisher to set your teaching agenda for you, though, you should try to create your own Scope and Sequence Chart for your ministry. On one axis put the age groups of your classes and the teaching settings, and on the other axis plot a timeline that reflects how far ahead you want to plan. Here's an example of what it might look like:

Table 5.2

	Winter 05	Spring 05	Summer 05	Fall 05	Winter 06	Spring 06
6th-8th Grade Sunday School	What is the Bible?	Life of Christ	Acts	Romans	1 & 2 Corinthians	Gal., Eph., & Phil.
6th-8th Midweek Study	Being part of worship	New beginnings	Friendship	Raising great parents	The future	Heaven
9th&10th Sunday	Pentateuch Part A	Pentateuch Part B	Joshua	Judges	Ruth	1 & 2 Kings
9th&10th Midweek	Stewardship	Growing in Christ	Materialism	Prayer	What is sin?	Christian history
11th&12th Sunday	Isaiah	Jeremiah	Lament.	Ezekiel	Daniel	Hosea & Joel
11th&12th Midweek	Service	Leadership	World affairs	Who am I becoming?	A Christian mind	Life after high school

SAMPLE SCOPE AND SEQUENCE CHART

You can see how a simple chart like this could be helpful in planning. The amount of detail you include should fit your needs and your ministry. I suggest planning like this with a group of volunteers, parents, and youth to get a variety of input and ideas.

You probably recognize a potential danger in using such a planning tool. You should never let what you've planned out become more important to you than the occasional need to be flexible. Sometimes you'll need to tweak or abandon even the best of plans due to unforeseen circumstances. When that happens, make the necessary revisions and move on. Planning is still vital, even when aspects of your plan do not end up as you expected.

While there is certainly a lot to consider in the curriculum puzzle, it's well worth the effort. What you teach and how you teach it sends a message. Understanding that should help you want to be more intentional. I am afraid most youth workers go their entire careers without planning more than a month in advance.

Summer 06	Fall 06	Winter 07	Spring 07	Summer 07	Fall 07
Col., Philemon, I & 2 Thess.	Pastoral Epistles	Hebrews	James & I & 2 Peter	John's Epistles & Jude	Revelation
Guys & girls	The media	Who is God?	Self image	Adolescence	Substance abuse
I & 2 Chronicles	Ezra & Nehemiah	Esther & Job	Psalms	Proverbs	Eccles. & Songs
Choices	Body image	Who is Jesus?	Emotions	Dating	Reaching out
Amos & Obadiah	Jonah & Micah	Nahum & Habakkuk	Zeph. & Haggai	Zech. & Malachi	Between the Testaments
What is the church?	Values	Sexuality	The world	Cults	The future

Now that you have a cursory introduction to what curriculum is and how to use it, the next chapter will discuss how to put together specific lesson plans.

FOR DISCUSSION

What might a ministry look like if Universal, Program, and Lesson Curriculum were planned out more intentionally?

Which of the four ideologies do you identify with the most and why?

What aspects of curriculum are most important for you to evaluate? What other criteria do you use?

What are some advantages in creating a Scope and Sequence Chart in your ministry? Do you think that is realistic?

ACTIVITIES

Write down some of the most important lessons you have learned in life. Now write down three specific lessons you learned in Sunday school as a teenager. How similar are the two lists? Why?

Evaluate the four ideologies in light of biblical evidence. Which seems most scriptural?

Ask a group of youth you teach to list ten things they learned over the past year by having you as a teacher. Tell them not to limit themselves to specific class lessons. Try to classify the list they create as explicit, overt, implicit, hidden, and null curriculum. What conclusions can you draw?

Gather some printed curriculum from three or four different publishers. Using the evaluation sheet on page 112 (or one you create on your own), find the strengths and weaknesses of each.

Create an ideal Scope and Sequence Chart for your ministry. How would you implement such a plan?

ENDNOTES, CHAPTER 5

59. Duckworth, J. (Ed.), (1989). *Hot Topics Youth Electives: School, Male & Female, Doubts.* Elgin, IL: David C. Cook Publishing Co., p. 5.

60. Most of these definitions, and some of the foundation for ideas in the rest of this chapter, are from Curriculum Design for Disciple-Making, a class I took in 1992 at Huntington College Graduate School of Christian Ministry with Dr. Dave Rahn. The first five are also listed in Pazmino, R. (1997). *Foundational Issues in Christian Education: An Introduction in Evangelical Perspective.* Grand Rapids, MI: Baker, pp. 223-224.

61. Huebner, D. F. (1982, July-August). From theory to practice: Curriculum, *Religious Education,* 77, p. 363.

62. Dewey, J. (1944). *Experience and Education.* New York: Macmillan, p. 16.

63. Miel, A. (1946). *Changing the Curriculum: A Social Process.* New York: Appleton-Century-Crofts, p. 9.

64. Cully, I. (1983). *Planning and Selecting Curriculum for Christian Education.* Valley Forge, PA: Judson, pp. 11-12.

65. LeBar, L. E. (1964). Curriculum in Hakes, J.E. (Ed.) *An Introduction to Evangelical Christian Education.* Chicago: Moody Press, p. 89.

66. The original source for this table came from my class with Dave Rahn at Huntington. He first was exposed to it in a curriculum development class in 1980 with Dr. Craig Hogan at Wheaton Graduate School.

67. Lynn, D. (2001). *Junior High – Middle School Talksheets.* Grand Rapids, MI: Zondervan Publishing House, p. 5.

68. Warden, M. (1999). *What's Your Point?* Cincinnati, OH: Standard Publishing, p. 8.

69. Jessup, D., Musick, H., & Kirgiss, C. (2002). *Guys.* Grand Rapids, MI: Zondervan Publishing House, p 12.

70. Bartlett, D. & Muir, B. (2000). *Talking the Walk.* Grand Rapids, MI: Zondervan Publishing House, p. 13.

71. *Quick Studies* series (1992). Elgin, IL: David C. Cook, p.6.

72. Retrieved August 22, 2002, from http://www.cookministries.com/curriculum/davidccook

CHAPTER 6

HOW CAN YOU PREPARE TO TEACH?

(A Step-by-Step Guide to Writing Lesson Plans)

"As I see it, there are two ways to prepare a lesson. Quite frankly, the way I learned to prepare is not the best way. A teacher can crank out a lesson as a matter of discipline (as I was taught), or a lesson can bubble forth from a life that is happily meditating on the truth of God. Preparation at its best does a little of each."

—JOSH HUNT[73]

* * * * *

Sure, we may laugh about it, but should we? You likely know some teacher who often prepares his lesson just a few minutes before class begins. Worse yet are those who do not even take a few minutes to look at the curriculum before class starts, trusting it to tell them exactly what to do. Occasionally teachers may have positive results with a lesson that was quickly thrown together. Unfortunately that just reinforces the erroneous and dangerous belief that they can do that most of the time and be great teachers.

The fact is this: Teaching effectively takes time and preparation. I often hear youth workers object to that notion by saying they prefer to let the Holy Spirit guide them. Others claim they do their best teaching under the pressure of time, so preparing ahead would cause them to be worse teachers. Those are both really excuses to be lazy.

I'd suggest that advance preparation actually enhances the work of the Holy Spirit in teaching. By following the suggestions in this chapter, the Spirit will have several opportunities over a few days to counsel you about your students, the subject matter, and how to teach. Keeping in mind that God already knows what will happen when you teach may help you realize that working on your lesson three days ahead of time can in no way hinder the Spirit's work.

There is a caveat to that, though. Some of us may tend to overprepare or rely on our human ability too much. Both extremes are inappropriate. Hopefully these ideas will help you strike a good balance.

A Step-by-Step Guide

The subtitle of this chapter promises a step-by-step guide to planning a lesson. I'll give you the steps right up front, in case you are a global, big-picture thinker. The rest of the chapter puts flesh on this outline.

How to Write a Lesson

1. Pray.
2. Know your students.
3. Know the subject you are to teach.
4. Write cognitive, affective, and action aims for the unit you are teaching.
5. Determine a sequence for the lessons.
6. Write one aim for each lesson.
7. Make sure the lesson aims support the unit aims.
8. Write your lesson plans:
   A. Gather your resources to learn about the subject.
   B. Determine the form your lesson will take.
   C. Write out the details for each activity.
   D. Read back through your lesson to see if it accomplishes your lesson aim.
   E. Let it sit for a day or so.
   F. Read back through it the day before you teach to make changes and improvements.
   G. Ask yourself, "If I am a student in this class, do I enjoy and learn something from this lesson?"
9. Pray.
10. Teach the lesson.

The Details

1. Pray

The most important aspect of the beginning, middle, and end of the teaching process is prayer. Pray for the students (individually and by name is great!) Pray that they would open to the Spirit's leading in their lives. Pray for yourself as you prepare. Pray for your sensitivity to the Spirit's guidance. Pray that what you plan will make an impact.

2. Know Your Students

I have heard many people ask the question "Do we teach a subject or do we teach students?" The academically correct answer is that we are supposed to teach both. In a sense, that seems the appropriate view for many reasons. Teachers must have a mastery of subject content and know how to communicate it effectively to students.

But what has always bothered me about that is that, without students, there is no one to learn. Whenever a group of adolescents gathers together, some of them are learning something, even if no one is purposefully teaching. The lessons may be poorly developed, and the conclusions could be totally wrong—but it is still learning. So as I see it, we can teach if there are students but no subject, but it is impossible to teach any subject without students to learn it.

That is why there are two chapters at the beginning of this book dedicated to knowing teenagers. Teaching must start with the students, their personalities, their needs, and their contexts before anything else.

THAT'S NICE IDEALLY, BUT...
What should you do when you're asked to teach on very short notice? I recommend having a few ready-to-go lessons tucked away in a file somewhere. Having a meaty, well-prepared lesson will help you compensate for the lack of time to custom tailor a lesson for the group you are teaching.

3. Know the Subject You Are to Teach

In youth ministry it is easy to love hanging out with kids and hate preparing to teach them. I don't think we object so much to the actual writing down of a plan as to taking the time necessary to learn a subject well enough to teach it to them.

Most of us are in youth ministry because we love teenagers. We love talking with them, playing with them, going to concerts with them, or just being with them.

Sitting at a desk reading books and taking notes to get ready to teach just doesn't fit in with that whole relational ministry thing very well. That's one of the reasons commercial lessons are so popular; all the information is already there, so you don't have to study very much.

The problem is that teens ask a lot of questions those curriculum guides don't address. Then what do you do? It is tempting to make up answers, since few students will know the difference. You could say you'll find out and get back to them, but you usually don't. You could even pass the buck by challenging them to research the answer for themselves and report to the class next week. But your youth are looking to you to know more than they do.

You don't have to pretend to know everything because that sends a negative message as well. You *do* need to study enough to be able to give thoughtful responses to your students. They deserve at least that much from you. That means having access to Bibles, commentaries, dictionaries, and other Bible reference materials as you prepare. You should also use the books and notes from whatever Bible or theology courses you've had.

4. Write Cognitive, Affective, and Action Aims for the Unit You are Teaching

Once you have a solid understanding of who you are teaching and the subject you will teach, then you need to map out plans for the series of lessons on that subject. Planning the topics and AIMS for each lesson in a series before you start the series is helpful in many ways.

- You can know the direction the series will take before you start. This helps you think about the specific topics or aspects of a topic you want to teach.
- If you create a Scope and Sequence Chart as discussed in the previous chapter, you can get a big picture of a year or more's worth of lessons. When you break that down into smaller series or units, then you can see the big picture for a specific set of lessons.
- If you want to do a series on the Psalms, for example, you can determine if you want to cover them chronologically, by the type of psalm, by author, by the way they are used in Scripture, or any number of other ways. When you decide, you can write the sequence out and see what each lesson should address.

After you know what subject you will teach, you should decide what you hope students will learn from it. Notice that I did not suggest that you should decide what you hope to teach. Such an approach is teacher-centered. It looks at teaching from the leader's standpoint and expects students to learn from what the teacher will do. If you place emphasis instead on what students should learn, you are focused on the teens as students. What you do as a teacher is determined by who the learners are and what they should learn.

To illustrate the difference, look at these two aims:

A) I will teach the students how to understand the Psalms.

B) Students will learn how to understand the Psalms.

Does the difference seem subtle? At first it is. Aim A declares what the teacher will do. Aim B expresses the desired result in the students. As a teacher, what is more important—what you intend to teach, or what the students actually learn? With well-written aims as a guide, your initial focus will make all the difference as you continue planning and concentrate on what the students will learn.

In order to write good aims, I believe it is helpful to consider the work of researcher Benjamin Bloom. He suggests a specific way of thinking about how people learn. BLOOM'S TAXONOMY divides the way people learn into three domains.[74]

One is the COGNITIVE domain which emphasizes intellectual or mental outcomes. This can include skills and abilities such as comprehending information, organizing ideas, analyzing and synthesizing data, applying knowledge, choosing among alternatives in problem-solving, and evaluating ideas or actions.

The second domain is called AFFECTIVE, which has to do with emotions, attitudes, appreciations, and values. This domain is demonstrated by behaviors indicating attitudes of awareness, interest, attention, concern, and responsibility, plus the ability to listen and respond in interactions with others.

Bloom's third domain is PSYCHOMOTOR learning, which has to do with physical skills including coordination, dexterity, manipulation, grace, strength, and speed. This domain shows that students can do something with what they have learned.

In aims written by educators, these three domains are often expressed as *know*, *feel*, and *do*. There is a logical sequence to these domains. True learning must involve change in all of these areas to be holistic and effective.

Think about a child learning to play piano. Before she begins lessons, she knows very little about a piano. As she progresses, she learns about the notes and how they relate to one another. Soon she can play "Mary Had a Little Lamb." But how did this happen? First, she gained some important knowledge about how the keys and notes work together. Second, she felt motivated to find a way for these notes to sound good together. Third, she demonstrated the ability to put the right notes in the correct order to play a song she recognized. That is learning.

Know, feel, do. This is how we change. The problem is that most teachers tend to plan for the knowledge domain and maybe skip to the action domain without considering the affective aspect of the learner at all. Simply having the knowledge will not motivate someone to real change.

Have you ever known someone with amazing natural ability who did little to develop it? People often say, "Oh, what a waste!" about such a talent and wonder why he never worked harder. The answer is simple, really. It's because he was never motivated; he never felt the desire.

This is especially true when it comes to teaching Christianity. There are many thousands of people who attend church and Bible studies whose lives are affected very little by their attendance. They have gained a lot of factual information. The cognitive learning has been very successful, but the affective domain is largely untouched—which results either in little actual life change or in disingenuous lives. That is why teachers must plan to reach the affective along with the cognitive and the psychomotor. Teaching that makes a difference has to change all three domains.

All that brings us back to writing those unit aims. In order to be student-centered and to include all three domains, I suggest you write goals specifically

VERBS TO USE FOR AIMS

Here are a few ideas of verbs to use as you write aims. Hopefully they will tweak your creative juices as you learn how to create good aims.

"KNOW" VERBS:

arrange, define, duplicate, label, list, memorize, name, order, recognize, relate, recall, repeat, state, classify, describe, explain, express, identify, indicate, locate, recognize, report, review, select, translate

"FEEL" VERBS:

accept, challenge, defend, dispute, judge, question, share, support, have confidence, be convicted, wonder

"DO" VERBS:

apply, choose, demonstrate, employ, illustrate, interpret, practice, schedule, solve, use, write, analyze, appraise, categorize, compare, contrast, criticize, distinguish, examine, experiment, question, test, arrange, assemble, compose, construct, create, design, develop, formulate, manage, organize, plan, prepare, propose, write worded. Something like "As a result of this unit, the students will…" would work. Write aims that begin with those words for each domain discussed above. To go back to the idea of teaching from the Psalms, a set of aims might look like this:

As a result of this unit, the students will…

> …recognize the different types of psalms.
> …know the way psalms were used in ancient Israel.
> …have confidence that Psalms is an important part of the Bible.
> …be convinced that Psalms should be a regular part of their Bible reading.
> …create a list of the worship psalms.
> …read through the Psalms in the next three months.

Notice that the first two aims are cognitive, the next two are affective, and the last two are action. This helps give some definition to what you hope to accomplish. Everything else you do should be measured against these aims.

You will want to write your aims in ways that make them most beneficial to your planning. Well written aims are specific, measurable, attainable, and challenging.

Writing an aim that is specific means that it has enough information to actually be helpful. Staying with our subject of Psalms, consider these two aims:

A) As a result of these lessons, students will feel closer to God.

B) As a result of these lessons, students will have confidence that Psalms is an important part of the Bible.

They are both affective, but the first one is too vague to be helpful. The second one indicates a specific emotion about a specific aspect of learning.

Measurable aims are those that can actually be evaluated fairly easily. When I have worked with students on this process in the past, writing measurable aims turns out to be more difficult than people think. Part of the reason may be because we tend to think in grandiose ideals. As an example, look at these two aims:

A) As a result of these lessons, students will understand Psalms.

B) As a result of these lessons, students will recognize the different types of psalms.

The second one is more measurable because there is a specific action involved that is observable. Most people I have worked with tend to write an aim like the first one, though. They rationalize it by saying that they really do want students to understand everything. After some discussion about developmental realities and teaching in digestible chunks, most eventually realize that the second aim would actually help them teach better.

For an aim to be attainable, it should be within the reasonable ability of the students to accomplish within the time the series will be taught. Look again at the two aims just above. Is it reasonable to expect a group of junior high students to understand the Psalms at the end of a six-week series? I know scholars who have dedicated a lifetime of study to the Psalms and still don't understand aspects of them. Most early adolescents will be able to at least begin to explain some of the differences in the types of psalms they read.

A difficult balance exists between making aims attainable and making them challenging. This is yet another reason for a teacher to know her students well. If you make your aims too easy to reach, then your lessons become boring. If they are too difficult, then students become frustrated. A well-written set of aims will be an important guide for the teacher to use in creating meaningful lessons that push the students to new levels of learning.

5. Determine a Sequence for the Lessons

Now that you know your students, know the subject you are to teach them, and have written aims for the unit, you need to decide how many lessons it will take and what you should teach in each lesson. Start this process by writing down the major aspects of the subject you have chosen.

As an example, let's stick with the Psalms idea. If you decide to teach according to the types of psalms, your topics could be broken down like this:

An introduction to Psalms

Psalms that are hymns

Psalms that are laments

Psalms that are for remembering

Psalms that are about trusting God

Psalms that are thanksgiving

Psalms that are wisdom

Psalms that are about kingship

This neatly creates a series of eight lessons for a unit on the Psalms. You could easily spend two lessons on hymns, combine a couple of the genres, or add in a concluding lesson—there is no one magical way to do this.

With this particular example, the order of the lessons may not matter very much. You could easily think of other topics where order would make a difference. If you are studying the life of Christ, you would likely want chronological lessons; but if you are looking at the teachings of Christ, you may want to start with the easy ones and work up to the more difficult ones. The key is to let the topics you choose determine the number and sequence of lessons. Do not try to artificially squeeze a survey of Christian theology into a four-lesson series.

6. Write One Aim for Each Lesson

Now that you know the order in which you will teach the lessons, you can decide on your goal for each one. When I learned to write lessons, conventional wisdom was that each lesson should have three aims—one know, one feel, and one do. After a few years of trying to write lessons that would accomplish three goals in 45 minutes, I determined that was too much. For the past several years, I have written one very good aim for every lesson I teach. It makes much more sense to work to accomplish one thing and to accomplish it very well.

Rather than working cognitive, affective, and psychomotor aims into every lesson, I plan one aim for each lesson that helps me accomplish my unit aims. In a six-week series, I will typically have two of each domain, but that is not always the case. I have found that it is easy for most of my lesson aims to center on the cognitive, so I always have to be careful about writing holistic goals.

That strategy seems to have made a difference in what students learn. I know it helps me feel less rushed as I teach. I have learned to take my time and focus on that one goal, rather than hurrying to cover all the material. I have noticed that many newer books on education are emphasizing the same idea—so I guess I was not the only frustrated teacher out there!

Using the lesson sequence from the Psalms, the weekly topics and aims might look like this:

Lesson 1: An introduction to the Psalms
Aim: As a result of this lesson, the students will explain what psalms are.

Lesson 2: Psalms that are hymns
Aim: As a result of this lesson, the students will recreate an ancient Jewish worship service using some hymn psalms.

Lesson 3: Psalms that are laments
Aim: As a result of this lesson, the students will defend the expression of laments to God.

Lesson 4: Psalms that are for remembering
Aim: As a result of this lesson, the students will list key events that are remembered in the Psalms.

Lesson 5: Psalms that are about trusting God
Aim: As a result of this lesson, the students will appreciate the challenges the psalmists had in trusting God.

Lesson 6: Psalms that are thanksgiving
Aim: As a result of this lesson, the students will express their thanks to God by writing their own psalms.

Lesson 7: Psalms that are wisdom
Aim: As a result of this lesson, the students will compare wisdom expressed in the Psalms to wisdom they hear from today's society.

Lesson 8: Psalms that are about kingship
Aim: As a result of this lesson, the students will recognize the importance of the kingship psalms.

Before you go on, evaluate these lesson aims. Are they specific? Are they measurable? Attainable? Challenging? If not, how would you change them?

7. Make Sure the Lesson Aims Support the Unit Aims
One other important step in the process is to evaluate your lesson aims against your unit aims. Remember that the lessons should accomplish the goals you

set for the series. To do this, look at each of your unit aims and ask which of your lesson aims accomplishes this goal. If you have a lesson aim that doesn't fit your unit aims, that doesn't mean it is not a valid objective, just that it does not fit this particular series. Save it and use it another time.

If you are going to accomplish anything intentional as you teach, you need to make sure your lessons take your students where you want them to go. Comparing your lesson aims to your unit aims will help you evaluate that.

8. Write Your Lesson

Finally, after reading more than halfway through this book on how to teach, you have arrived at the section on actually writing lessons! The truth is that this is the easy part. Once you have done all the preliminary work, the rest practically falls into place. Unfortunately, rather than starting at the beginning, most youth workers want to skip right to this part. That's why most of us don't teach very well.

Once you get to this stage of planning, you are ready to think about the specific information you want to teach and how you will teach it. But what kind of teacher do you want to be? How do you think teachers, students, and subject matter should interact? The way you think about this may be helped by considering various METAPHORS for teaching.

Metaphors allow you to use ideas that are already familiar to you to help break open a new idea you are trying to grasp. This section will consider teaching metaphors including assembly-line worker, farmer, medical doctor, pilgrim, salesperson, coach, observer,[75] relay runner, sage, and guide.

For the teacher who operates as an ASSEMBLY-LINE WORKER, education is all about doing his part to put the right components of knowledge into the student. He sees his role as one in a series of steps designed to create an end product—which, for the most part, should look like all the other products. His role is objective, set, necessary, and offers little tolerance for flexibility. He teaches what he is told to teach using the tools he is given.

The FARMER, however, is much more of a nurturer. He believes his role as an educator includes meticulously sowing, watering, fertilizing, and harvesting. As a sower, he must understand enough about both his subject matter and his students to know what, when, and how to plant. He pays attention to his students' development so he knows when they need extra help or encouragement. He also realizes he cannot do everything. One of the most frustrating things about being a farmer is that even if one does everything correctly, there are many outside forces that have a say in how crops grow. This is true for the teacher as well.

A teacher who sees herself as a MEDICAL DOCTOR takes another distinctive approach. She works to understand the student so she can diagnose, treat, and cure a variety of problems. This approach to education takes on the view that the teacher needs to "fix" students in some way. She sees problems that need addressed, so she teaches topics to meet those needs. She builds relationships so she can better understand her students and thus help them with their specific issues. The role of the student here is fairly passive and centers on doing what the doctor prescribes.

An even different approach is that of the co-traveling PILGRIM. While she has more experience and likely more knowledge than her students, she sees her role more as one who shares her own journey and encourages students. Her agenda is not content-driven, but growth-driven. Whatever she can do to help students mature and experience God is what she desires. The students in this metaphor must take a lot of ownership over their own development, because the pilgrim is on a journey that cannot be too influenced by others.

The SALESPERSON is a familiar metaphor that secular society has applied to church teachers, birthing a cacophony of televangelist jokes. In this view, education is primarily about getting students to buy what the teacher has to sell. That may be salvation, theological positions, ministry philosophies, or a plethora of other ideas. For the salesperson, the end justifies the means. Whatever he can do to get others to accept the message he is hawking is okay, because he has the most important goal in mind. The student's role here is to evaluate whether or not to accept what the teacher is selling.

A currently popular metaphor is that of teacher as COACH. What makes this so attractive in youth ministry is that a good coach understands her sport, knows how to motivate and teach her athletes, and is a master at encouraging, prodding, and chastising them at just the right moments. Part psychologist, part parent, part policeman, and part friend, the coach knows her role. She has times to teach and nurture, but when the game is on, she must stand on the sideline, trusting that her team remembers and executes what she has taught them. This leads to moments of extreme joy, pride, frustration, and grief.

A much more extreme metaphor is that of the OBSERVER, who mainly watches students grow with very little influence. Much like perennial wild flowers that bloom whether they are cared for or not, the students of the observer are left to their own devices to mature. Occasionally she might prune or shape in order to make the students grow in specific ways, but typically she is a passive spectator in the educational process. She may provide a series of options that students may work at on their own pace if they desire, but she is not upset if they make slow progress or go in a different direction altogether.

The teacher who is a RELAY RUNNER wants to pass off his knowledge to his students so they will eventually pass it on to their own students someday. He will likely not add to what was passed to him, but will take very seriously his duty to guard and deliver it unscathed and well-protected. Part of the relay runner's responsibility is to understand his role in the ongoing task of teaching and learning. As a learner he takes the knowledge passed on from those who came before him. As a teacher he hands it off to those who come after.

A SAGE is a teacher who sees his role as imparting his learned wisdom on whoever will listen. He has studied and worked hard to learn all he knows, and he has failed, in his eyes, if he does not share that with students. The sage learned from other sages, added to what he was taught, and is now prepared to teach others. Even if students do not understand everything he shares immediately, they will grasp enough of it to make a difference. There is little room for question asking or creativity as the sage teaches, because he has so much content to cover.

As a GUIDE the teacher leads the way, sharing important information and creating learning opportunities that are practical and challenging. She believes she needs to provide interactive methods to assess how her students are doing. By forcing students to get their hands dirty in real-life activities and being there to clarify, encourage, and rescue if needed, she allows learners to prove to themselves that they are maturing and that what they learn matters.

Do you see yourself in one or more of these metaphors? Be aware that the way you shape your lessons is affected by the role you perceive yourself to play as teacher.

There are surely many other ways to think about how teachers use curriculum to educate students. These metaphors are not meant to be exhaustive, but illustrative of a variety of practices. Nor do I want you to think that anyone adopts one of these metaphors all the time. Most teachers use curriculum in different ways depending on the situation, topic, and students they are dealing with at a given time.

A. Gather your resources to learn about the subject.

To begin the actual planning of the lesson, you need to gather whatever resources are helpful to you. These might include notes you've made as you studied the subject, curriculum you purchased to help guide you, or other sources of information on the topic.

My office often looks like it has been ransacked as I am preparing a lesson. Sometimes I pull every related resource off my shelves and scatter all the notes I can find. In the past few years, I've done more of my research using the Internet, so now I have added that information in a separate pile. All of this just helps me glean the most important, helpful material that applies to my students, the lesson topic, and my lesson aim. I usually wind up with a couple of pages of notes and lots of ideas.

You may work with material differently, but the idea should be the same. Gather whatever information is helpful to you and write down notes on what will help you accomplish your lesson aim.

B. Determine the form your lesson will take.

Once you know the specific content of your lesson, you are ready to start writing it out. One helpful strategy I learned in college has helped me through many different teaching contexts in the past 20 years. It is known as the HOOK-BOOK-LOOK-TOOK (HBLT) method.[76] While the rhyming name of this idea may sound goofy, I believe it is an amazingly effective and sound way to write lesson plans. Each of the four parts of the HBLT approach has a specific purpose and flow.

The HOOK is the beginning of the lesson that grabs the students' attention. It is usually three to five minutes long and somehow gets the class thinking on the same page. For some students, it answers the question, "Why should I pay attention?" Good hooks can be engaging questions, video clips, songs, skits, games, or other activities. Many educators believe it should tie directly into the lesson, but I don't believe it has to—especially if it is a very short activity.

In the BOOK portion, students are introduced to the topic or biblical text. It can be five to ten minutes long. This part addresses the question, "What are we going to study, and what do I need to know about it?" Too often I see classes in which a student reads the Scripture out loud, then the teacher expounds on it for a period of time. While this may be the quickest way to share information, it is not necessarily the most effective. One challenge is to be creative in how the passage is shared. Responsive reading, dramatic reading, or listening to an audio recording are a few of the many alternative ways to do this.

As part of the book portion, teachers need to find a way to help students understand the biblical context and meaning of the verses. Again, there are many ways to accomplish this other than lecture. Chapter 8 has an extensive list of methods that can help you come up with creative ideas.

The third section of the lesson challenges students to take a LOOK at what the Scripture might mean in their lives. It is the application portion that answers, "What does this say to me?" It is also typically the longest part of the lesson and involves more than one activity or method. Teachers can have several approaches to this part that are all effective. I tend to think it is the most difficult, though, because it requires teachers to think about how to reach as many students as possible with the activities.

The key part of the lesson is the TOOK, because it issues a specific challenge to students to do something with what they've learned. It is the "So what?" aspect of the lesson and answers the students' questions about how, specifically, their lives should change because of what they have learned. Since this part comes at the end and a lot of lessons go longer than intended, the took often gets left out. This is a major problem, since life change is supposed to be the point of teaching. Without the took, students have some new information, but they don't know what to do with it.

Whatever challenge you plan as the took, it should be specific and immediate. I like to create challenges the students have to implement immediately. For exam-

> **HELP! I'M USING PURCHASED CURRICULUM!**
>
> Not to fear, you can still adapt those commercial lessons to fit this model. In fact, most canned lessons you can buy are already written with something very similar to the HBLT approach. Look for these elements:
>
> 1. The opening activity
> 2. Introducing the Scripture passage
> 3. Exploring the passage to learn what it means
> 4. Applying the passage to the students' lives.
>
> Once you have identified these components, then you can begin to evaluate how closely the written material coincides with the goals you have for your group. Rather than starting from scratch, your major task is rewriting it to suit your students.

ple I might say, "My challenge to you today is to explain to your parents over din-
ner what an imprecatory psalm is and give them an example." That way they immediately apply what we've discussed, and I can ask them about it the next time we're
together.

Granted, HBLT is not the only effective strategy for planning to teach, but I
think it is especially helpful for those who are fairly new at writing lesson plans.
Once you master this method, I encourage you to try others.

C. Write out the details for each activity.

After you choose the appropriate methods for each part of your lesson, you
are ready to think about the details. They might include thinking about how long
each activity should take, what materials you will need, and exactly what you should
say for instructions or questions. Planning out these details will help you be even
more at ease as you teach and will make sure you purposefully clarify everything you
do. It can help you avoid a situation where you ask everyone to fill out their work-
sheet, and you forgot to make copies.

D. Read back through your lesson to see if it accomplishes your lesson aim.

When everything is written out, go back and read through your lesson again.
Then reread your lesson aim. Does the lesson do what you originally planned for
it to do? If not, then determine what needs to be tweaked and change it. If it does,
then you are ready to forget about it for a day or so.

E. Let it sit for a while.

To really plan effectively, this whole process needs to start several days in
advance. The process of writing the lesson plans out should be finished at least
three days before you teach them. This gives your brain time to chew on what you've
planned.

F. Read back through it the day before you teach to make changes and improvements.

After a couple of days, go back and read through what you have written. See
what doesn't make sense or what new ideas pop into your head. This gives you a
chance to correct problems or be more creative. It also helps you become more
familiar with your lesson.

On the day you teach a lesson, you should find at least 15 minutes to go through your plans one last time. Another chance to tweak and become more familiar with what you've planned will only help.

G. Ask yourself, "If I am a student in this class, do I enjoy and learn something from this lesson?"

As a final step, I always ask myself if my students will learn something from what I have planned. This requires me to be objective and think from their point of view. Neither is easy or automatic. You might like what you teach, but if the students don't, then your teaching is not effective.

9. Pray.

Not as a last resort, but as a reminder that you are teaching only through the power of the Holy Spirit.

10. Teach the lesson.

Now it is finally time to teach the lesson. This is when all the preparation makes the biggest difference. A well-planned and well-thought-out lesson will always be better than one thrown together at the last minute. Always.

A DISCLAIMER, A CONFESSION, AND SOME MUSINGS

As part of the process of writing this text, I asked several people I trust to read through it and offer suggestions. I wrote this chapter knowing full well that this traditional approach to teaching does not fit well with contemporary POSTMODERN thinking. So here's my disclaimer:

WARNING: THIS CHAPTER MAY NEED TO BE FILTERED THOUGH POSTMODERN LENSES.

But here's my confession: I still like and use the HBLT approach to lesson planning. Though it may be MODERNISTIC, I have not seen anything better—nor even anything as good. What I have seen recently, though, are youth workers, steeped in postmodern youth ministry teaching strategies, who fail miserably in

CAUTION!

Even a well-written lesson plan needs to be altered on occasion. If your lesson isn't going well, if there's a more pressing issue that needs to be addressed, or if you realize that you've done a poor job planning it, then abandon ship and do something else.

I've had lessons when I've said, "Okay, this isn't working. Time for plan B. Who wants to suggest a plan B?" Almost always someone in the group comes up with an idea that was better than my original lesson anyway.

That should be the exception rather than the rule, though.

their attempts to share the absolute truth of God's Word. These failures are often shrouded in attempts to be a storyteller who connects with students on a transparent and emotional level.

I fear that one of the failures of youth ministry has been the dichotomizing of our roles as relational pastors with our biblical command to be disciplemakers. Jesus is the ultimate model for us as we both build relationships with teens and disciple them in all truth so they will obey what the Word commands. Teaching the truth does not require us to turn off the relational aspect of our ministry. But it also does not permit us to forsake the teaching of truth for fear of alienating immature believers. Great teaching is both highly relational and truth-driven. To truly meet the biblical expectation to teach holistically, nothing less can be accepted.

For Discussion

Does this chapter make writing a lesson too complicated? How likely is it that following these suggestions will actually help you teach better?

What is the role of spontaneity in teaching? How does having a detailed lesson plan help or hinder that?

How much do you agree with the assertion that effective learning happens through the interaction of the cognitive, affective, and psychomotor domains? What are some personal examples to support your position?

Which of the teaching metaphors do you most closely identify with and why? Can you think of others?

Activities

Look at some published curriculum. Evaluate how well it uses aims for the series and for each lesson.

With that same curriculum, determine how much background information on the Scripture or subject it shares for teachers. Is it adequate to be able to teach the lesson and answer important questions students may have?

Write unit and lesson aims for whatever class you are currently teaching, using the guidelines from this chapter. After you begin teaching the series, evaluate how helpful that process has been.

Go to a few people you believe to be excellent classroom teachers. Ask them if they write aims and how they plan lessons.

Write a series of lessons that teaches volunteers to plan a unit and write lessons. Use the suggestions and steps in this chapter as you write.

ENDNOTES, CHAPTER 6

73. Hunt, J. (1998). *Disciple-Making Teachers*. Loveland, CO: Vital Ministry, p. 111.
74. Barton, L. G. (1994). *Quick Flip Questions for Critical Thinking*. San Clemente, CA: Edupress.
75. For more on these first seven ideas, see Pleuddeman, J. E. (1989). Metaphors in Christian Education, *Christian Education Journal* 10:1, pp. 39-47.
76. Richards, L. O., & Bredfeldt, G. J. (1998). *Creative Bible Teaching: Revised and Expanded*. Chicago: Moody Press, pp. 154-159.

CHAPTER 7

WHAT METHODS SHOULD YOU USE TO TEACH?

(The World's Most Comprehensive List of Teaching Strategies)

*"The teacher who wishes to be really effective will be sure that
his teaching is characterized by variety."*
—KENNETH GANGEL[77]

*   *   *   *   *

Are you feeling challenged yet? Maybe even a bit overwhelmed? That's understandable—teaching adolescents is an incredibly important and complex task. But I hope you are also feeling encouraged, because it is possible to learn to teach well. It takes time and effort. There is a lot to know and understand. But it's well worth it.

Here's a brief review of what has been covered so far:

- What is teaching and why does it matter? (To create a framework for understanding why teaching well matters.)
- Who are adolescents? (To better understand what is happening in and to the adolescents you teach.)
- Who are *your* adolescents? (To give you a way to learn more about the unique teens God has given you.)
- How do kids learn? (To explore various learning theories so you can know that not all kids learn the same way.)
- What should you use to teach? (To help you think more intentionally about the curriculum you use.)
- How can you prepare to teach? (To help you put together the nuts and bolts of a lesson.)

That leads us to this chapter, which will help you think about the specific methods, strategies, activities, and ideas to employ as you teach. (A quick note: This chapter is chock-full of lists and ideas; it's really more of a reference tool than fun fireside reading. You should approach it knowing it is not written like the other chapters.)

Coming up are chapters that will help you evaluate your teaching and better understand how Jesus taught, as well as a number of tips for great teaching.

What is a Teaching Method?

Anything a teacher uses to accomplish her goals with a group of students is a method. Sometimes called strategies, methods are simply the how (as in "How am I going to get the students to learn about God's covenant with Abraham?") that grows out of the what (as in "What should the students learn about God's covenant with Abraham?")

All teachers use methods every time they teach. It is impossible not to use methods. Even those who lecture every minute of the lesson are using a teaching method called lecturing.

How to Choose a Good Method

There is no perfect teaching strategy for a given situation. One of many good options will do. Of course, several poor options are also available, so how do you know? Here are a few ideas:

Know your group. You have to know the teens you are teaching very well in order to pick the best methods. Some groups love discussion, and others don't. Some groups are very artistic, while others value mental challenges.

Know your aims. What you hope students will take away from each aspect of the lesson should also shape your decision. Cognitive aims are usually not best accomplished through a service project. Personal application requires something other than recitation.

THE WORLD'S WORST TEACHING METHOD

What is the absolute worst teaching strategy in the world? Lecture? Osmosis? Memorization? Exams with 100 multiple-choice questions? Long essay questions? Anarchy?

The answer is...none of the above. The world's worst teaching method is the one you always use, no matter what it is or how well you do it.

Ever heard the maxim, "Familiarity breeds contempt"? That applies to teaching as well. When the same thing happens over and over again, we tend to turn our brains off. For maximum learning, our brains must be fully engaged.

If you don't know what your favorite teaching method is, ask your students—they'll know. Then make sure you don't use it for a month, or at least use variations of it.

Know your setting. The method you choose must fit with the room and resources available. Don't decide to use a greased watermelon relay to teach teamwork if your kids will be in good clothes and you'll be meeting in a small room shared by the church treasurer. Don't plan to show a video clip if you are not sure about the availability or quality of a TV and VCR/DVD player.

Know yourself. You also need to have a good handle on who you are and what methods you could lead well. Creating a sculpture of the Last Supper might be a great way to help youth visualize that setting. But unless you or another leader can help the class create a decent sculpture, the method will actually take away from the message.

THE DISCUSSION MONSTER

I have to admit my bias. I love discussion. As a teacher I use some type of discussion in almost every single lesson I teach, and I think you should too. Yes, I know the sidebar on the previous page warns against using any one method too much, but discussion is more than a method. It is, to coin a term, a METAMETHOD—an overarching category of many related submethods. Discussion is so varied as to its uses, aspects, layers, and complexities that it is more than just one method. I would also say that the various arts, student projects, and even special trips and events are also metamethods.

Because of my belief that discussion is so important, I want to take this chance to expand on it at some length, beginning with advantages and disadvantages.

Advantages of Discussion

I have some very good reasons why I like to use discussion so much. From what I have learned, here are some key ones:

Students want to talk. When I started in youth ministry, I was convinced youth came because I was so great and funny and wonderful. How wrong I was. Students come primarily because of each other. They want to talk to each other, and they want to hear from each other. Leading a great discussion during a lesson is my way of using their natural tendencies to accomplish my teaching aims.

Discussion engages brain cells. A thoughtful response to a well-formulated question requires the use of gray matter. When a teacher crafts great questions, students are encouraged to use their God-given minds to engage with the subject at hand. It helps make learning active rather than passive.

It can enhance communication skills. As teachers our goal is not just to make sure youth are "getting it" as we teach, but to help make them better people all around. Leading a good discussion will aid the development of students' verbal communication skills. By encouraging young people to think about what they want to say and say it clearly, teachers create better communicators.

Teachers can assess learning during the discussion. The quality of the responses should help teachers understand how well youth are progressing toward the lesson aim. Discussion gives you a chance to evaluate on the fly and either go back and review more—or go in a whole new direction if need be.

Discussion invites learning from multiple sources. One of my favorite aspects of a good discussion is that it allows students to learn from everyone else, not just me. If I have a class of 20 students, then there are 20 other sets of experiences, thoughts, and opinions available besides mine. How selfish and arrogant of me to think that my input is the best or most important. Plus, sometimes kids can explain something to each other much better than I ever could.

Potential Problems with Discussion

Discussion does have its drawbacks, though. Some hazards to be aware of include the following:

Discussion can take up too much time. Anytime a teacher opens the door for discussion, there is potential for it to get out of hand. Sometimes it takes longer to wrap up the discussion or to get to the main point than you anticipate.

Discussions sometimes ramble off the subject. Both students and teachers are often guilty of this. Teens easily go off on tangents, because they tend to think so randomly. A good discussion leader needs to learn how to redirect at such times.

Individuals can dominate discussion. No matter how hard you try to avoid them, there is at least one "discussion hog" in every group. Teenagers crave attention, and some take advantage of group discussion to make sure everyone knows they are there.

Introverts and other process thinkers may be left out. On the other side of the continuum are the shy students who rarely, if ever, say anything during discussions. That is too bad, because they are often the process thinkers who have the most valuable nuggets to contribute.

Discussion can hide a lack of preparation. Because teens enjoy talking, it is easy to open class with a question and just let them go with it for a while. This means a teacher could go in totally unprepared and no one would ever know. A good teacher never uses discussion to mask a lack of preparation.

It only works well with smaller groups. Discussion needs to be deep and intimate to have an impact for most students. That cannot happen in a large group. I know a lot of teenagers who tell me they like going to churches with large youth groups so they can just talk with their friends and not participate in anything deep. That is not a good learning environment.

Types of Questions

For most people, leading a great discussion does not come easily or naturally. It takes work, just like most other aspects of teaching. What your students get out of a discussion has everything to do with the quality of the questions you ask. In leading a discussion, it is helpful to know that there are many different types of questions.

CLOSED QUESTIONS or Factual Questions: These ask for definite answers. They have a limited number of correct responses—usually only one. Yes-no, true-false, and recall questions all fit this category. If you were teaching a lesson about the Fall of Adam and Eve, some examples would be:

> *Where did Adam and Eve live before the Fall?*
> *Did they listen to the serpent's temptations?*
> *What tree did he convince them to eat from?*

OPEN QUESTIONS: In contrast to closed questions, "open questions" are those that have more than one potential answer. There are many different styles. Open questions can fit into any of the following groups:

INTERPRETIVE QUESTIONS: These questions require students to make sense of information:

> *Why would the serpent want to tempt Adam and Eve?*
> *What are some reasons God might have prohibited them from eating from that one tree?*

How likely is it that Adam and Eve thought about the consequences of their action?

THOUGHT QUESTIONS: These require students to think beyond the specific information in the lesson:

Since Adam and Eve had it made in the Garden of Eden, why would they even think about disobeying God?

What other characters in Scripture can you think of who were tempted so directly?

Which of those characters were able to resist temptation?

EVALUATION QUESTIONS: These push students to figure out why something happened, the result of an action, or how it could have been different:

What might have happened if Adam would have resisted Eve after she ate the fruit?

Why did some other people in the Bible successfully resist temptation?

How did Adam and Eve's choice affect all aspects of creation?

APPLICATION QUESTIONS: These allow students to think about how the subject matter might make a difference to them:

How has Adam and Eve's choice affected you?

What are some examples of how you were tempted this week?

What can you learn from how others resist temptation?

Bloom's Taxonomy and Discussion Questions

I mentioned earlier the work of Dr. Benjamin Bloom. His theories of cognitive learning have provided me with a lot to think about as I form discussion questions. Keep in mind that cognitive learning is demonstrated by information recall and other intellectual skills such as comprehending information, organizing ideas, analyzing and synthesizing data, applying knowledge, choosing among alternatives in problem-solving, and evaluating ideas or actions.

Bloom categorized cognitive learning into six levels, which are addressed individually below. Visually, it may help to think of Bloom's Taxonomy like a staircase. Each level builds on the previous one in a fairly sequential order. He sees simple recall or recognition of facts as the lowest level. Thinking ability increases through more complex and abstract levels to the highest order, which is classified as evaluation.

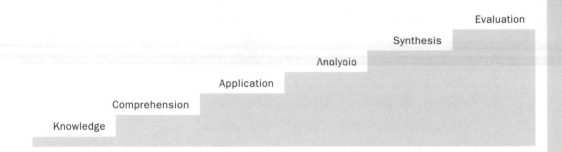

Many educators have worked to apply Bloom's ideas to discussion questions. The following is a summary of one of the more successful attempts, along with some specific questions that could be used in the lesson on Adam and Eve from above.[78]

Level 1: Knowledge

Students recount previously learned material by recalling facts, terms, basic concepts and answers. This is the first step in a cognitive progression that helps students begin with a foundation of knowledge and move to integrative thinking. Key words in questions at this level include: *who, what, why, when, omit, where, which, choose, find, how, define, label, show, spell, list, match, name, relate, tell, recall,* and *select.*

Questions might begin with the following: What is…? How is…? Where is…? When did…? How did. . .? How would you explain…? Why did…? How would you describe…? Can you recall…? How would you show…? Can you select…? Who were the main…? Can you list three…? Which one…? Who was…?

From our Adam and Eve lesson, Level 1 questions could include: Who are the key people involved in this passage? What was God's one prohibition for Adam and Eve? How did the serpent trick Eve?

Level 2: Comprehension

Students demonstrate understanding of facts and ideas by organizing, comparing, translating, interpreting, giving descriptions, and stating main points. Key words in questions at this level include: *compare, contrast, demonstrate, interpret, explain, extend, illustrate, infer, outline, relate, rephrase, translate, summarize, show,* and *classify.*

Questions might begin with the following: How would you classify the type of…? How would you compare…? How would you contrast…? Will you state or interpret in your own words…? How would you rephrase the meaning…? What facts or ideas show…? What is the main idea of…? Which statements support…? Can you explain what is happening…? What is meant…? What can you say about…? Which is the best answer…? How would you summarize…?

From our Adam and Eve lesson, Level 2 questions could include: Explain why Eve listened to the serpent. Rephrase what the serpent said to her. Interpret Adam's response to Eve.

Level 3: Application

Students solve problems by applying acquired knowledge, facts, techniques, and rules. Key words in questions at this level include: *apply, build, choose, construct, develop, interview, make use of, organize, experiment with, plan, select, solve, utilize, model*, and *identify*.

Questions might begin with the following: How would you use…? What examples can you find to…? How would you solve…? How would you organize _____ to show…? How would you show your understanding of…? What approach would you use to…? How would you apply what you learned to develop…? What other way would you plan to…? What would result if…? Can you make use of the facts to…? What elements would you choose to change…? What facts would you select to show…? What questions would you ask in an interview with…?

From our Adam and Eve lesson, Level 3 questions could include: What other strategies could the serpent have used on Eve? Think of other examples of people being tempted. How have you experienced such a temptation?

IS THERE AN HBLT TIE HERE?

A student pointed out that this taxonomy might be a good way to think about writing lessons as well. He saw levels 1 and 2 fitting in with Book, 3 and 4 corresponding to Look, and 5 and 6 relating to Took. That makes some sense to me. There's definitely a long-term goal to move students from Level 1 to Level 6, but attempting that in each lesson seems more difficult. What do you think?

Level 4: Analysis

Students examine and break down information into parts by identifying motives or causes, as well as making inferences and finding evidence to support generalizations. Key words in questions at this level include: *analyze, categorize, classify, compare, contrast, discover, dissect, divide, examine, inspect, simplify, survey, take part in, test for, distinguish, list, distinction, theme, relationships, function, motive, infer, assume*, and *conclude*.

Questions might begin with the following: What are the parts or features of…? How is _____ related to…? Why do you think…? What is the theme…? What motive is there…? Can you list the parts…? What inference can you make…? What conclusions can you draw…? How would you classify…? How would you categorize…? Can you identify the different parts…? What evidence can you find…? What is the relationship between…? Can you make a distinction between…? What is the function of…? What ideas justify…?

From our Adam and Eve lesson, Level 4 questions could include: Why would Adam eat the fruit knowing what God had said? What is it about the way God made us that allows us to give in to temptation even when we know we shouldn't? Dissect what the serpent said to Eve that was so effective.

Level 5: Synthesis

Students compile information in a different way by combining elements in new patterns or proposing alternative solutions. Key words in questions at this level include: *build, choose, combine, compile, compose, construct, create, design, develop, estimate, formulate, imagine, invent, make up, originate, plan, predict, propose, solve, suppose, discuss, modify, change, improve, adapt, minimize, maximize, delete, theorize, elaborate, test, improve,* and *change.*

Questions might begin with the following: What changes would you make to solve…? How would you improve…? What would happen if…? Can you elaborate on the reason…? Can you propose an alternative…? Can you invent…? How would you adapt _____ to create a different…? How could you change (modify) the plot (plan)…? What could be done to minimize (maximize)…? What way would you design…? What could be combined to improve (change)…? Suppose you could _____ what would you do…? How would you test…? Can you formulate a theory for…? Can you construct a model that would change…? Can you think of an original way for the…?

From our Adam and Eve lesson, Level 5 questions could include: What might have happened if Adam had refused to eat the fruit? If I were Satan, in what ways would I tempt you? How could God have made us so that we were stronger in resisting temptation?

Level 6: Evaluation

Students present and defend opinions using a set of criteria to make judgments about information, the validity of ideas, or the quality of work. Key words in questions at this level include: *award, choose, conclude, criticize, decide, defend, determine, dispute, evaluate, judge, justify, measure, compare, mark, rate, recommend, rule on, select, agree, interpret, explain, appraise, prioritize, support, criteria, prove, disprove, assess, influence, perceive, value, estimate, influence,* and *deduce.*

Questions might begin with the following: Do you agree with the actions…? with the outcomes…? What is your opinion of…? How would you prove…? disprove…? Can you assess the value or importance of…? Would it be better if…? Why did the character choose…? What would you recommend…? How would you rate the…? What would you cite to defend the actions…? How would you evaluate…? How could you determine…? What choice would you have made…? What would you select…? How would you prioritize…? What judgment would you make about…? Based on what you know, how would you explain…? What information would you use to support the view…? How would you justify…? What data was used to make the conclusion…? Why was it better that…? How would you prioritize the facts…? How would you compare the ideas…? How would you compare the people…?

From our Adam and Eve lesson, Level 6 questions could include: Defend the serpent's desire to get Eve to eat the fruit. Evaluate your own ability to resist temptation. Assess the people you spend the most time with and their influence on your decisions.

Tips for Leading Great Discussions

Whether or not you try to adopt Bloom's levels as you write discussion questions, there are several important tips to keep in mind.

- Build on what students already know, then move to what they don't know or need to learn.
- Assess student learning by evaluating their responses to questions.
- Take care in how you phrase questions so that they ask what you really want to know.
- React to answers in such a way that students know you have heard their response.
- Never make fun of what a student says.
- Emphasize thought over recall.

- Arouse interest and curiosity by asking thought-provoking questions.
- Focus attention on where you want the discussion to go.
- Reinforce ideas by rephrasing questions and responses.
- Use both correct and incorrect answers to teach.
- Probe deeper by asking students to explain what they have said or by asking them to respond to each other.
- Ask questions in a logical sequence that moves toward your lesson aim.
- Start with easier, factual questions.
- Plan questions ahead of time.
- Restrict each question to one idea.
- Ask questions throughout the lesson.
- Make sure questions are age-appropriate.
- Ask students what they think about an idea as well as how they feel about it.
- Arrange the room so students can see one another's faces.
- Don't reveal your own ideas or opinions too soon (or it will cut off discussion).
- Allow responses from multiple students instead of getting just one.
- Address wrong answers appropriately.
- Bring discussion to an end before it dies.
- Make your students feel like they are the experts.
- Avoid irrelevant, insulting, or vague questions.
- Don't feel like you have to expound on every answer or response.
- Encourage teens to disagree with you and with each other.
- Don't fear silence!
- When a student asks you a question, turn it back to the group by asking what someone else thinks before you respond.

There are many other things to be aware of when you lead discussions, but these are among the key ones. You will learn more as you gain experience and see the rewards of a great discussion.

While discussion is a great foundation for teaching, you'll want to use a variety of other methods in every lesson you teach. There are many wonderful sources for getting ideas. Although what follows is only one such source, it is...

The World's Longest List of Teaching Methods

The following list includes more than two hundred teaching methods, with a brief explanation or example of how you could use each one. Remember, you have to know your group and your topic very well to choose the appropriate method. Each of these can be changed and adapted in different ways.

1. Acrostic: Use the letters JOHN to describe the Gospel of John. (Jesus-centered, On-the-go, Holy, Nurturing)

2. Action songs: Put actions with lyrics to better understand or memorize.

3. Add a Verse to a Song: Take an existing song and add new lyrics to it.

4. Adopt a Mission or Missionary: Put your lesson on world missions into action.

5. Advance Organizers: Tell the class what you will be teaching over the next few lessons so students can see the topics fit together.

6. Adventures: From white-water rafting to solving a mystery, these special events can push students to new aspects of learning.

7. Agree/Disagree: Individually or in groups have students explain why they agree or disagree with statements you make.

8. Allegory: Write a story about the life of Job using symbolic characters.

9. Apprenticeship: Pair each teen with an adult to learn about service.

10. Attention-getters: Any activity that gets kids to focus on one person or thing.

11. Audio Clip: Play a snippet of a song or interview to make a point.

12. Banners: Song of Songs 2:4 says, "His banner over me is love." What might that look like?

13. Bible Covers: Students make their own to express themselves.

14. Blackboard: Use a chalkboard or dry-erase board to write ideas or points.

15. Blogs: Web-based journaling.

16. Brainstorming: Ask kids to think of ways to get involved in church. This is about the quantity of ideas, not the quality.

17. Brochure: Create a pamphlet inviting people to hear Paul speak at the Areopagus.

18. Bulletin Board: Create a display showing the dimensions of Solomon's Temple.

19. Bumper Stickers: Create stickers with catchy slogans to encourage people to read their Bibles.

20. Buzz Groups: Have groups of three to five kids discuss a question for just a minute, then ask them to share what they discussed.

21. Can of Worms: Make a controversial statement and have the students discuss it.

22. Case Study: Find a real-life story to illustrate a point and have the class discuss choices that were made.

23. CD Art: Use puff paint to decorate a CD.

24. CD Label Art: Design a CD label that communicates the main point of the message.

25. Celebrity Interview: Imitate Madonna after she witnesses David's slaying of Goliath, or Scooby Doo after he sees Jesus heal a blind man.

26. Cell Phone Frenzy: Use the games on cell phones to have a fun contest.

27. Character Portrayal: Teach about the crossing of the Red Sea dressed as Moses.

28. Chat Room: Specify a time each week to discuss a topic.

29. Circle Response: Ask everyone in the room to respond to the same question.

30. City as Text (a.k.a. Walkabouts): Take the class on a walk around your town or neighborhood to highlight an aspect of your lesson.

31. Class Project: Everyone works together to complete one task.

32. Cloud of Witnesses: Invite older adults to share about their own faith journeys.

33. Coat of Arms: Have each teen create one to represent key aspects of his life and personality.

34. Collage: Using different media and poster board, represent body-image messages in current popular shows and movies.

35. Colloquy: Create a conference at which the class presents its research and shares about the 10/40 Window.

36. Comic Strip: Draw a strip of the 12 spies sent to scout the Promised Land.

37. Commercial Jingle: Rewrite popular jingles to promote prayer.

38. Contemporary Parallel: Rewrite Jesus' triumphal entry to Jerusalem as if he were entering Washington D.C. today.

39. Contests: Who can find all the references to light in the Gospel of John?

40. Contrast: Consider the differences between Jesus' encounter with the Rich Young Ruler and his encounter with Nicodemus.

41. Conversation: Specifically guide questions and responses.

42. Costume Lesson: Everyone dress as their favorite disciple.

43. Create a Church: What would your perfect church be like? Include ministries, pastors, worship, buildings, and so on.

44. Create a Web site: Make a site about your topic that other youth could access on the Internet.

45. Crossword Puzzle: Make one using all the names of Jesus in the Bible.

46. Cultural Framing: Study the Proverbs from the point of view of the original audience.

47. Data Gathering: Find as much information as possible about the walls of Jerusalem as you study Nehemiah.

48. Debate: Halloween—Satan's holiday or a fun way to get candy? Help students get resources.

49. Debriefing: After any type of experience, it is good to ask, "What did you think about that?" or "Why did that happen?"

50. Decorate the Door: Introduce your new topic by plastering the classroom door with hints about the subject.

51. Demonstration: Invite someone in to show the group how to make tents.

52. Devil's Advocate (as if he needs another one): Deliberately take an opposing viewpoint.

53. Dialogue: Write a conversation that Noah might have with Jonah.

54. Diary, Log, Journal: Have teens write daily thoughts about how they see God at work around them.

55. Digital Camera: Use a few to tell a story on the view screens.

56. Discourse: Write a speech that Samuel might have given as he explained why God chose David to be king.

57. Discussion: Nothing helps students learn like a great discussion.

58. Disk or CD Sent Home: Put homework or daily thoughts on a computer disk to send home with each student.

59. Display/Exhibit: Create a series of posters about the minor prophets.

60. Drama/Skit: Write a short play that reveals the main point.

61. Drawings/Doodles: Sketch the scene described in the lesson's Scripture reading.

62. Drill and Practice: To memorize something, repeat it over and over and over and over and…

63. Duct Tape: It has a million uses; surely some of them are with teenagers.

64. E-mail Study/Prayer: Send an e-mail to students the day before the lesson to give them something to think about. Include prayer items.

65. Encrypt a Message: Create your own code to make a statement or share a verse.

66. Epitaphs. How do you want to be remembered?

67. Estimate the Cost: How much would it cost Noah to build the ark today?

68. Examples: Use contemporary examples to explain Scripture.

69. Expanding Panel: Each new panel reveals the next part of the story.

70. Experiments: Create a hypothesis and test it, just like in chemistry.

71. Feasts: Celebrate the Passover with a traditional Jewish meal.

72. Field Trip/Road Trip: Take the class "on location" for a more realistic setting.

73. Film Talk Back: Watch a movie and discuss the contents and message.

74. Finger Plays: Make little paper puppets that fit around fingers to recreate Samson's crushing the Philistines.

75. Fish Bowl: Have three or four teens sit in the middle and have a discussion while everyone else watches silently from the outside, then switch roles.

76. Flash Paper: Magicians use it for tricks; teachers use it as an object lesson.

77. Focus Group: Select a few kids to give feedback.

78. Frieze: Paint an entire wall to visualize a story.

79. Games: Steal a good idea or make one up.

80. Graffiti: What might the Israelites have written on the walls of Pharaoh's palace?

81. Graph/Chart: Create a bar graph to illustrate the lengths of Paul's missionary journeys.

82. Group Drawing: Everyone contributes.

83. Group Presentation: Work together to research, write, and present a topic.

84. Grow a Plant: Many object-lesson possibilities.

85. Guest Speaker: Invite a pastor from another denomination to discuss what their congregation believes.

86. Holidays: Invent a new one, based on your lesson. (I love Ehud Day!)

87. Human Slides: Describe a scene and have students create a picture using other youth as props.

88. Humor: Finding the right joke or funny story can be tricky, but is quite effective.

89. Hyperbole: An exaggerated statement to make a point, such as, "It is easier for a camel to pass through the eye of a needle than for a rich man to enter the kingdom of heaven."

90. Hypothesis Forming: Create a statement that makes a guess about the outcome of what is being studied.

91. Illustrations: Find a good story to make a point.

92. Inductive Study: Let the Scripture speak for itself.

93. Infrared Tag: Use the IR beam function on cell phones and PDAs to send messages during lessons.

94. Instant Photos: Use an instant camera to play a game or tell a story.

95. Internet Camera: Use a camera to connect live with some individual or group that might be a good resource for your lesson.

96. Internet Search: Using a thorough search engine, plug in key words to help look up relevant information.

97. Interview: Have students talk to someone with a unique background to help with the lesson.

98. Jewel Case Treasure: Decorate the covers of empty CD cases and put something inside to represent the lesson.

99. Jigsaw Presentations: Divide your teens into groups of three or four and have each group research and then report on different aspects of your topic.

100. Jigsaw Puzzle: Put a story or illustration on a board, then cut it up and have the students put it together.

101. Learning Centers: Create different activities that students rotate through.

102. Lecture: The old standby can be effective when done well.

103. Letter Writing: Write a real letter to someone the students know or a mythical letter to a historic figure.

104. Library: Use a church, college, or public library to look up information.

105. List: Think of all the things the Hebrews complained about in the Book of Exodus.

106. Litany: Create a worship litany and compare it with what you're used to.

107. Lyrics: Analyze lyrics of a song or hymn.

108. Magic: Nothing like a little prestidigitation to get attention.

109. Marketing Plan: How could Christians in Ephesus attract Diana worshipers?

110. Maxim: A short saying that communicates truth, such as, "No one can serve two masters."

111. Memo: Have students write a quick note after the lesson to explain what they think you've just taught.

112. Memorization: Can be a good beginning point.

113. Metaphor/Simile: God's grace is like the sky because it's beautiful and endless.

114. Mission trips: Close to home or far away, they are a great way to stretch students.

115. Mobile: Cut out figures or symbols and hang them together with string.

116. Mock Trial: Was Judas guilty of treason or impatience?

117. Models: Using clay or Play-Doh, make models that explain the lesson.

118. Monologue: One person giving a prepared or memorized speech.

119. Montage: Similar to a collage, but using only one form of media.

120. Multiple Senses: Discuss Adam and Eve's first day outside of the Garden by asking, "What did they smell, taste, feel, hear, and see differently than the day before?"

121. Mural: A painting that tells a story.

122. Music: Few things connect with teens as deeply.

123. Musical Commercial: More than just a jingle, it's a full production.

124. Name That…: Animal from the ark, Mosaic Law, Beatitude.

125. Natural Occurrences: Observe birds as they fly south or leaves as they change color and ask what this tells us about God.

126. Neighbor Nudge: In pairs, discuss a question very briefly.

127. Newscast: Do news, weather, and sports from the day of Pentecost. ("There's a chance of raining tongues of fire this afternoon…")

128. Newspaper Headlines: From the *Jericho Daily News* the day after the wall fell.

129. Online Bible Quiz: Use a Web site to create a fun review.

130. Open-Ended Question: One that has no specific answer.

131. Open-Ended Story: Tell a partial story and have the class create different endings.

132. Oral Reports: Give students each a chance to share what they have learned.

133. Outline: Find the major points of a book of the Bible and outline it.

134. PDA Note Sharing: Have teens beam messages, questions, or notes about the lesson to you and each other.

135. Painting: Big or small, it's always fun.

136. Panel Discussion: Invite a few "experts" in to share about a special topic.

137. Pantomime: If you can get your youth to do something without talking.

138. Parable: Make up your own to share a theological truth.

139. Paradox: Two things that don't seem to make sense together, like "If you want to be first, you need to be last."

140. Paraphrase Hymn: Rewrite a song to update it or clarify a point.

141. Paraphrase Story: Rephrase the main points of a story in your own words.

142. Participation: Involving students to help you teach a part of the lesson.

143. Peaks and Valleys Graph: Have students plot their spiritual ups and downs starting at childhood and relating to other events in their lives.

144. Personal Experiences: Share how a point from the lesson has had an impact on your life.

145. Personalize Scripture: Students rewrite I Corinthians 13 substituting their names in the place of the word love.

146. Personification: Giving human attributes to something that is not human.

147. Plays: More involved than skits since they are longer and take more planning.

148. Poetry: Can be used or written for almost any topic.

149. Point of View: What is an astronomer's take on the birth of Christ? Or a sailor's view on the story of Jonah?

150. Posters: To display a story, explain a concept, or promote an event.

151. PowerPoint Games: There are many good games available in stores and on the Internet.

152. Praise: Directed toward God as part of a lesson or directed toward students as encouragement.

153. Prayer: Not just to bless the lesson, but as an actual teaching experience.

154. Problem-Solving: Create a theological or real-life dilemma and challenge teens to solve it biblically.

155. Puppets: There's nothing like putting your hand in a sock with lipstick on it to bring out creativity.

156. Question-Answer: After a lecture or presentation invite the class to ask questions based on what was shared.

157. Question Box: Sometimes kids are too shy or embarrassed to ask questions, so allow them to write anonymously and put the questions in box.

158. Quiz: An occasional quick five-question quiz can give you a helpful sense of how much students are grasping.

159. Radio Review: Analyze a program from a local radio station (Christian or secular). What worldview is it preaching? How can students evaluate it?

160. Reaction Panel: Choose three adolescents to give their individual reactions to the topic as you present it.

161. Read a Classic: Choose a classic Christian book to study together.

162. Readings: Dramatic readings can often set the tone for a great lesson.

163. RealPlayer Video Lesson: Using the RealPlayer program (or other similar software) make a movie to introduce a point or to combine clips.

164. Rebuke: Jesus used this very successfully. You should set it up ahead of time.

165. Repetition: Doing something over and over is still a good way to learn.

166. Reports: Even written reports can be fun and helpful.

167. Review: Briefly go over what was discussed at the previous meeting. (You should probably do this every time you teach.)

168. Review a Song or Book: A good way to teach critical analysis.

169. Role Play: To help put a theory into practice and discuss how it could be done.

170. Scale Model: Recreate the Ark of the Covenant or the city of Jerusalem.

171. Scrambles: Jumble Scripture, parts of a story, a chronology, books of the New Testament, etc.

172. Scripture Search: Find the left-handed judge!

173. Scripture to Video: Recreate a Bible story as realistically as possible.

174. Sermon: Have the class write one together.

175. Service Projects: Rake leaves, wax a floor, paint a building, wash dishes, do laundry, gather eggs…

176. Sign language: Learn a verse or a song in sign.

177. Simulation Games: As close as possible to the real thing, with time of discussion afterward.

178. Slide Show: Use presentation software to create a series of slides with pictures and captions.

179. Song Comparison: Look at lyrics from artists with two different worldviews. Or compare a hymn with a contemporary worship song.

180. Song Writing: Create your own, individually or as a group.

181. Special Request: Study whatever the youth ask for.

182. Spontaneous Inquiry: Sometimes a student raises a question that just can't wait, so dig in right away.

183. Start a Business: What businesses would the Israelites need after settling in the Promised Land?

184. Sticky Notes: Use various sizes and shapes of Post-its to create teams or share information.

185. Storytelling: In almost any fashion, it's always a hit.

186. Story Writing: Fiction, nonfiction, historical, biographic, etc.

187. Student Activity Book: To give them something to follow along with. Buy one or create your own.

188. Student Reviews: Of your teaching, of the topic, of the church, of anything.

189. Student Teacher: Have one of the leadership teens teach at least once a month.

190. Summary: Tell the story of King Solomon in less than fifty words.

191. Survey: Have the class ask adults how many cities they know in which Paul started churches.

192. Sword Drill: Who can find Bible verses to read fastest?

193. Symbol: Think of something simple to represent something complex.

194. Symposium: Bring together "experts" to offer a series of seminars.

195. Tag-Team Teaching: One person does the intro, another does the Bible teaching, another leads discussion, someone else does a game.

196. Talk Show: With a host, an emcee, and special guests to interview.

197. Teachable Moments: When something unexpected happens, look for a way to learn from it.

198. Temporary Tattoos: Washable art with a message.

199. Testimonies: Invite students or adults to talk about the impact God has had on them.

200. Time Capsules: Leave a legacy for future youth.

201. Time Line: Trace the life of Paul through Acts and the epistles.

202. TV/Play Script: Write it just like you were going to perform it.

203. Version Variations: Read from the NIV, KJV, NASB, NCV, Message, etc., and talk about the differences.

204. Video Clips: This is easier than ever using a DVD.

205. Video Production: Also easier than ever with editing software available on most newer computers.

206. Web Discussion Groups: Set up a discussion room so students can participate at any time.

207. Who's Who: Create a list of important prophets and do a short biography of each.

208. Wire Sculpture: Use pipe cleaners.

209. Word Association: What pops into your head when I say "sacrifice"?

210. Word Picture: Use as many adjectives as possible to describe the scene when Peter cut off the centurion's ear.

211. Work Days: Spend a whole day doing a service project.

212. Workshops: Demonstrations with the opportunity for the youth to try it themselves.

213. Worship: There's much to learn from what you do and what you don't.

214. Write a Newspaper: Beyond the headlines, including comics, sports, and classifieds.

215. Write a Prayer: As a response to the lesson.

216. You Might Be a…: Pharisee if…; false prophet if…; serpent in the Garden if…

217. Youth Talent: Invite teens to share a special gift or ability.

Look for even more ideas on the Web at www.teachingyouth.com.

FOR DISCUSSION

Which types of methods do you use a lot?

Discussion is presented as a metamethod. What are other categories of metamethods you can think of?

Is too much importance placed on discussion here?

What are some other benefits or problems with discussion that aren't mentioned here?

ACTIVITIES

Visit various teaching settings and take note of the variety of teaching methods used. Compare the methods you observe with the attitudes of the students in those classes.

Write a series of four lessons using a variety of activities. Incorporate Bloom's six levels into your discussion questions.

Interview great teachers you know about their favorite methods. Do you notice any similarities in their responses?

ENDNOTES, CHAPTER 7

77. Gangel, K. (1974). *24 Ways to Improve Your Teaching*. Wheaton, IL: Victor Books, p. 10.
78. Barton, L. G. (1994). *Quick Flip Questions for Critical Thinking*. San Clemente, CA: Edupress.

CHAPTER 8

HOW CAN YOU KNOW IF YOU ARE MAKING A DIFFERENCE?

(Effectively Evaluating Your Teaching)

"Students may correctly answer all the questions in their Sunday school workbooks without being related to Christ. It is easy to feel successful when we have put on a smooth program, but the crucial question is, what is happening to the people? The test of our teaching is the changed lives of the person."

—LOIS E. LEBAR[79]

*   *   *   *   *

Chuck was a mechanic with whom I worked at a factory several years ago. One day he confided in me that he had found some spots on his arms the week before. His family had a history of various cancers, and Chuck was afraid he had a form of melanoma. I suggested he go see the company nurse to set up a doctor's appointment. He said he couldn't do that. Over the next several days when I pressed him about it, he kept saying that he didn't want to worry his wife, or that he didn't have time, or some other excuse.

Eventually his spots worried him so much that he finally agreed to go see the nurse. After he left his work station to walk to the nurse's office, I anxiously waited for him to return. Less than 20 minutes later he returned, holding out his arms for me to see. The spots were gone.

"It was splatter from the new grease we're using on the machine," he chuckled. "The nurse had seen a couple of other guys with the same thing, and she had a cleaner that took it right off. I don't have cancer after all!"

A lot of people I know are afraid to see a doctor because they fear something is dreadfully wrong with them. They would rather not know than have their fears confirmed. The problem is that our worst fears are very rarely realized.

I know a lot of youth workers who refuse to evaluate their teaching for the exact same reason: They are afraid they really are horrible teachers, and they would rather not know that. They fear asking others for feedback on their teaching because of what people might say. Maybe they'll have to change everything they do. Maybe they are so bad that they'll be asked to stop teaching altogether. They would just rather not know.

For some teachers, evaluating their effectiveness is as scary as going to see a doctor. But it shouldn't be like that. When done well, evaluation will help accentuate what you do well, identify areas for improvement, and ultimately result in greater effectiveness—so that more lives are touched for the sake of the kingdom.

WHY EVALUATE?

Teaching youth is a high and holy calling that is an extreme privilege. Those of us who have the honor of getting to help a group of teenagers learn to love and obey Christ's commands have an obligation to do that well. While there is not a specific scriptural command to teach youth well, there are plenty of admonitions to do everything we do the best we can do it. For example, 1 Corinthians 9:19-24 states:

> Though I am free and belong to no man, I make myself a slave to everyone, to win as many as possible. To the Jews I became like a Jew, to win the Jews. To those under the law I became like one under the law (though I myself am not under the law), so as to win those under the law. To those not having the law I became like one not having the law (though I am not free from God's law but am under Christ's law), so as to win those not having the law. To the weak I became weak, to win the weak. I have become all things to all men so that by all possible means I might save some. I do all this for the sake of the gospel, that I may share in its blessings. Do you not know that in a race all the runners run, but only one gets the prize? Run in such a way as to get the prize.

This is only one of many places where Paul commands Christians to do whatever it takes to make a difference. For the purpose of this chapter, a good paraphrase might say:

Though I am free to teach as I wish and do not have to be accountable to any-one, I make myself a teaching servant to everyone, to win as many as possi-ble...But I choose to try to teach in all ways to all people so that by all possi-ble means I might save some. I do all this for the sake of the gospel, so that I may share in its blessings. Do you not know that in youth ministry all the youth workers teach, but only some are great at it? Teach in such a way as to be a great teacher.

Later in 1 Corinthians Paul goes on to say, "If then I do not grasp the mean-ing of what someone is saying, I am a foreigner to the speaker, and he is a for-eigner to me. So it is with you. Since you are eager to have spiritual gifts, try to excel in gifts that build up the church" (14:11-12). The interpretation of these verses too often is narrowly focused on the gift of tongues, but it applies to any form of communication. If my students do not grasp the meaning of what I am saying, then I may as well be speaking Chinese. If I am eager to have spiritual gifts (and I am), then I want to excel in gifts that build up the church. Teaching well, by its very nature, edifies and builds up people.

Assessing your teaching effectiveness will have several important, if potential-ly scary, outcomes:

You will learn what others think about your teaching. This is the most obvious and the most intimidating aspect of the evaluation process. Any time you open yourself up to comments from others, there is the potential for deep emotional scarring. (I'm only partially kidding about that.) When you are going through an evaluation, there is a big temptation to take comments personally. What others think is important, at least to a point. Your most important task is not to get students to like you, but to motivate them to change. I believe that most youth workers are much more con-cerned about the former. You need to find out what people think about your teaching so that you can take that into consideration as part of the assessment process.

You will learn how much impact your teaching has. By asking the right questions and seek-ing the appropriate information, you can know if your teaching is helping to change lives. I established in the first chapter that changing lives is why we teach. If your teaching does not do that, then you should find out why—so you can fix the problem and become more effective.

You will identify what you do well. Even the least experienced teachers do many things very well. Sometimes aspects of teaching just come naturally because of God-given gifts or personality traits. Other times teachers have worked very hard on what they do, and that effort pays off. It is good to know those areas in which you are very strong so you can take advantage of them.

You will identify areas where you can improve. On the other hand, even the most experienced teachers are weak in some areas. Good evaluations will identify what could be improved and help teachers know how to develop. No one does everything right, and no one does everything wrong. Every teacher can improve in some areas.

Others will know that you want to improve. Allowing yourself to be evaluated shows that you know you can improve and you want to find out how. Teachers who think they have it all together tend to put off teens, who seem to have a special sense for detecting arrogance and hypocrisy. People respect those who show a teachable attitude.

Others will see an improvement in your teaching. When you go through a good evaluation process and use the results to change, better teaching will result. If you are teaching better, others will notice. Plus, it's nice to get those "Your discussion leading skills have really improved this month" comments.

You set a positive example that others will want to follow. As a Christian leader, others will follow what you do. When maturing believers know that the youth pastor has been evaluated and that it has helped improve his teaching, they are more likely to be open to it themselves. It also shows the youth that you know you have something to learn—and that alone sets a good example.

Keep in mind that a good evaluation can help teachers teach better, which will result in more learning, which leads to life change, which creates great disciples, which is what youth ministry is supposed to be all about.

WHAT TO EVALUATE

There is more to this process than asking students what they think about your teaching, and there is more to evaluate than just the teacher. A thorough assessment should include all of the following:

The Teacher: Evaluation always should include the teacher, but too often it doesn't include anything else. To focus only on the teacher is to ignore many other factors that affect learning.

The Teaching Environment: Pay attention to the classroom environment. Is it conducive to learning? Look for visual and aural distractions. Some kids can shut them out to pay attention, but many cannot. Also consider the temperature of the room, colors, chairs and tables, posters, availability and condition of teaching aids such as dry-erase/chalk boards, overhead projectors, TV/VCR/DVDs, and computers. (Note: It is not important to have all of these aids, but what you have should be in good working order).

The Goals: Why does your ministry have Bible studies, small groups, discipleship groups, Sunday school, or any other teaching opportunity? If it has no purpose, then why does it exist? If it does have a purpose, is that purpose being fulfilled? Is there a better way to accomplish the goal? Asking these questions will help you assess the very nature of your teaching ministry.

> Teaching is like selling; you can't have a sale unless someone buys. You haven't taught unless someone has learned.

The Curriculum: Evaluate what is being taught using the three levels of curriculum from the earlier chapter. Do not just look at the printed materials you use, but assess your long-term plans and your Scope and Sequence Chart. Is it still valid? What should be tweaked? How has it helped, if at all? You need to make sure that what you are teaching is what you had planned to teach.

The Students: Along with assessing who is teaching, where teaching is taking place, why you are teaching, and what is being taught, you also need to consider who is being taught. Think about how your youth are divided into classes. Does that division make the most sense? Is there a better way to create classes? Also examine the students themselves. How are their attitudes toward the class? Are they ready to learn? Are they doing all they can to make the class effective?

How to Evaluate

By this point you might be feeling a bit overwhelmed. With everything else you have to do in your ministry, this whole idea looks pretty time-intensive. And that's true: A good and thorough evaluation process takes time because there are several aspects to it. Here are some suggestions for how to make the process a bit more organized and less nebulous.

The most common form of evaluation usually involves having someone watch you teach, then share some thoughts about what was observed. That may elicit a few helpful comments, but it is really inadequate by itself. Consider some other aspects of observations that can help your evaluation process:

Observing Yourself: What do you think of your own teaching? What compliments and criticisms do you get from teens? With what aspects of teaching do you feel most comfortable? Which are most difficult? Watching a video of yourself teaching can help you identify your own strengths and weaknesses.

Parents' Observations: What do the parents of your teenagers say about your teaching? What do they say their kids say? Do they see an impact from your teaching? What do they think about the subjects you teach? What suggestions do they have?

Other Adults' Observations: Who else should you ask to observe you? Are there great teachers you know who could come and watch you teach a couple of times? What suggestions do they have?

Students' Observations: As important and helpful as the opinion of others may be, what the youth think of your teaching is really most important. Teachers in any setting are often reluctant to open themselves to their students' critiques. Often they do not believe student evaluations are accurate. Years of research show that, when the right questions are asked in the right way, student feedback is both accurate and helpful. Asking your teens to help you become a better teacher also shows that you value them. Whatever your motivation, students need to be involved. You should do this both formally and informally.

Formal Evaluations

At least once a year you should have your students fill out an evaluation of you. Create a survey instrument that seeks specific information that will give you valuable feedback. Avoid questions or statements that can be answered yes/no, true/false, or agree/disagree. Below are some statements that get to the heart of your teaching. They can be answered on a scale such as:

Always	Almost Always	Usually	Sometimes	Not Very Often	Never
6	5	4	3	2	1

Note that for some questions 6 would be the best answer, but on others 1 would be the best. This helps you determine if all those high scores were from students who actually read the questions. Here are the items:

- Sarah seems well prepared.
- Sarah knows the Bible well.
- Sarah explains ideas so I can understand them better.
- Sarah teaches in a lot of different ways.
- Sarah plays favorites with some students.
- Sarah keeps my attention when she teaches.
- Sarah keeps the attention of the rest of the class.
- Sarah teaches topics that are interesting to me.
- Sarah asks good questions.
- Sarah lets us participate during class.
- Sarah talks too much during class.
- Sarah helps me know how the Bible applies to my life.
- Sarah's teaching challenges me to change.
- Sarah is a creative teacher.
- Sarah thinks she knows everything.
- Sarah seems to want to be a good teacher.
- I know more about God because of Sarah's teaching.
- I am bored when Sarah teaches.
- I am a growing Christian because of Sarah's teaching.
- I want to learn more about the Bible because of Sarah's teaching.

You should also include a few open-ended questions that will allow students to express their opinions in more detail. I always like to ask:

- What is the best thing about Sarah's teaching?
- What do you like least about Sarah's teaching?
- Name three things that are different about you because of what you have learned from Sarah.
- If you were Sarah, how would you teach differently?
- What else would you like to say about Sarah's teaching?

You should not be in the room when students are filling out the evaluations. Even if you are not looking at what the youth write, your presence in the room will influence them. Ask someone else to hand out the evaluations and collect them.

I strongly suggest you have someone else tally the results and type up the comments. That way you are not tempted to try to figure out who said what about you.

Informal Evaluations

On a regular basis you should ask your students a few evaluation questions just to see what they are thinking. You could ask questions like these:

- How do you like this topic?
- Was last week's discussion helpful?
- How could I make this clearer for you?
- What are you doing with what we are studying?
- What would you like me to do differently?
- Am I making any sense?
- What do you not understand?

Asking the right questions of a variety of people will give you some helpful information to use in the evaluation process. The next challenge is figuring out how to understand what people have said about your teaching and what to do about it.

What to Do with Evaluations

One of the best ways to ensure that an assessment process will be fruitful is to have others helping you. I hope you are in a situation where you have someone else or a group of others who can help you understand the evaluations you've received. The key is to look for information that identifies problems, patterns, and issues to be addressed. Again, I believe asking the right questions is the key. Try these:

- What positive comments seem to be most common?
- Do the evaluations from parents and other adults agree with those of the students?
- What are the weakest aspects according to each group?
- Of the strengths, which seem to be most important?
- Which of the weaknesses are most important to address immediately?

These questions need to be asked about the teacher, learning environment, curriculum, goals, and students. If the people assisting with the process are insightful, critical thinkers, you should feel confident that the conclusions from the evaluations are accurate and helpful. The next step is to prepare to make whatever changes are necessary.

MAKING CHANGES

Change often comes slowly and painfully, but it does not have to. When suggestions for change are accompanied by good data (like a formal evaluation process), change often dictates itself.

One church I served had a very helpful Christian Education Committee to supervise and encourage me. They decided it was time to do a thorough evaluation of our Sunday school curriculum, so I created some evaluation tools, set a date for a teachers' meeting, and prepared for the process.

Before too many days passed, I heard grumblings that several teachers were not at all happy about evaluating the curriculum. They had taught it for as long as they could remember and were perfectly happy with it. There was no need to even consider change. When the committee reaffirmed our plan to do the evaluation, the unhappy teachers made it clear they would show up en masse to make sure no one decided to switch curriculum.

The day of the evaluation meeting, I had gathered sample materials from six different publishers and spread the materials out in a room by grade levels, and had evaluation surveys ready to hand out. After a brief introduction to the various publishers and some instructions about how to proceed, the evaluation began. In addition to the group of teachers determined to hold the status quo, there was another group of newer and more open-minded teachers. I was ready for battle.

Oddly enough, the unexpected happened. After a few minutes of examining one of the curriculum samples, I noticed some of the old guard gathered in an animated discussion, so I edged closer to listen in.

"My, look at this," said one. "I've been looking for these types of ideas," added another. "Wow, this looks like fun," commented a third.

Before long, they were feverishly taking notes on the evaluation sheets (which were very similar to the one I shared in the chapter on curriculum). After an hour, I called everyone back together to compare notes.

"Well, what did you think?" I asked. The response was surprising and nearly unanimous. They decided that the evaluation sheets showed a clear advantage in changing curriculum companies. Those who didn't strongly support the change said they would be happy either way. The next Monday I placed an order with our new supplier of Sunday school materials.

As it turned out, they chose the company I would have selected if the decision had been entirely up to me. But if I would have suggested that change and insisted on implementing it unilaterally, my tenure there would have ended quite prematurely. The impetus for change was based on our agreed upon, objective, evaluation tool. I took no credit.

The same experience repeated itself in a situation involving a teacher that many people wanted removed from a certain class. We did an evaluation of every teacher using the same methods for each one. The results were shared with each individual. Without uncomfortable coaxing or creating a scene, the teacher in question volunteered to find another ministry. "It looks like I'm not a very good teacher," she observed.

While she decided to stop teaching, other teachers identified their own areas of weakness to work on. The result was not only better teaching, but more teachers. We discovered that people were happy and even eager to volunteer when they found out there was a system to help them teach well. Most people want to do a good job at whatever they volunteer to do. Teaching is no exception. Those teachers who objected to being evaluated eventually quit on their own.

The key seems to be identifying specific items that need to be improved and creating strategies to make those improvements. For instance, when I started teaching college, I tried to fit in and be cool by exchanging barbs with the students in class. The evaluation from the dean that first semester was glowing. When he observed my class, everything was great. The comments from the students were more telling, though.

Several students complimented my teaching, but fried my sarcasm. I talked to another professor I respected, and he suggested that I target that as something to change the next semester. On the first day of class, I shared the concern with my students and asked them to hold me accountable. Whenever they heard me being sarcastic or sharing even good-natured ribbing with a student, they were to say something. It worked amazingly well. The evaluation helped me identify something specific to change, determine a definite way to change it, and ask for accountability. I have used such an evaluation model for my own teaching in college and in my work with youth ever since. It is very effective.

To recap, here's how evaluation could work:

1. Invite evaluation
2. Examine all aspects of the teaching situation
   a. The teacher
   b. The environment
   c. The curriculum
   d. The goals
   e. The students
3. Have others help in the process
   a. Supervisors
   b. Parents
   c. Other adults
   d. Students
4. Do formal and informal evaluations
5. Examine all the information from all the sources
   a. Look for key strengths and weakness
   b. Identify areas to address
6. Make plans to change which are
   a. Specific
   b. Observable
7. Evaluate regularly to keep improving

CONTINUING TO IMPROVE

Once you see the benefits of good evaluation, I hope you will want to keep a regular schedule for yourself and other youth teachers. In addition to the process explained above, there are other ideas you can take advantage of to improve your teaching effectiveness.

Observe Others: One of my favorite ways to learn about teaching is to observe great teachers. When I was doing my doctoral program, my statistics professor amazed me with her teaching skills. She was engaging, creative, caring, clear, and knowledgeable. Plus she used a variety of teaching techniques and methods to help those of us who were statistically challenged to succeed. I learned a lot about statistical methods in the two courses I took from her, but I learned at least as much about teaching.

Find people who are excellent teachers and watch them teach. Look for what they do and how they do it. See what aspects of their approach you might be able to emulate. Most will be flattered and honored that you would like to observe them.

Talk To Others: When you talk to other youth ministers, rather than comparing attendance numbers, complaining about difficult kids and parents, and bragging about your latest creative activity, ask them what they are teaching and how they are doing it. You can learn a great deal from conversations with other teachers where you share teaching ideas, philosophies, methods, and approaches. I often pick up new tips, strategies, or ways of thinking about teaching in such dialogues.

Attend Conferences: Maybe more than any other Christian profession, youth ministry offers a dizzying array of conference and workshop opportunities. From classes at Christian colleges to denominational gatherings, from regional one-day conferences to national multi-day conventions, there are numerous ways to hear great speakers with valuable experience that can help you teach and minister more effectively.

Don't just attend the most popular conferences with the most well-known speakers. I encourage my students to get into the habit of rotating their attendance patterns (unless they have the budget and time to attend four or five different ones each year), so they can take advantage of as many unique events as possible. Often the smaller gatherings with youth ministry practitioners no one has ever heard of offer valuable learning opportunities at much more affordable prices.

Read: A regrettable characteristic of youth workers is our collective aversion to reading. I suspect it has a lot to do with the fact that we tend to be people-oriented and would rather hang out with whoever we can find than curl up with a good book for a couple of hours. Early in my youth ministry career, I had to force myself to read. People I respected kept telling me I needed to read more to be well-educated and to touch peoples' lives more effectively. I was skeptical, but I decided to schedule two hours a day, three days a week, to read. I asked people I knew for suggestions and dug in. I read current and classic literature, Christian and secular, nonfiction and fiction—but very little that was youth ministry oriented.

As an extreme extrovert, disciplining myself to read regularly required a lot of self-control, but I found that it very definitely paid off. Not only was I a better youth pastor because of my reading, but I could also kick tail at Trivial Pursuit!

Regardless of how you decide to do evaluations, just make sure you do them regularly. It may be painful at times, but the reward of changed lives is worth it.

For Discussion

Why are most people apprehensive about being evaluated in just about any situation?

What are some other ways to evaluate besides the ones suggested here?

How do you think teachers in your ministry context would react if someone tried to institute a thorough evaluation process? If your ministry already does a thorough evaluation, what difference does it make?

Does this chapter make evaluation seem too mechanical to you? If so, how could it be done in a way that makes more sense for you?

Activities

Do a Bible study on the idea of evaluation. Look for situations in which some type of assessment is done and try to discern why.

Go to a few people you consider to be great teachers. Ask them if you can sit in on a couple of their teaching sessions. Also ask them about their ideas on evaluation.

Interview the principal of a local school about how the teachers there are evaluated. Ask about the strengths and weaknesses of that method, as well as the difference good evaluations can make for teachers who want to improve.

ENDNOTES, CHAPTER 8

79. LeBar, L. E. (1981). in Graendorf, W. C. (Ed.) *Introduction to Biblical Christian Education.* Chicago: Moody, p. 168.

CHAPTER 9

HOW MIGHT JESUS TEACH TEENS TODAY?

(A Few Observations and Suggestions)

"But if anyone causes one of these little ones who believe in me to sin,
it would be better for him to have a large millstone hung around his neck
and to be drowned in the depths of the sea."
—MATTHEW 18:6

"He also told them this parable: 'Can a blind man lead a blind man?
Will they not both fall into a pit? A student is not above his teacher, but everyone
who is fully prepared[80] will be like his teacher.'"
—LUKE 6:39-40

*   *   *   *   *

"Jesus was a master teacher."
"Jesus was the best teacher who ever lived."

Throughout my education and experience in ministry, I have heard many different people make these claims, or very similar ones. I also believe they are true, even though there is no hard evidence to support them. Because I think Jesus truly was the best teacher in history, it is vitally important to pay attention to how Jesus taught. He always had the right words to say at just the appropriate moment. He knew his students well enough to know how to push them to grow in just the right ways at just the right times.

It's tempting to discount our own potential to be great teachers, since Jesus had a bit of an advantage—after all, he is fully God and everything. But being a believer in the truth of the Bible, I also know that Jesus meant what he said in John 14:12-14:

> I tell you the truth, anyone who has faith in me will do what I have been doing. He will do even greater things than these, because I am going to the Father. And I will do whatever you ask in my name, so that the Son may bring glory to the Father. You may ask me for anything in my name, and I will do it.

Trying to do what Jesus did without the power and authority Jesus had would be futile. However, the Lord promised that every person who believes in him and asks for his help will be able to do not only what he did, but much more. Wow! Now that's a promise I need to claim.

In the passage the modern church refers to as the Great Commission, Jesus "commissions" his followers to make disciples as they go about living their daily lives by baptizing and teaching (Matthew 28:19-20). This isn't just any old teaching. Jesus commands us to teach disciples to "obey everything I have commanded." Not to teach them to memorize it. Not to teach them to know it. Not to teach them to feel good about it. Our commission is to teach them to *obey* Jesus' teachings. And not just the ones we like or are comfortable with, but *all* of them.

Sounds like an impossibly daunting task for mere mortals, right? It is. That's why Jesus said we would have to do it through faith in him, with the help of the Holy Spirit, by bathing our teaching in prayer. (See chapter 1 for more on the Spirit's role in teaching.) Yes, it is a huge responsibility, but one the Lord has given us the means to accomplish—if we do it as he says.

SOME OBSERVATIONS ABOUT JESUS' TEACHING

To try to better understand how Jesus taught, I spent time reading the Gospels and making notes about those occasions in which he seemed to be specifically teaching a group or individual. I did not focus on times when Jesus performed miracles (although he did use some of those to teach, and I took note of those), or other situations that were not primarily teaching. What I learned was very eye-opening.

Whom Jesus Taught

Jesus taught everybody who would listen to him. He even tried to teach people he knew wouldn't listen, but he still gave them the opportunity. You could say that Jesus' teaching career began at age 12, when he stayed in Jerusalem to hear the rabbis teach and ask questions. When his parents expressed their concern, he tried to teach them about his priorities: "Didn't you know I had to be in my Father's house?" (Luke 2:41-50).

Jesus taught John the Baptist a bit more about who he was and what his mission was to be in Matthew 3:13-17. John did not think it proper to baptize Jesus, but Jesus insisted because, "It is proper for us to do this to fulfill all righteousness" (3:15). Then John consented.

Jesus even tried to teach Satan. Matthew 4 records the temptations of Jesus in the wilderness. Jesus was aware of Satan's tricks, even his inappropriate use of Scripture. Jesus knew Scripture well enough to stand up to this temptation. The Lord wanted Satan to know not primarily who he was (Jesus never said, "Hey, don't mess with me. Don't you know who I am?"), but that he rested in his knowledge of God through Scripture. Satan has no authority over someone with such convictions. We can learn a lot from this encounter, but Satan seems to be clueless.

On other occasions Jesus taught very large crowds, maybe up to 20,000 at times. There also seems to have been a group of perhaps a few hundred that followed him from place to place listening to him. There was also the group of disciples, which evidently numbered about 70 or so, and were the most devoted followers of Christ. He often would teach them separately and send them out to share and to heal. Out of this group of disciples, Jesus called 12 apostles, to whom he gave authority to do special ministries at various times. These were the ones closest to him during his ministry years.

Even within this group of 12, there were three Jesus called to share special events with him. These unique opportunities helped prepare Peter and John especially for their key roles in the beginning of the Christian church. Jesus may have spent more effort on Peter than any other person. It's hard to know what Peter had that Jesus decided to use, but Peter was the subject of many of Jesus' most difficult and personal lessons.

Then there were the religious leaders. The Pharisees, Sadducees, scribes, rabbis, and chief priests all heard Jesus teach, asked him questions, interacted with him, and had to decide how to respond. Most reacted poorly. Some decided to believe what he said, or at least gave him a chance to prove his claims.

Jesus even spent time with the outcasts of ancient Israel. He chose to interact with Samaritans, women, lepers, sinners, tax collectors, thieves, the blind, the demon-possessed, and many others. The Lord shattered social barriers that had been virtually impenetrable for centuries in order to share the Good News he had brought. Israel had never seen anything like it. Jesus taught everyone, without regard to status, health, ethnicity, or gender.

What Jesus Taught

As I studied what Jesus taught, I was surprised by a few of my findings. For example, Jesus taught topically the vast majority of the time. In fact, there is only one incident when he begins with Scripture. That is when he goes to the synagogue on the Sabbath and is handed the scroll of Isaiah (Luke 4:16-21). He finds a passage to read to the crowd and declares that he is the fulfillment of the prophecy.

Jesus does quote or allude to the Hebrew Scriptures many other times. When he does, it is typically to support a point he is making or to discuss how he is fulfilling specific prophecies. The fact is that Jesus usually taught topically.

Another interesting discovery was that Jesus emphasized what we might call theological teaching. As I noted the subjects of Jesus' teaching, three topics appeared most frequently. His own purpose and ministry, the nature of God, and explaining faith were his most discussed topics. He taught about who he was and what he was to do in more than 110 passages in the Gospels. The nature and work of God is discussed in more than 80 passages. Faith, belief, and what they mean in the lives of those who follow him is Jesus' topic in about 45 passages.

Other theological subjects Jesus focused on include the church, the end times, eternal life, God's will, hell, the Holy Spirit, judgment, human nature, praise and worship, prayer, Scripture, resurrection, righteousness, the Law, the Sabbath, Satan, sin, and salvation.

One of my most unexpected findings was how often Jesus challenged his listeners to live up to a higher standard than they had been. In more than 40 passages, Jesus teaches about the high expectations he has of his followers. Along with the many times Jesus taught about how Christians should act and treat others, these passages make it obvious that our behavior is a major concern of his teaching.

Below I have listed the subjects of Jesus' teachings as I noted them in my study. I have no delusions about this list being unabridged or comprehensive. I am also quite sure that some will claim it is inaccurate—and it may well be. Nonetheless, it was a fascinating study that I would strongly encourage you to try yourself at some point. We have a lot to learn from Scripture, and we should not rely on others to tell us what it says.

Subjects of Jesus Teachings
(with references)

Adultery (Matthew 5:27-28,32; Luke 16:18)

Bad teaching (Matthew 16:12, 18:5-6; Mark 9:42; Luke 11:52, 17:1-3)

Being born again (John 3:3-21)

Celibacy (Matthew 19:11-12)

Church (Matthew 16:18; 18:17)

Commitment (Matthew 8:19-22, Mark 10:21, Luke 18:22)

Discipline (Matthew 18:15-17)

Divorce (Matthew 5:31-32, 19:8-9; Mark 10:11-12; Luke 16:18)

End times (Matthew 24:1-25,46; Mark 13:7-37; Luke 12:35-40, 17:22-37, 21:9-28; John 6:44, 16:19-23)

Enemies (Matthew 5:44)

Eternal life (Matthew 19:17-26; Mark 10:29-30; Luke 16:19-31, 18:30; John 3:15-16; 5:24; 6:27,47,51,58; 10:28; 12:25,50)

Eyes (Matthew 6:22-23; Mark 8:18; Luke 10:23-24, 11:34)

Faith/belief (Matthew 8:10-12,26; 10:32-33,40; 12:30; 13:3-33; 14:27-31; 17:20-21; 21:21-22; Mark 4:3-8, 13-20, 40; 5:34, 36; 9:23; 11:22-24; Luke 7:9,50; 8:5-15,25,47,50; 12:8,31; 16:31; 17:6,19; 18:42; John 3:11-18; 5:24; 6:27,29,35,47; 7:37-38; 8:24; 10:37; 11:26,40; 12:44-46; 13:19-20; 14:9-12; 16:27; 20:29)

False prophets/teachers (Matthew 7:15-20,21; 24:4-5,11,23-24; Mark 9:39-41; 13:5-6, 21-22; 21:8)

Fasting (Matthew 6:16-18, 9:15-16)

IS THAT IT?
Please keep in mind that what is recorded in the Gospels is only a small percentage of all that Jesus said and did. (See John 20:30-31 and 21:25.) The Holy Spirit inspired the biblical writers to record those things that would accomplish God's ultimate purpose. Jesus undoubtedly taught many more things in many more settings and many more ways than what we read about in our Bibles.

I am also confident that nothing essential or important to our faith or growth as disciples has been omitted.

Following him (Matthew 16:24-25, 19:28-30; Mark 10:21; Luke 11:23)

Forgiveness (Matthew 6:12,14-15; 9:6; 12:31-32; 18:22,35; Mark 3:28-29; 11:25; Luke 7:47; 11:4; 12:10; 17:3-4; 20:23)

Freedom (John 8:30)

Giving to the needy (Matthew 6:3-4,42; 25:35-45; Luke 11:41; 12:33)

God's nature (Matthew 5:34-35,45; 6:6, 8-9,11-15,18,26,30,32; 7:7-8,11; 10:28,30; 11:25-30; 16:27; 18:14; 19:26; 20:23; 26:55; Mark 10:18,27; 13:32; Luke 6:35-36; 10:21-22; 11:2-4,13; 12:5-7,24,28,30-32; 15:7,10,11-32; 16:15; 18:19,27; 20:38; 22:29; John 3:16-21; 4:23-24; 5:17,19-47; 6:27,32-33,44-46,57-58; 7:16,28-29; 8:18,26,29,40,50,54; 10:15-18;25-30,38; 12:26,28,44-45,49,50; 13:31-32; 14:1-2,6-7,9-21,23-24,26,28,31; 15:1-10; 16:15,27-28; 19:11)

God's will (Matthew 6:10, 7:21, 10:29, 12:48-50; Mark 3:35; John 7:17)

God's Word (Matthew 24:35; Mark 13:31; Luke 21:33; John 5:38-39, 8:51, 10:35)

Good works (Matthew 5:16, 6:1, 7:16-21, 10:40-42, 12:33, 21:43; Mark 4:24-25; Luke 6:27,43-45; 17:7-10; John 15:8)

Heart (Matthew 6:21,35; Mark 7:19,21; Luke 6:45; John 14:27)

Hell (Matthew 7:13, Mark 9:48-49, Luke 12:5)

His purpose (Matthew 5:17; 9:6; 12:39-42; 16:4,27-28; 17:9,12,22-23; 19:28; 20:18-19,28; 23:39; 24:30-31; 25:31-33; 26:1,29,32,64; Mark 1:38; 2:10,17; 8:31; 8:38; 9:31; 10:33-34,39-40,45; 14:25,28,62; Luke 4:43; 5:24,32,35; 7:22-23; 9:22,44; 10:22; 11:20,29-32; 12:8-9,14,40,49-51; 13:32-33; 17:25; 18:31-33; 19:10; 20:9-18; 21:15,27; 22:15,27,29,37,69,70; 23:3; 24:26,44,46,49; John 2:19; 3:14-18; 4:10,14,26,34-38; 5:17, 19-47; 6:27, 35-40,44-51,53-58,64,65; 7:33-34; 8:15-18,21,27-29,40,42,50,55-56,58; 9:5,37,39; 10:7-18,25-30,38; 11:25-26; 12:7-8,23,26,27,31-32,35-36,44-50; 13:8,12-20,31-33,36; 14:1-4,6-7,9-21,27-31; 15:1-26; 16:4,5-16,25-28,33; 18:36-37; 20:17,21)

Holy Spirit (Matthew 10:20; 12:31-32; Mark 13:11; Luke 11:13; 12:10,12; John 3:5-8; 6:63; 7:38-39; 14:16-17,26; 15:26; 16:7-15; 20:22)

Hospitality (Matthew 5:47, 10:40-42; Mark 9:37; Luke 9:3-5;48)

Human nature (Matthew 5:36, 7:11, 10:31; Luke 12:6-7,24-26,28; John 3:19, 8:23)

Humility (Matthew 18:4,10; 20:26-27; 23:11-12; Mark 9:35, 10:43-45; Luke 9:48, 11:43, 14:11, 18:10-14, 22:25-27)

Hypocrisy (Matthew 5:20; 6:1-2,5,16; 7:5; 15:3-20; 23:1-33; 24:51; Mark 7:6-13; 12:1-12,38-40; Luke 6:41-42; 11:39-52; 12:1,56; 13:15; 18:10-14; 20:46-47)

Innocence (Matthew 10:16)

John the Baptist (Matthew 11:7-14, 17:11-13; Mark 9:12-13; Luke 7:24-28; John 5:31-36)

Joy (John 15:11, 16:24)

Judging (Matthew 7:1-5; Luke 6:37-38,41-42; 22:30)

Judgment (Matthew 7:1-5,23; 21:44; 24:50-51; 26:24; Mark 12:40; Luke 6:37; 10:12-15; 11:50-51; 12:5,9-10,45-48; 13:28-30; 19:11-27; 20:47; John 5:22,27,29-30; 12:31,47-48)

Kingdom of God/heaven (Matthew 6:10; 7:14; 11:11-12; 12:25-28; 13:24-33, 44-50; 16:19; 18:3-4,23-35; 19:14,23-24; 20:1-16; 21:31,33-44; 22:1-14,30; 23:13-14; Mark 1:15; 4:11,26-32; 9:1; 10:14-15,23-25; Luke 10:9,11; 11:20; 12:32; 13:18-21; 13:28-30; 15:4-7; 16:16-17; 17:20-21; 18:16-17,24-25,29; John 3:3)

Knowing culture (Luke 12:56)

Lawsuits (Matthew 5:25,40; Luke 12:58-59)

Learning from God (John 6:45)

Lending and borrowing (Matthew 5:42, Luke 6:35)

Looking for signs/miracles (Matthew 16:2-4; Mark 8:12; Luke 11:29; John 4:48, 14:11)

Love (Matthew 5:44,46; 22:37-39; Mark 12:29-31; Luke 6:27; 7:41-42; 11:42; John 13:34-35; 14:21, 3-24,28-31; 15:9-13)

Lust (Matthew 5:28)

Making a difference (Matthew 5:14-16)

Marriage (Matthew 19:4-6,11-12; Mark 10:6-9)

New ways (Matthew 9:16-17, Mark 2:21-22, Luke 5:36-39)

Oaths (Matthew 5:33-37)

Obedience (Matthew 7:24-27; 12:48-50; 19:17,21; 25:14-30; Mark 3:35; Luke 6:46-49; 8:21; 11:28; John 12:47-48; 13:14-17; 14:12-21,23-24; 15:10-14,20)

Paying ministers (Luke 10:7)

Peace (John 14:27)

Perfection, wholeness (Matthew 5:48; 19:21)

Persecution (Matthew 5:11-12,44; 10:17-23,35-40; 24:9; Mark 13:9,11-13; Luke 6:22; 10:3; 12:52-53; 21:12,16-17; John 15:18-25; 16:2-3,33)

Perseverance (Matthew 10:22; 11:6; 24:10,13; 26:41; Mark 13:13; Luke 11:8,24-26; Luke 13:6-7; 18:1-8; 21:19,34-36; John 8:31; 15:4-10; 16:1)

Power of God's people (Matthew 18:18-19)

Praise/worship (Matthew 5:16, 21:16; Luke 19:40; John 4:21-24, 5:41-44, 13:31-32)

Prayer (Matthew 5:44, 6:5-13, 7:7, 21:22, 26:41; Mark 9:29, 11:24-25, 14:38; Luke 6:28, 11:2-4, 5-10, 18:1-8, 22:46; John 14:14, 15:7, 16:23-24)

Priorities (Luke 9:60,62; 10:41-42; 12:15,34; 15:4-10)

Raising expectations (Matthew 5:17,18-22,28-30,32,34,37,39-42,44; 6:1,16,20,24; 10:34-40;

11:12; 18:7-9; 20:26; Mark 4:24-25; 8:34-38; 9:35,50; Luke 5:10; 6:27-36; 9:23-26,60,62; 11:35-36; 12:33-34,48; 14:26-27; 19:45-46; John 13:14-17, 34-35)

Reconciliation (Matthew 5:23-26, 18:15; Mark 9:50; Luke 12:58)

Rejection (Luke 10:16)

Relationships (Matthew 10:24,35-40; Mark 3:33-35; Luke 8:21; 11:11-13; 14:26; John 15:12-17)

Repentance (Matthew 11:20-24; 21:32; Luke 13:3,5; 15:7,10-32; 17:3-4; John 5:14)

Resurrection (Matthew 22:30-32; Mark 12:24-27; Luke 14:14, 20:34-38; John 5:21,25,28-29; 6:40,44,54)

Revenge (Matthew 5:38-39)

Rewards (Matthew 5:46; 6:1-2,4-5,16, 18; Mark 10:29-31; Luke 6:23,35; 8:18; 10:19-20; 12:8,31,44; 14:14; 18:30; 19:11-27)

Righteousness (Matthew 5:19-20, 7:12; Luke 11:33-36; John 3:19-21)

Role of the Law (Matthew 5:18)

Sabbath (Matthew 12:1-12; Mark 2:27-28; 3:4; Luke 6:5,9; 13:15-16)

Sacrifice (Matthew 16:24-28; Luke 14:26-27,33; 21:3-4; John 12:25; 15:13)

Satan's nature (Matthew 5:37, 6:13; Luke 13:16)

Scripture, proper use of (Matthew 4:7, 21:16, 22:29; Mark 12:24; Luke 4:21; John 5:39, 10:34-35)

Serving (Matthew 6:24, 20:26-27, 25:40; Mark 9:35, 10:43-45; Luke 10:30-37, 22:26-27; John 12:26, 13:14)

Sharing the gospel (Matthew 24:14; Mark 13:10, 14:9; Luke 24:47; John 4:35-38)

Shrewdness (Matthew 10:16; Luke 16:8)

Sin (Matthew 5:29-30, 6:12; Mark 7:20-23, 9:43-47; John 8:34, 9:41, 15:22-24)

Speech (Matthew 5:21-22, 12:36-37; Luke 6:45)

Teaching (Matthew 13:52, 18:6; Luke 6:39-40)

Temptation (Matthew 6:13)

Things done in secret (Matthew 6:18, 10:26-27; Mark 4:22; Luke 8:17, 12:2-3)

Trust (Luke 16:10-12; John 12:36; 14:1)

Truth (John 8:32)

Wealth (Matthew 6:19-21, 19:23-24; Mark 10:21-25; Luke 6:20, 24; 12:21; 16:9,13)

Who is truly blessed (Matthew 5:3-11)

Whom he wants (Matthew 9:13, 18:12-14; Luke 14:26-27; John 4:23-24)

Who will be saved (Luke 13:24-27; 14:16-24; John 10:9)

Worry (Matthew 6:25-34; Luke 12:22-26)

How Jesus Taught

Even more than what Jesus taught, how he taught has been studied and discussed for a long time. Many authors have attempted to enumerate the various teaching methods Jesus used. In 20 years of ministry and teaching, I have probably read dozens of books, essays, and articles about the teaching ministry of Jesus, and his methodology was the primary focus of most of them. While methodology is important, I am afraid that this focus has caused us to overlook other aspects of Jesus' teaching as recorded in the Gospels.

Any cursory reading of Jesus' ministry would reveal that he taught through lecture, asking questions, challenging his listeners, telling stories, using objects, and giving assignments. The Lord was never satisfied with a shallow understanding of any subject, and we shouldn't be either. Digging a bit deeper reveals a few other insights about how Jesus taught.

Jesus encouraged critical thinking. Jesus often challenged those around him with questions that required critical thinking. On one occasion, some tax collectors had approached Peter, asking if Jesus paid the two-drachma tax. When Peter saw Jesus after that, Jesus asked him a very difficult question about kings collecting taxes (Matthew 17:25). A more famous occurrence was when he asked the priests about the authority of John's baptism (Matthew 21:25). Other examples are in Matthew 21:31 and 22:43-45, as well as Mark 12:35-37; Luke 7:41-42, 20:3-4, and 41-44; and John 6:5-6.

Jesus was concerned that his followers learn *how* to think about a variety of issues. If he had cared only about sharing facts, he would have taught much differently. Critical thinking, problem solving, and real-life application were his goals.

Jesus taught with clarity. Jesus did not want to leave his disciples—especially the 12 he called out—unnecessarily wondering about the meaning of what he taught. He struck a balance between just giving information and challenging his students to dig for meaning. For that reason Jesus often clarified or restated what he'd said in a larger context. In Matthew 13:10-17, the disciples ask Jesus why he speaks to the crowds in parables. Jesus explains that the disciples have been granted knowledge of the mysteries of heaven, but the crowds do not have that same privilege. Jesus took the time to explain why he taught differently in various settings.

On other occasions, Jesus would tell a story to the multitudes, but wait until he was with only the disciples to explain the meaning. This is the case, for example, with the parable of the tares in Matthew 13:36-43. The disciples even expressed appreciation to Jesus when he would explain clearly to them (John 16:29). After his resurrection, Jesus made sure to teach plainly and patiently so the disciples were clear on the meaning of all they had witnessed (Luke 24:27).

Jesus used comparison and hyperbole. Sometimes it appears as if Jesus used language to separate those who understood from those who did not (e.g., John 16:25). His explanation to the disciples that some hear and comprehend and others don't, plus the use of the phrase, "Those who have ears, let them hear," seem to attest to this. Jesus used comparison, METAPHOR, SIMILE, HYPERBOLE, and other figures of speech quite often to communicate specific ideas to only a select portion of his audience. Apparently he knew that some would catch his message and others would not. Consider the following examples:

"To what shall I compare the kingdom of heaven?"

"The kingdom of God is like..."

"If anyone comes to me and does not hate his father and mother, his wife and children, his brothers and sisters—yes, even his own life—he cannot be my disciple."

"It is easier for a camel to go through the eye of a needle than for a rich man to enter the kingdom of God."

"If your right eye causes you to sin, gouge it out and throw it away."

"I tell you the truth, unless you eat the flesh of the Son of Man and drink his blood, you have no life in you."

All of these quotes from Jesus are examples of ways that Jesus used symbolic or figurative language to teach.

Jesus used criticism. Jesus was always nurturing, positive, and reassuring—treating the disciples, the crowds, and others around him with a gentle touch, right? Wrong. It is amazing how often Jesus used harsh words, called names, and chastised people, even his closest friends. He used words and phrases like "Woe to you" (Matthew 11:20-24), "You of little faith" (Matthew 16:8-11), "Satan" (Matthew 16:23, Mark 8:33), "unbelieving and perverted generation" (Matthew 17:17, Luke 9:41), "robbers" (Matthew 21:12-13), "hypocrites" (Matthew 23:13-15,23,25,27,29), "blind guides" (Matthew 23:16,17,24,26), "fools" (Matthew 23:17), "serpents" and "brood of vipers" (Matthew 23:33), "wicked" (Luke 11:29), "foolish" (Luke 24:25), and "liar" (John 8:55) to address hearers from Pharisees to apostles.

Jesus also regularly rebuked and corrected those listening to him. In Mark 7:18 Jesus rebukes his hearers for not understanding what he is saying. In a more popularly known incident from Mark 8:32-33, Peter has the nerve to rebuke Jesus for saying he must suffer and die, then Jesus rebukes Peter right back and calls him "Satan." I don't think Jesus was being very sensitive to Peter's self-esteem at that moment.

Do not start to believe Jesus' use of criticism can be used as an excuse for calling our junior highers names when they get on our nerves. If I ever find out that one of my middle school daughter's teachers called her Satan, you'd better believe I'll be sharing how upset I am about that. Clearly, though, Jesus was not as concerned with positive affirmations as our contemporary society and conservative church is.

Other characteristics of Jesus' teaching. Jesus' teaching got him into trouble with the Jewish religious leaders of his day. One of the most common descriptions of Jesus' teaching was that he taught "with authority" (Matthew 7:29, Mark 1:27, Luke 4:32). Why was this so amazing to those who heard Jesus teach? Scholars can't say for sure—but evidently all the other teachers were wimps in some way. Maybe they quoted lots of other teachers as they spoke. Maybe they taught in third person. Maybe they were not challenging or knowledgeable. Maybe they were just uninspiring. Somehow Jesus communicated confidence and authority when he spoke. The masses loved it. The leaders were threatened by it.

Jesus' teaching also had passion. One specific incident in a synagogue on the Sabbath is recorded in Mark 3:1-5. A man with a withered hand was present, and Jesus approached him. After asking the man to stand, Jesus asks the crowd, "Is it lawful on the Sabbath to do good or to do harm, to save a life or to kill?" No one answered him immediately, which made Jesus mad. Verse 5 indicates the hardness of their hearts angered him. The Greek word used for anger here, οργης (*orges*) is not a mild word. It communicates passionate wrath. Jesus felt deeply about what he was teaching and his ministry. He desperately wanted listeners to understand. I believe people with open eyes could see that and appreciated that about him.

Where Jesus Taught

We all know Jesus never taught in a formal church building or at a Christian college. He did teach in the equivalent of a church or college setting for the first century, though. The synagogue was the center of life and activity for Jews of Jesus' day. It was not only their house of worship, but also the local school, a community gathering place, and a center for philosophical discussion.

But Jesus did not limit his teaching ministry to the official religious buildings. No, he went out and taught wherever people would listen. As a result, Jesus taught from town to town, in public and in private, in homes and along roads, on hillsides and on seashores, to large masses and to individuals. Jesus was never limited by the walls of a facility.

Jesus taught everywhere he went. He was not dependent upon dry-erase boards, overhead projectors, or computers. He used the sand under his feet if he needed to write something. The world was his classroom.

When Jesus Taught

In the same way Jesus was not limited by where he taught, he was not limited by when he taught, either. Jesus taught whenever people came to him. If he had a message for people who did not come to him, then he went to them. Just think of vertically challenged Zacchaeus up in that Sycamore tree. All he wanted was a glimpse of the teacher everyone was talking about, but he wound up with a personal encounter when Jesus approached him. Jesus taught personally whenever he could.

One of the most frustrating things about Jesus to the religious leaders was that Jesus taught and healed on the Sabbath. The four Gospels record at least 14 occasions when Jesus taught on the Sabbath. He wanted the Pharisees to understand that the Sabbath was given for the good of humanity, but people are not bound by their laws for the Sabbath. Teaching, healing, sharing, laughing, and so on, are all permissible anytime.

As much as Jesus seemed to enjoy freaking out the religious hypocrites, he also seemed to delight in freaking out the disciples. Why else would he sleep through a typhoon, walk up to their drifting boat on the surface of the water, and call a man who had been dead three days out of his tomb clothes? At times of crisis when a typical person would be losing it, Jesus shows up, calm as can be, with a nugget of truth to share. Perfect. No time is a bad time to teach.

How People Responded

Just as is the case with any other teacher, people responded to Jesus in a variety of ways. Some were positive, some were negative, and some just reacted. Many hearers came to believe in Jesus as the Christ; others accused him of being from the devil. Most often though, those who heard Jesus teach are said to have been amazed or astonished (Matthew 7:28, 8:27, 12:23, 21:20, 22:33; Mark 1:27, 2:12, 6:2, 10:32, 12:17; Luke 4:22,32,36; 20:26; John 7:15). It seems they had never heard anything quite like what Jesus was saying and how he was saying it.

This amazement led to several different responses. Some wanted to know more, so they asked questions of him. Occasionally listeners would express delight (Mark 12:37, Luke 13:17), praise God (Mark 2:12), or just listen intently (Luke 19:48). Others wondered among themselves if Jesus could be the one they had waited for (Matthew 12:23). Many decided he was Messiah and expressed their belief (Matthew 14:33; John 6:68-69; 7:31,40-41; 8:30; 9:38; 11:27; 16:30), some asked for faith to be increased (Luke 17:5), and many even left everything and followed him (Matthew 8:1, John 8:12). Several simply wanted to do something in response (Luke 23:5).

Others were skeptical and responded in a variety of more negative ways. Some expressed anger (Luke 4:28, 6:11), fear (Matthew 8:34; Mark 4:41, 10:32), or offense (Matthew 15:12; Mark 6:3; Luke 11:45,53; 13:17; 16:14; 20:19; John 6:61). Many tested him in an attempt to trap him (Matt 16:1).

Maybe it shouldn't surprise us, but nowhere in the four Gospels do we read that people were bored by Jesus or indifferent to what he was teaching. His teaching always elicited a response of some type. Jesus' teaching was powerful, memorable, and life-changing. So what might this mean for us as we teach teenagers?

SOME MISTAKES TO AVOID WHEN TRYING TO TEACH LIKE JESUS

Certainly there are many nuggets we can pan from what we know of Jesus' teaching ministry. Below are some common mistakes youth teachers may make by misinterpreting certain aspects of Jesus' teaching. The list is followed by some important implications I think we should glean from it.

Don't think that you can't teach like Jesus, because he's God and you're not. As discussed earlier, Jesus promised us, his followers, that we could do the things he did, and even greater things, because of our belief in him. Several times in the Gospels Jesus is said to have known what people were thinking. I don't believe that power is necessary in order for us to teach with the insight Jesus did.

God wants and expects us not just to teach adequately, but to teach very well. To help us accomplish great teaching, he has provided some divine assistance for us. That help is in the person of the Holy Spirit. The Spirit will help if we ask and allow it. We have the same Spirit today that Jesus promised almost 2,000 years ago. You can teach like Jesus.

Don't give up on teens who you think aren't listening. Jesus kept trying to teach the religious hypocrites, even though he knew what they were thinking. We don't know what our kids are thinking, and we never know for sure that they are not listening.

Over the past 20 years of my ministry, I have had many students who I thought were not paying any attention. But later a lot of them asked a question or showed some other evidence that they had been with me a lot more often than I thought. We need to give teens the benefit of the doubt rather than a series of ultimatums. Perseverance and patience are vital for teachers as we work with adolescents. Trust in the ministry of the Holy Spirit more than your own.

Don't treat your church leadership the way Jesus treated his. Not because Jesus was wrong, but because he had a different time frame and purpose than you do. He knew he had a limited amount of time to share his message. He also knew that speaking to the leaders as he did would get him killed.

Your ministry will not thrive if you call your elders hypocrites or drink a Dr. Pepper in the sanctuary just to show that you can. In fact, it will likely end.

There is a time and a place for sternly addressing ministry leaders. I have done it myself on rare occasion. Some wisdom and discernment are appropriate here, and those qualities come only with age and maturity.

Don't rely on others to tell you what to teach and how to teach it. Learn to think and study for yourself. I have seen too many times when an unwitting volunteer is handed a class to teach and a quarterly or a book to teach from, yet still flails aimlessly because he lacks specific direction. Teach whatever you are teaching for a specific purpose.

Just because the church bought curriculum for you to use doesn't mean you are married to it. Get to know your students and their needs, then select or adapt materials to teach them accordingly. See the chapter on curriculum for more on this.

Don't eliminate Bible study or memorization because the Gospels do not record Jesus doing it. History records that the primary teaching method of ancient Jewish culture was rote memorization. There is little doubt that, as product of first-century Judaism, Jesus would have memorized the Torah. His use of Hebrew Scripture also shows a great command of not just the words, but the meaning, so Jesus obviously studied (see Luke 2:52). In his teaching, Jesus almost always taught topically, but that doesn't mean it is wrong to teach any other way. A good study through Isaiah, Luke, or I Corinthians can be great with teenagers. In fact, we need to be modeling to them how we read and study the Bible ourselves. Leading such a study is one very effective way to do that. The danger here is in relying totally on topical studies with young people and using the Bible to proof text your beliefs. Strike an appropriate balance.

Scripture memorization can be great when used as a tool rather than an end. While the New Testament never records that Jesus commanded or even encouraged his followers to memorize Scripture, it is clear that the Lord relied heavily on a thorough knowledge of the Word during his ministry. Mastery of any subject matter does not need to include memorization of it, but it does require a working knowledge of what it is, what it means, and how to understand it. I know a lot of people who can quote Scripture easier than they can name the members of their own family. A great many of them have very poor Christian witnesses. I also know a lot of wonderful believers who can quote only a few of the Top Ten Bible verses, but whose commitment to Christ and Christian growth is more than apparent.

Don't limit yourself to only the methods Jesus used. While Jesus used a wide variety of ways to teach, he did not use every possible strategy. Just because it's not in the New Testament does not mean you cannot use it. Scholars do not know a lot about how other great teachers of the ancient Near East taught their students, so we can't say Jesus was doing more or less than his contemporaries.

While we have many recorded incidents of people being amazed at Jesus' teaching, it was due to his authority (as discussed above) rather than his methodology. You might infer then that Jesus was using many of the same strategies that other great teachers were using. Otherwise people might have declared their amazement with his object lessons or complex parables. Regardless, I am convinced that the Lord would certainly be using video cameras, the Internet, DVDs, and whatever else he could to communicate his message to today's youth.

Don't call your students names when they seem thickheaded. I know Jesus did this on occasion, but that does not give us authority to do so. Telling your high schoolers that theirs is an unbelieving and perverse generation likely would not be beneficial to your ministry. Honestly, it is difficult for me to know why Jesus used some of the harsh language that he did.

Right or wrong, we live in a much more sensitive time and culture. We need to recognize that reality. I have known several teens who were hurt by the way a youth leader spoke to them. Sometimes that hurt was because those youth were overly sensitive. More often, though, it was because the youth leader thought he was being funny. I have even heard adults use the excuse that insults are their "love language." Words hurt kids more than they let us know. We need to be extra cautious about the words and tone we use to communicate with them.

Don't think you have failed if some students don't like your teaching. It is easy to assume that Jesus was 100 percent successful as a teacher. Not true. Jesus, the Master Teacher, had students that didn't listen to him. Even one of his chosen few betrayed him. We are not called to a higher level of success than Christ was. In fact, we are not called to succeed at all. We are simply called to be faithful to God.

Hold yourself to high standards, but make sure they are realistic. No one can tell you how many of your teenagers should be dramatically moved by your every lesson. Sometimes some will, and sometimes many will. There will be days when no one is moved. (Now, if no one is ever listening, that's another story...)

SO HOW MIGHT JESUS TEACH TODAY'S TEENAGERS?

Jesus would teach to make disciples. This is our command directly from the resurrected Lord. We are not to make Baptists or Wesleyans or Episcopalians, but disciples. (No, that's not the same thing.)

Making disciples means sharing the gospel with youth who need to hear. It means teaching them the story of the God who created them, loves them, and yearns to have an eternal relationship with them. It means teaching them what

Scripture says and how to obey everything in it. It means not being satisfied with teaching a good lesson to a bunch of nice kids. It means challenging them to Christian maturity and helping them learn how to live in and have an impact on a world that is desperately lost and in need of the Savior. It means a lot of work.

We are too easily satisfied when teens seem to like us and parents are happy that their children want to come back next week. The disciples Jesus made ministered in the spiritual trenches of Judea and Samaria and beyond. They attacked false prophets. They were persecuted, which means more than not being allowed to pass out fliers in school. They were beaten and killed for their faith. That is the type of disciple Jesus still wants.

Jesus would teach obedience to God's commands. This is our ultimate goal—that our students would be obedient to God. I'll take the risk of beating on this point too much, because Jesus does and so do many other biblical authors. In fact, the idea of obedience appears in nearly 250 references. That's why I pointed out in chapter 6 that I don't believe any lesson is complete until students know what to do with it.

It's so easy to get sidetracked by emphasizing memorization, attendance, and conformity. Those may be good things, but they are not the primary reason we teach youth. Check these out:

- "Hear, O Israel, and be careful to obey..." (Deuteronomy 6:3)
- "Be strong and very courageous. Be careful to obey all the law my servant Moses gave you." (Joshua 1:7)
- "Unlike their fathers, they quickly turned from the way in which their fathers had walked, the way of obedience to the LORD's commands." (Judges 2:17)
- "To obey is better than sacrifice." (1 Samuel 15:22)
- "He commanded Judah to seek the LORD, the God of their fathers, and to obey his laws and commands." (2 Chronicles 14:4)
- "I obey your statutes, for I love them greatly." (Psalms 119:167)
- "Obey me, and I will be your God and you will be my people." (Jeremiah 7:23)
- "The LORD thunders at the head of his army; his forces are beyond number, and mighty are those who obey his command." (Joel 2:11)
- "If you want to enter life, obey the commandments." (Matthew 19:17)
- "Blessed rather are those who hear the word of God and obey it." (Luke 11:28)

- "If you obey my commands, you will remain in my love..." (John 15:10)
- "For it is not those who hear the law who are righteous in God's sight, but it is those who obey the law who will be declared righteous." (Romans 2:13)
- "And, once made perfect, he became the source of eternal salvation for all who obey him." (Hebrews 5:9)
- "Remember, therefore, what you have received and heard; obey it, and repent." (Revelation 3:3)

Jesus would teach obedience, because that is what Scripture emphasizes. Knowing God is important, since you must know him to obey him, but knowledge alone is incomplete. Understanding God might be nice, but it does not need to come before obedience. In fact, I can think of many occasions when I obeyed God without understanding why. Feeling close to God is important to today's youth. That's fine—until they decide it is hypocritical to obey if they do not feel like it.

Jesus would teach everyone, especially those who might not be welcomed by traditional churches. Focusing primarily on the "good Christian kids" who attend church every Sunday may be easy, but it is not biblical. Jesus set such a groundbreaking example with regard to relationships that we are compelled to follow it. As a result, you should take the time and effort to teach those kids who are outside the norm for you and your group.

One way to do this is to look at what needs exist in your school or community. Then fill these gaps by offering a class in something unique that would especially target the outcasts and marginalized. The teens in your area may not include tax collectors, prostitutes, lepers, or Samaritans, but you have contemporary equivalents. Shy, low-income, hard to get along with, drug-dealing, single-parent, low GPA, smelly, and prejudiced teenagers all need to know the love of Christ.

A favorite praise song of the youth group I teach has been "Breathe Deep," by The Lost Dogs. It lists dozens of types of people that often have a hard time finding acceptance in our modern evangelical churches. The chorus is brilliantly profound yet simple. It repeats, "Breathe deep, breathe deep the breath of God." Those on the fringes of adolescent society need to hear this invitation. They are the too-often overlooked souls who are crying out for God's unconditional love. Our ministries should be going to them.

Jesus would teach in a variety of settings. I used to compartmentalize my ministry. Sunday school and youth group were the times for teaching. Pool parties were for fun, mission trips were for service, and church was for worship. It took a while for me to realize how wrong I was. Now I look for teaching opportunities everywhere I go.

This has become very annoying to my college students, the youth at church, and to my own kids. I just see learning opportunities everywhere I turn. Think about all the various occasions Jesus used to teach. In order for this to happen, though, you have to force yourself to break out of the restrictive box in which you've placed education. Learning should be both formal and informal, both structured and unstructured, both planned and spontaneous.

I often wonder if the disciples grumbled when Jesus would start in on something new when they were trying to relax.

"Jesus," one of them might whine, "we're supposed to be resting, remember? Can't you lay off the teaching for a while?"

Surely that had to happen. Teaching should not just be something you do, teaching should become part of who you are. When that happens you, too, will see opportunities in every tree, traffic jam, and ball game.

Jesus would teach different groups differently. Think about the adolescents you teach. Are they all alike? Do they all like the same activities, enjoy the same food, or cheer for the same teams? Neither do they all learn alike. Jesus taught the multitudes differently than he taught the 12. Learn from that. Despite what you might read in ads for printed curriculum, one size does not fit all when it comes to teaching.

Use your powers of observation and common sense to consider how you might need to adjust your lessons for different individuals, contexts, or sizes. Have specific goals for your various teaching settings. Go so far as to call out a few teenagers (like Jesus called some disciples to him) and have special teaching times with them. Determine who you really connect with most and put an emphasis on deeply discipling one or two youth.

Jesus would teach theologically. As discussed in chapter 1, too many youth growing up in church today don't understand much about God or the Bible. And most certainly do not have a personal commitment to the Christian life. That is because we have emphasized teaching cultural hot-button issues or feel-good topics over theological ones. We need to fix that.

Jesus taught more about theological issues than anything else. Over half of his teaching topics were primarily theological in nature. A common objection is that teens are bored with theology. The problem isn't your kids or theology. It's either that you are trying to teach it the way you were taught (yawn) or that you just don't know how to make it palatable for them. Don't teach systematic theology the way you learned it in college. Teach biblical, practical theology that speaks to the way kids encounter God in their daily lives.

You can learn a lot about how your young people want to be taught if you'll just ask them. I have always found that, when it comes to theology, youth only trust the Bible. Because of that, I love to break out all the study aids I can and help them do a thorough study as I guide them. Their self-discovered insights and probing questions create better lessons than any printed curriculum you'll ever find. Teens are very theological, just maybe not the same way you are.

Jesus would teach to raise expectations. Most churches have some type of membership. This membership often has some requirements or expectations: "Members are to tithe at least ten percent." "Members must be involved with at least one of the ministries of the congregation." "Members will commit to pray for the staff regularly." "Members should attend at least one worship service a month." I think Jesus would scoff at these. They simply do not reflect New Testament Christianity. This is reflected in what we ask of our youth.

For some reason we have gotten away from expecting a lot from today's Christian adolescents. We are afraid failure might hurt their self-esteem. We've dumbed down Christianity to the point that it is almost unrecognizable when compared to biblical faith.

Demand a lot from your teens. Push them hard. They need to understand what Christian commitment is and how to live it out today. Kids love to be pushed in this way. That's why competitive sports, music programs, and other activities typically draw the best out of them.

Remember the movie *Stand and Deliver*? It was based on a true story about Jaime Escalante, a calculus teacher at a tough East Los Angeles high school. Escalante took a group everyone else gave up on and taught them how to pass a rigorous standardized test. In one scene, a group of teachers is discussing these students and how hopeless they are. Escalante expresses his confidence that he can teach them when everyone else has failed. When his fellow teachers asked him why, he replies,

"Ganas"—the Spanish word for desire. He explains that someone's desire will push him to meet the level of expectations others have for him. I believe this is the spirit that most youth workers are missing when it comes to nurturing teens.

Jesus would teach to increase critical thinking. "I've never thought about it that way before." I love it when students say that. One of the greatest accomplishments of Jesus as a teacher was getting those around him to think. He was clearly bothered by the mindless obedience of the Jewish people to the instructions of hypocritical religious leaders. I believe a great many churches are at the same point today.

Go back to chapter 1 and re-read some of the comments by the "Amazing Apostates". Notice how many of them express frustration that critical thinking and questioning were discouraged. God wants us to think for ourselves. He is not interested in an army of identically programmed religious robots. Teach your students to think for themselves. Write questions and create projects that force them to interact with a subject and wrestle with its truths. Avoid answering your own questions, and instead encourage teens to interact with Scripture and each other. Don't make everything obvious. Use riddles, metaphors, and hyperbole like Jesus did.

Jesus would teach with authority. Where does your authority come from when you teach? Consider who you use or quote most often. "According to Dobson…" "Swindoll says…" "In McDowell's latest book…" Each of these men has a wonderful ministry and valuable insights to share, but they are not your authority. I have noticed it in lessons or sermons I hear as well as the papers I read. Some people quote others so often that I wonder if they have any original thoughts at all.

You have the authority of Christ when you teach—so act like it! I am tired of listening to mild-mannered, mealy-mouthed youth leaders lecture teenagers for an hour, using everybody's ideas but their own. The truth you have to share comes straight from the Holy Spirit. Name it and claim it, but do not tame it.

Jesus would teach so students respond. If your kids file out of class and never think again about what they just discussed, you have failed. If you want to teach to make a difference, then teach as if your teaching makes a difference. Give your students something to do as a result of your lesson.

I am always amazed at how often I sit in on a lesson and am left wanting more, because it is incomplete. Usually that happens when the teacher has prepared well and shared some interesting insights, but doesn't follow through with an application or a challenge. Often I get the sense that the teacher thinks she's hit a walk-off home run when it's really just a long fly ball. The Christian faith is a *practical* faith. God wants his truth to make a difference in our lives. As teachers, we need to help teenagers discover how their faith matters.

Which brings us back to the "So what?" of the lesson. This does not have to be something big. Jesus had many creative approaches that pushed the disciples to respond. He told the rich young ruler to sell all he had. He told several people to go and sin no more. He challenges others to share what they've heard. He asks some to wait and pray. Chapter 6 has more on this.

Jesus would teach holistically. Considering everything this chapter discusses about Jesus and his teaching, it is obvious that he taught to have an impact upon the mind, heart, soul, attitudes, and actions of those who were listening. Teaching that does any less is incomplete. A quick look at Jesus' interactions with Peter shows us this.

Jesus taught Peter theological truths. He also addressed Peter's emotions, for example when Peter cut off the ear of soldier on the night Jesus was betrayed. He shaped Peter's soul when, after Jesus had been transfigured, Peter wanted to build three monuments. Jesus called Peter to action when he asked Peter three times, "Do you love me?" and then challenged Peter to feed and tend his flock.

God created adolescents in his image, which means they are multidimensional young men and women. Jesus would undoubtedly teach in a way that would mature all of those dimensions.

The Ultimate Reward

Jesus promised an amazingly great reward for those whom he taught. Listen to his words from John 13:17: "Now that you know these things, you will be blessed if you do them."

Similar words echo in John 14:21: "Whoever hears my commands and obeys them, he is the one who loves me. He who loves me will be loved by my Father, and I too will love him and show myself to him."

Learning from Jesus and obeying what he taught results in receiving God's love and blessing to the fullest extent. We can obtain that by obeying him. Our students can receive that as well, but it is our responsibility to learn from Jesus and teach our youth what he has commanded.

For Discussion

Which aspects of Jesus' teaching ministry have had the greatest impact on you?

What surprises you about the topics Jesus taught? Anything missing that you assumed he addressed or emphasized?

How do we determine when Jesus (or any other person in Scripture), was using figures of speech or exaggeration, and when he was being literal? How can we teach youth to determine that for themselves?

What are your experiences with Scripture memorization? What are the positives and negatives of encouraging it with adolescents?

Is this chapter too hard on current youth ministry practices? What is your assessment of what and how you were taught as a teen?

What theological truths are essential to teach young people? Are there different points of theology that should be taught or re-emphasized at various ages?

Activities

Do your own study of Jesus' teaching. Read through the Gospels and start making notes about what you notice. When you are finished, go back through what you have written and make some of your own conclusions.

Go to a library and do some research on critical thinking. Find out what teachers and researchers are discovering about how to help people think better and more deeply. Brainstorm how to apply this to youth ministry.

Keep a journal for a few weeks to make note of teaching opportunities that occur outside of your usual educational settings.

Find some sample youth curriculum at a local church or bookstore. Read through it and determine if you think Jesus would teach from it or not. How would it need to be revised to more closely match his expectations?

ENDNOTES, CHAPTER 9

80. Most translations have *train* in the place of *prepare* in this verse. I believe *prepare* is a better contemporary rendering, though. The Greek word here is κατηρτισμενος δε which carries the idea of having been made complete. Our use of the word *train* today is much too loose. I trained my puppy to housebreak him. He was taught a conditioned, unthinking response. That is not the idea Christ is communicating here. Christian teachers are not to train other Christians. We are to teach them to be complete in Christ. There is autonomy and intelligence in that process. I recoil at the term *teacher training* for the same reason.

CHAPTER 10

WHAT OTHER TEACHING TIPS SHOULD I KNOW?

(A Lot of Other Important Issues that Didn't Fit Anywhere Else in the Book)

*   *   *   *   *

For every teacher in any teaching setting there are seemingly thousands of issues to consider as you seek to make your teaching effective. Each of the previous chapters have focused on one major issue. This chapter is where you can find a few dozen other ideas (some major and others minor), that will help you enhance the impact you have on students. These are in no particular order.

DISCIPLINE

In almost any group you will have at least one teen who is disruptive and likes to cause trouble. Here are some tips for dealing with discipline:

- Deal with discipline issues before they begin by building a relationship with kids. In a positive relationship, most youth will not want to disappoint or upset you.
- Work with parents. Know the names of parents and make sure the teens know you have a relationship with them.
- Spread out the adult volunteers. Don't let them all sit together in the back.
- If someone is causing a disruption as you teach, slowly move toward them as you talk. The closer proximity of the teacher will make most youth check their behavior.
- Talk outside class with kids who are causing chronic problems, just to make sure they know they are a problem.
- If a teen is regularly being disruptive, then tell him and his parents that he may not return until his behavior improves. This sends the message to the

other students that you want to teach them. Most are upset with friends who cause problems and will be happy you are taking a stand. Make sure to spend more individual time with the one you remove, though; he and his parents still need ministry.

SETTING UP THE LEARNING ENVIRONMENT

Teachers communicate a lot to students by the way they arrange the learning environment. Tables and chairs in rows facing the front indicate that the teacher is the center of attention. To foster discussion, make sure the adolescents can see one another's faces. Arranging chairs in a circle or horseshoe, orchestral seating, or randomly spread out chairs can all accomplish this.[81] If you will be writing on a board or using a TV or screen that students need to see, make sure they can see it easily.

TEMPERATURE, WINDOWS, AND OTHER DISTRACTIONS

Often adults forget how easily adolescents get distracted. Pay attention to the following items:

- The room temperature should be between 68 and 72 degrees. If kids are too warm, they'll be drowsy. If they are too cool, they'll be thinking about how cold they are.
- If there are windows in the room, including in the doors, make sure that you face them and most of the teens do not. Otherwise, any time someone walks or drives by, or when it snows or rains, their attention easily shifts from the lesson to the windows.
- Excessive noise can be a problem. Banging furnaces, a loud neighboring class, or a blaring sound system can all cause attention problems.
- When there is a distraction, ignoring it is like spitting into the wind. You are better off saying something about it quickly, then redirecting the focus. That at least lets the class know you are aware of the distraction.

USING AUDIOVISUAL AIDS

Almost anytime you can find a way to use media to enhance the lesson, kids will learn more. Be aware of these issues:

- Make time to set up and try out your media before you have to use it. This allows you to do trouble-shooting, if needed, before the lesson. I have seen many good teachers become frustrated with a video or CD because they didn't try it out or cue it up before class.
- When using TVs, make sure there is no distracting glare off of the screen. That usually means the screen needs to be pointed away from windows and lights and toward the center of the group.
- When using audio, make sure the volume is appropriate for all to hear easily without distracting other nearby groups.
- When playing a song, always have the lyrics available on either a projection or a sheet of paper. Most kids can't pay attention to the words if they don't have something to follow.
- When writing or projecting words, make sure they are large enough for people in the back to see them easily. This is true for using an overhead projector or PowerPoint as well.
- When you are done with a point and want the students to pay attention to you or each other, you need to turn off or darken the projection.
- No matter what you want students to see, be sure all of them can actually see it. That means you can't stand in front of it.

SIZE OF THE GROUP

For larger classes, consider breaking up into smaller groups for activities or discussion. For smaller classes, try to meet in a space that is appropriate for the number of students. Plan your activities and methods so you can be flexible (that means always having a plan B) if a lot more or a lot fewer teens show up than you'd expected.

NATURE OF THE SETTING

Where you meet makes a difference as well. Consider the following:
- A small-group Bible study should be more intimate and more discussion-oriented with less structure.

- A class that meets on Sunday morning should probably not include a lot of physically active games that might make teens sweat or prevent those in dress clothes from participating.
- An indoor class should take advantage of the setting and not involve activities that might break something.

MIXING GUYS AND GIRLS

Your adolescents live in a coed world and need to learn how to get along as Christians in that world. For that reason, I believe it is appropriate for guys and girls to meet together most of the time. At least once or twice a year it is a good idea to have a series of lessons or special activities that are gender-specific. There are also some topics that are better taught to a group of the same sex in order to foster more open discussion and application.

A large number of youth ministries rely on small groups as the primary means of teaching and building formal relationships. Most of these ministries seem to divide the groups by gender. I have talked with many youth leaders and teens who tell me how important that same-sex safe haven is for their growth. It's easy to see why that could be true.

So the setting and purpose of the teaching are important considerations as you decide whether it is best to mix genders. But keep in mind that a ministry that always has the guys and girls separate is going to have a much tougher time being holistic.

FOCUS ON THE TEENAGERS AS INDIVIDUALS

When a green-haired, eye-brow-studded, dog-collar-wearing, chain-belted kid walks into your group, it's easy to comment on her appearance. Don't do it. Focus on her name, where she lives, or what music she likes. Get to know her personally without making assumptions based on what you see (1 Samuel 16:7).

ERASING

When erasing a chalk or dry-erase board in front of a group, use a vertical motion rather than side-to-side. It's a butt wiggle thing. Teens notice that stuff.

The Teachable Moment

Teachable moments occur when, in the midst of the daily routine of life, something happens that helps you reflect on an aspect of God's truth. Too often people look for these opportunities only in times of crisis. While difficulties and struggles certainly can present us with teachable moments, so can a softball game, fixing a meal at home, folding laundry, driving on a rainy day, or any number of other regular experiences.

The fact is, teachable moments happen daily if you look for them.

Handouts

Having handouts for students to read or write on is usually a good idea. Make sure they are readable, though. If the print is small, do not use florescent papers or inks because they tend to hurt the eye. Don't hand them out until you are ready to use them, otherwise they become distractions. Make sure you have enough copies for everyone so students aren't distracted by sharing. Ask kids or volunteers to pass around the handouts so you can focus on the class.

Using Bibles

Should you ask kids to bring their own Bibles to use? Should you have a supply to pass out for those who don't bring them? Should you assume they won't bring Bibles and just print out the passage for everyone? I don't know that there's one correct way to answer these questions, but you should think about them and make your decision purposefully.

Flexibility

I don't know what the single, most important quality to possess in youth ministry is, but flexibility has got to be very close to the top of the list. Don't be so married to your goals and plans that you cannot adjust to the unexpected. Always have a plan B—even if plan B is just to abandon plan A. This is another great reason to have a trusted team of volunteers. Use their insights and creativity to allow you to be more flexible. Keep asking yourself, "In ten years, how much of this will really matter?" and don't sweat the small stuff.

CREATIVITY

Youth workers often pride themselves in being outrageously creative. Teaching is a great context in which to practice that creativity. Be very careful, though, about being too creative. Yes, that is possible.

Early in my ministry with Youth for Christ, we were taking a group of high schoolers to Florida for spring break. Someone on staff dreamed up an idea for a very cool activity called "The Tax Game." The more the staff worked on it, the more excited we got. It had action, problem-solving, and fun, while requiring strategy and some luck. As we set the game up and explained it to the kids, we were more than a bit disappointed to see the blank stares and lukewarm reception for our incredibly creative game.

We were so excited about our new game that we forgot high school students don't do or understand taxes. Collecting deductions and avoiding penalties meant nothing to them. We were caught up in our creativity and not thinking about our context.

STUDENTS WITH DISABILITIES

Even the smallest groups may have students with some type of disability. Large groups undoubtedly do. Don't just think that if you can't see a disability, then none exist. Dyslexia, reading or listening-comprehension problems, and social anxieties can be just as problematic for teens as blindness, mobility difficulties, or hearing loss. Talk with experts (parents, teachers at the local schools, or a disabilities resource person at a local college) to find out how to adapt your teaching appropriately.

EQUIPPING VOLUNTEER TEACHERS

Never recruit a volunteer and just throw her into a class with some purchased curriculum and say, "Let me know if you have any problems." Always take time to require new volunteers to observe and learn before they teach.

Your Voice

Be aware of how your voice projects. It is your job to communicate well with the students. That means you may have to learn how to speak louder or softer, project better, or talk less when you teach. Don't expect teens to adjust to you.

Volunteer Involvement in the Lesson

When one person is teaching, the other adults in the room still have important roles to play. Here are some:
- Spread out and sit among the youth rather than together.
- Be aware of distractions and try to take care of them before they become problems.
- Encourage quieter students to make a comment or ask a question.
- Rarely (as in almost never) respond to a comment or question unless the person leading specifically asks the adults to respond. Remember, the lesson is for teens.
- Move toward kids who are talking or causing problems.
- Never be a problem to the leader. The role of the other adults is to facilitate the teaching.

Arrive Early

This is especially true when you have some setting up to do. Plan well ahead for teaching aids and get them ready and tested out before students arrive. You and the other adults should greet each teen as he or she arrives. You cannot do that if you're messing with a CD player or making copies.

The key is that by arriving early, you have more time to spend talking with the students. When you typically arrive just on time, or even late, you are sending the message that either you are not prepared or you'd prefer to spend the minimum amount of time necessary with them.

DON'T BE DRIVEN BY THE CURRICULUM

I have seen too many teachers plow through a lesson because they feel they have to get through everything. To paraphrase a famous saying, "Curriculum is made for the students, not students for the curriculum." Make sure the needs of your students come before the instructions in the material. That might mean taking two weeks to do a lesson, because students want to talk more in depth about something than you'd anticipated.

KNOW WHEN TO SCRAP YOUR LESSON

Sometimes no matter how hard you plan, you need to throw out your agenda. If you get into a lesson and it becomes obvious it is not connecting with the students, you need to find out why. Don't be afraid to admit that you wrote a poor lesson. It will happen. Also, sometimes the students are dealing with something you can't know about ahead of time. It may be a problem with a family or friend, illness, last night's basketball game, a great worship service that just ended, the prom, or any number of other issues.

"DECHURCHIFY" YOUR LANGUAGE

Pay attention to the vocabulary you use. Proclaiming that, "God's propitiatory atonement for reconciliation was fulfilled through the substitutionary sacrifice of the blood of the Lamb," may be true, but those words will block any message to most youth. "When Jesus died, he paid the price God requires so we can have a relationship with him," is just as true, plus it is understandable. You will still have to explain conceptually why that is true and what that means, but at least your religious multi-syllabic oratory won't be a verbal stumbling block.

INTEGRITY, INTEGRITY, INTEGRITY

Adolescents will learn from you those things that you model in your own life. They have great hypocrisy detectors that are finely tuned. You must be a leader with integrity, period.

Dividing Students into Groups

Some people believe it is best to divide groups randomly to separate friends from each other. Others think it's best to let the teens divide themselves so they are happy with who's in their group and more likely to participate. Actually, there may be times when either of these approaches is preferable. Think ahead of time about why you want to divide the class into smaller groups. The purpose of the activity should dictate how you divide the youth. Counting off by numbers, drawing names from a hat, teacher assignment, or student choice are all appropriate options depending on the context.

New Students and Visitors

Don't ignore first-timers when they come to class. If they came with someone, have that person introduce them. If not, then make sure you greet them in some way. Hopefully you have a team of youth and/or volunteers who will make them feel at home, introduce them around, and get some basic information.

Copyright Issues

Legal matters related to the use of copyrighted materials in religious settings are very complex. You will find a variety of interpretations of what you can and cannot do legally. In fact, some court cases seem to contradict each other. We are bound to follow the laws of the land (Romans 13:1-5), so that means we must know the laws and their implications. Here are a few items to keep in mind as guidelines:
- *Fair use* is a term that allows people to make a copy of something in specific circumstances. You can almost always make a single copy of something you have purchased for a teaching setting. That includes making copies for an overhead or PowerPoint presentation, or to read aloud in class.
- You may make one copy of something for each student to use if you include the copyright notice and if it is under a certain limit (ten percent of the entire work, one chart, graph, or illustration of a work, a poem of not more than two pages, etc.)

- You may not make copies of something to avoid paying for it. That includes reproducing student workbooks, burning CDs, or copying videos.
- Showing commercial videos is a sticky subject. Most carry a legal disclaimer stating they are for home use only. In most cases, it is probably okay to use a short clip to make a point or spark discussion. It is never legally permissible to show an entire entertainment video in a setting outside the home without paying a "public performance video license fee." Movie studios have successfully sued schools and organizations for violating that law.
- If your church or organization holds a license from Christian Copyright Licensing International (CCLI), that only gives you permission to use songs and lyrics (with proper acknowledgment) from the participating publishers, none of which are secular.

MAKING RULES

If you feel a need to create rules for your classroom, ask your students for ideas. That way they have ownership and the right to enforce their rules. Otherwise it sets you up in an adversarial role by imposing regulations on them. I have always found that groups of teens are harder on themselves than I would be when it comes to creating rules.

THE TOP TEN TRAITS OF GREAT TEACHERS

Decades of educational research have identified several traits of effective teaching.[82] The following ones are most important to teaching in youth ministry. (Not all great teachers do all of these, and few do any of them well when they first teach):

- *Great teachers make sense to the students.* This means avoiding lessons that are vague, too complicated, or too broad in scope. This reinforces the idea that a great teacher needs to plan effectively and speak intentionally.
- *Great teachers use a variety of instructional methods.* This helps keep interest and forces teachers to be creative.
- *Great teachers are focused on the topic.* It is easy to get off track when teaching,

especially in the midst of a good discussion. Great teachers recognize this and help the class refocus.

- *Great teachers involve students in the lesson.* Often called "student engagement," this idea refers to connecting learners to the subject actively.
- *Great teachers know if students are "getting it."* This occurs through constant evaluation during and after the lesson.
- *Great teachers use student ideas.* Encouraging youth to participate in class by using, acknowledging, applying, and summarizing their comments and suggestions helps them have ownership in the learning process.
- *Great teachers put each lesson in context.* This includes helping students understand how each lesson fits with what has come before and what will come after it.
- *Great teachers ask questions.* Have I mentioned that enough yet?
- *Great teachers probe their students' minds.* This means asking students to clarify or expand on what they or another student said.
- *Great teachers are enthusiastic.* The emotional side of teaching well is sometimes overemphasized, but is nevertheless important. Students respond positively to teachers who show enthusiasm about what they are teaching.

TEACHING CONTROVERSIAL TOPICS

People often ask me, "What should I teach my kids about controversial stuff?" From homosexuality to abortion, from women in ministry to "just war," youth and teachers alike seem to be vexed by tough subjects. Too often we try to find Scripture to tell us what to think about such issues. What I encourage is to help your students use Scripture to learn how to think, period. That way they can be transformed by the renewing of their minds (Romans 12:2) and learn to have the mind of Christ in all things (1 Corinthians 2:16). Teach youth how to think, and they will be able to figure out what to believe.

BUILD UP, NEVER TEAR DOWN

Memorize Ephesians 4:29: "Do not let any unwholesome talk come out of your mouths, but only what is helpful for building others up according to their needs, that it may benefit those who listen." Have it tattooed on your forehead, make it your life's theme verse, require your volunteers to know it in eight languages, model it to your teenagers, and expect them to abide by it as well. All the time. No exceptions. None.

READ, READ, AND THEN READ SOME MORE

Magazines, newspapers, books, and Web sites are all great sources not just to learn about youth and teaching, but to learn about anything. The more you learn, the more you know, you know?

COMMUNICATE WITH PARENTS AND CHURCH LEADERS

A few times a year you should let parents and those in leadership at your church know what you are teaching. This shows that you have a plan and want them to be informed. You might be reluctant to publicize this quarter's study on The Ten Grossest Things in the Old Testament, but communication is always good. Don't feel like everyone has to agree with what you're teaching.

ENDNOTES, CHAPTER 10

81. For several more ideas about how to arrange chairs, as well as a lot of other great ideas for teachers, see Dockery, K. (1999). *The Youth Worker's Guide to Creative Bible Study, Revised and Expanded.* Nashville, TN: Broadman & Holdman.
82. Borich, G. D. (1996). *Effective Teaching Methods (3rd edition).* Englewood Cliffs, NJ: Merrill, pp.10-33.

READ THIS LAST!

Now that you have finished reading this book, don't think you have learned everything you need about teaching. Far from it. Keep learning about teaching. I want to encourage you with two final thoughts:

Long after your students have forgotten any specific lesson you taught, they will remember you and what you modeled. That is not an excuse to teach poorly or without preparation. It is a caution to keep your priorities straight.

You are not called to be successful as the world defines success. You are called to be faithful in the ministry God has given you. The number of teens who flock to your class has little bearing on that. Some ministries have lots of kids, not because they are faithful, but because their goal is to have lots of kids. Your goal is to change lives for the sake of making disciples.

May you eagerly seek God's blessing as you teach.

GLOSSARY

ABSTRACT Existing only in the mind.

ACCOMMODATIOIN Allowing or making room for something new.

ADOLESCENCE The developmental transition period between childhood and adulthood.

ADOLESCENT GROWTH SPURT The rapid change in height that occurs during adolescence.

AFFECTIVE Having to do with emotions and motivations.

AIM A goal or purpose to achieve in teaching.

ANALYTIC LEARNER A student who prefers to learn by gathering all pertinent information and thinking logically through an idea.

ANOREXIA NERVOSA An eating disorder in which a person eats significantly less than is necessary.

APPLICATION QUESTIONS A type of open question designed to help students understand the difference an issue makes in their lives.

ASSEMBLY-LINE WORKER A metaphor that depicts teaching as the systematic assembly of a student, in which one process leads to the next.

ASSIMILATION Accepting an idea and blending it in with other accepted practices or beliefs.

ASYNCHRONICITY IN GROWTH When various aspects of development occur unevenly. (for example, One arm may grow faster than the other or emotional maturity may outpace physical growth.)

AUDITORY LEARNERS Students who understand the world primarily through their sense of hearing.

AUTONOMY The cognitive realization that one is an individual.

AVOIDANT Preferring to process information in one's head, rather than through shared activity.

BI-POLAR MODELS Learning-style theories that have two extremes.

BLOOM'S TAXONOMY A way of understanding the levels of thinking, developed by Dr. Benjamin Bloom.

BODILY-KINESTHETIC INTELLIGENCE The natural ability to use one's body in a physical or athletic way.

BOOK In the HLBT technique, the part of a lesson that communicates the actual text of Scripture to students.

BULIMIA An eating disorder in which a person habitually vomits after eating.

CEREBELLUM The part of the brain located near the back that develops information-processing skills.

CIRCADIAN CLOCK A biological function that determines the body's need for sleep.

CLASSROOM ENVIRONMENT The setting for teaching, including everything from the temperature to the color of the walls to the furniture.

CLIQUE A close group of peers, usually few in number, who share a common interest and are often exclusive.

CLOSED QUESTIONS Questions that have few possible answers (i.e., yes/no or true/false).

COACH A metaphor that sees teaching as helping students learn, but allowing them to actually live with encouragement and direction, but without much interference.

COGNITIVE Concerned with intelligence and thought.

COGNITIVE FLEXIBILITY The ability of the brain to consider potential outcomes of a situation.

COLLABORATIVE Able to work together with another person or group.

COMMERCIAL CURRICULUM Lesson material that can be purchased from a publisher.

COMMON SENSE LEARNER Someone who relies primarily on her own intuition to draw conclusions.

COMPARTMENTALIZE To keep separate and unrelated.

COMPETITIVE Involving individuals or teams pitted against each other, as in games or contests.

CONCRETE Focused on that which is practical and tangible.

CONJUNCTIVE FAITH The fifth stage of Fowler's faith development theory in which individuals can understand opposing points of view simultaneously.

CONVENTIONAL MORAL REASONING The second of Kohlberg's three stages of moral reasoning in which moral decisions are made based on societal norms.

CONVERGENT Coming together into a single point of focus. Convergent thinkers learn by linking new information to old information.

CULTURAL EXEGESIS The process of learning about a culture in order to minister in that culture.

CURRICULAR IDEOLOGIES Beliefs about the purpose curriculum has in the teaching process.

CURRICULUM Anything that helps someone learn.

DEPENDENT In learning, preferring the presence and close guidance of a teacher.

DETACHMENT The process of an adolescent separating emotionally from parents.

DIVERGENT Differing from something. Divergent thinkers seek alternate applications for new material as it is learned.

DOGMA The specific and strongly held beliefs of a group of people.

DYNAMIC LEARNER A student who learns by doing.

EARLY ADOLESCENCE The period between ages 10 and 14, usually corresponding to sixth, seventh, and eighth grade.

EPISTEMOLOGY Having to do with the nature of knowledge.

EXEGESIS Research and interpretation.

EXISTENTIAL Having to do with the nature of existence.

EXPLICIT CURRICULUM The plans or expectations of a teacher that are clearly expressed to students.

EXTROVERT A person who prefers interaction with others and their social environment.

FALSE-SELF BEHAVIOR When teenagers choose to engage in an activity that is opposed to their natural personality.

FARMER A metaphor that understands the teacher as one who imparts information and nurtures its growth.

GLOBAL Applying to all situations or people.

GOD-ESTEEM Psychologically, understanding one's value through the eyes of God rather than other people.

GUIDE A metaphor that understands the teacher to be one who shows the way.

HEDONISM The pursuit of pleasure.

HIDDEN CURRICULUM Learning goals that are not expressed to students.

HOLISTIC Relating to all aspects of a person; concerned with wholes or complete systems rather than parts.

HOOK In the HLBT teaching method, the first part of a lesson that gets the students' attention.

HOOK-BOOK-LOOK-TOOK (HBLT) A specific organized method of planning a lesson.

HUMANISTIC An ideology of teaching that emphasizes addressing the needs and maturity of students.

HYPERBOLE A figure of speech that involves exaggeration of reality.

IDENTITY ACHIEVEMENT When an adolescent comes to a satisfactory understanding of who he or she is.

IDENTITY CONFUSION (OR IDENTITY DIFFUSION) When an adolescent has a variety of self identities and is unsure which is his or her true self.

IDENTITY FORECLOSURE When an adolescent makes a premature decision about whom he or she is.

IDENTITY VS. IDENTITY DIFFUSION Erikson's developmental stage that describes the primary psychosocial conflict of adolescence.

IDEOLOGY A system of beliefs that guides one's activities and decisions.

IMAGINARY AUDIENCE The adolescent belief that others around them are paying special attention to the details of their lives.

IMAGINATIVE LEARNER Students who learn best by thinking through issues and ideas.

IMPLICIT CURRICULUM That which is learned and is implied by the stated goals.

INDEPENDENT In learning, preferring to work alone or at one's own pace, rather than under a teacher's close direction.

INDIVIDUATION The process of an adolescent's becoming more independent.

INDIVIDUATIVE-REFLECTIVE FAITH The fourth stage of Fowler's theory in which a person takes ownership of faith.

INTERPERSONAL INTELLIGENCE The natural ability to understand and relate to others.

INTERPRETIVE QUESTION A style of open question that requires students to find the meaning and nuances of an issue or idea.

INTRAPERSONAL INTELLIGENCE The natural ability to understand oneself deeply.

INTROVERT Preferring solitude and reflection to social interaction and involvement.

INTUITIVE Relying on direct perception rather than reason or reflection.

INTUITIVE-PROJECTIVE FAITH The first stage of Fowler's theory in which individuals are influenced by the images and attitudes they are given by others.

KINESTHETIC LEARNERS Students who must be in motion to learn most effectively.

LATE ADOLESCENCE The final stage of adolescence, typically recognized as the years between high school graduation and full adult maturity.

LEARNING STYLES (or LEARNING PREFERENCES) The complex and varied ways in which individuals learn best.

LESSON CURRICULUM The plan and materials used to teach an individual lesson.

LINGUISTIC INTELLIGENCE The ability to communicate well through the written or spoken word.

LOGICAL-MATHEMATICAL INTELLIGENCE The ability to understand and manipulate numerical, logical, or sequential information.

LOOK In the HLBT method, the part of the lesson that guides the students through deeper interpretation and application of the text or subject.

MARGINALIZED People who are not accepted or welcomed by the majority of the people in a culture.

MEDICAL DOCTOR A metaphor in which the teacher's role is to diagnose and fix problems or meet needs in students.

MENARCHE The event of first menstruation.

METACOGNITION The awareness of one's ability to think and the thinking process.

METAMETHOD A large category that includes several similar teaching methods (e.g., skits, role plays, and musicals are part of the metamethod of drama).

METAPHOR A figure of speech using one word or idea to describe another for the purpose of comparison.

METHODOLOGY The ideas, tools, and strategies used to teach.

MIDDLE ADOLESCENCE The second of three adolescent stages, usually understood to coincide with the high school years.

MODERNISTIC Describing a way of thinking in which beliefs and propositions are measured and analyzed primarily by objective, scientific means.

MULTIPLE INTELLIGENCES A theory proposed by Dr. Howard Gardner that seeks to explain the differing aptitudes that individuals possess.

MUSICAL INTELLIGENCE The natural ability some people have to compose, perform, and/or interpret music and its components.

MYSTICAL Not perceptible to the intellect or senses.

MYTHICAL-LITERAL FAITH The second stage of Fowler's faith development theory in which human traits are attributed to God and interpreted literally.

NATURIST INTELLIGENCE The natural ability to relate to and understand God's creation.

NEGATIVE IDENTITY When an adolescent assumes an identity obviously objectionable to his or her family or other significant adults.

NEW AGE MOVEMENT A broad range of philosophies and religious beliefs that see all experiences as spiritual in some way.

NULL CURRICULUM What students learn or assume from what is not taught.

OBSERVER A metaphor that understands the teacher's role to be watching the learner grow from a distance.

OMNIPOTENT Infinite in power, as God.

OPEN QUESTION A question that has a variety of possible responses and must be answered in several words or sentences.

ORTHODOX Commonly and/or historically accepted as true and right.

OVERT CURRICULUM Teaching that is obvious to the learner, whether intended by the teacher or not.

PARTICIPATIVE A learning style in which a group is active together as opposed to watching or listening to one person.

PERSONAL FABLE The adolescent belief that no one has ever had their same experiences and therefore cannot understand them.

PILGRIM A metaphor for teaching in which teachers see themselves on a journey alongside their students.

POSTCONVENTIONAL MORAL REASONING The third of Kohlberg's three stages, occurring when a person understands society's rules and conventions to be relative and dependent on a variety of factors.

POSTMODERN A currently popular way of thinking that understands truth to be relative and subjective.

PRAGMATIC Practical; having a specific use or purpose.

PRECONVENTIONAL MORAL REASONING The first of Kohlberg's three stages of moral reasoning, typically associated with childhood, in which the practice of making moral decisions is based on the likely reward or punishment.

PREFRONTAL CORTEX The very front of the brain immediately behind the forehead, responsible for long-term thinking and believed to be still maturing in adolescence.

PRESERVATION A teaching ideology that sees teaching as the way to pass on cultural norms and expectations from one generation to the next.

PRIMAL FAITH The base of Fowler's stages in which trust is placed in caregivers and is mixed with hope and love.

PROGRAM CURRICULUM Long-term plans for teaching in a specific context (e.g., one-year teaching plans or requirements to graduate with a given college degree).

PSYCHOMOTOR Concerned with action, particularly physical action.

PSYCHOSOCIAL MORATORIUM When adolescents put development of identity on hold to experience freedom from the responsibility of adulthood.

PUBERTY The physical stage of adolescent development in which the genitals mature and the individual becomes capable of reproduction.

RANDOM Without particular order or sequence.

RAPID EYE MOVEMENT (REM) The deepest and most productive moments of sleep, so named because the eyes move up and down and side to side very quickly.

RECEIVED CURRICULUM What the student actually learns from a given experience or lesson.

REFLECTIVE Thoughtful, pondering, not quick to answer or decide.

RELATIVISM The belief that truth is not absolute and depends on individuals or circumstances.

RELAY RUNNER The metaphor for teaching that depicts the teacher as handing off knowledge so that students can take it further.

RITES OF PASSAGE Specific events or rituals that mark the passage from childhood to adulthood.

ROMANTIC The teaching ideology that believes students should be allowed to grow on their own with a minimum of influence.

SAGE The teaching metaphor that believes the teacher should impart wisdom to the student.

SALESPERSON The metaphor in which the teacher must convince the student that the subject is important enough to learn and study.

SCOPE AND SEQUENCE CHART A long-term plan, typically two or three years, that lays out what each age group will be studying in a given setting.

SELF-ESTEEM How a person feels about whom he or she is.

SELF-IDENTITY Who a person perceives himself or herself to be.

SELF-RELIANCE The ability to function independently.

SENSORY MODEL A way of understanding learning styles based on visual, auditory, tactile, and kinesthetic modes.

SEQUENTIAL Characterized by order and logic.

SHEMA A Hebrew word meaning *hear*, commonly used to refer to Deuteronomy 6:4-9.

SIMILE A figure of speech that compares one word or phrase to another typically using *like* or *as*.

SPATIAL INTELLIGENCE The natural ability to evaluate relationships of objects, spaces, and/or distances.

STORM AND STRESS The theory that adolescence is characterized primarily by very straining experiences and emotions.

SUBJECTIVE Relative to individual interpretation or experience.

SYNTHESIS The combining of multiple ideas or items to form a whole.

SYNTHETIC-CONVENTIONAL FAITH The third stage of Fowler's theory in which faith is shaped by and in relationship with others.

TACTILE LEARNERS Those who learn best by physical touch.

TEACHABLE MOMENT A time when people are most open to learning or change, often associated with an unusual experience.

TOOK In the HBLT method, the part of the lesson in which students are presented with a specific challenge or activity to change as a result of the lesson.

TRANSCENDENTAL A teaching philosophy focused on meditation and spiritual disciplines.

TRANSMISSION The sharing and passing on of knowledge or culture, often with the purpose of preserving that information.

UNIVERSAL CURRICULUM Anything that is learned, whether it is planned or not.

UNIVERSALIZING FAITH The sixth and last of Fowler's stages in which people translate their faith into living for the sake of others with little regard for their own hopes and desires.

VISUAL LEARNERS Those who learn best by seeing information or objects.

WICCA A belief system that includes worship of nature, belief in a natural balance of good and evil, and the practice of spells and incantations.

REFERENCES

Altemeyer, B., & Hunsberger, B. (1997). *Amazing Conversions.* Amherst, NY: Prometheus Books.

American Demographics (2000, March). Ithaca.

Atkinson, H. (2001). *Teaching Youth with Confidence.* Wheaton, IL: Evangelical Training Association.

Barna Research Group (2002). April 23 news release.

Bartlett, D., & Muir, B. (2000). *Talking the Walk.* Grand Rapids, MI: Zondervan Publishing House.

Barton, L. G. (1994). *Quick Flip Questions for Critical Thinking.* San Clemente, CA: Edupress.

Benson, P. L., Galbraith, J.& Espeland, P. (1998). *What Teens Need to Succeed.* Minneapolis, MN: Free Spirit Publishing.

Blender (2000, June/July).

Bomar, J., & Sabatelli, R. (1996). Family system dynamics, gender, and psychosocial maturity in late adolescence. *Journal of Adolescent Research*, 11.

Borgman, D. (1997). *When Kumbaya is Not Enough.* Peabody, MA: Hendrickson.

Borich, G. D. (1996). *Effective Teaching Methods, third edition.* Englewood Cliffs, NJ: Merrill.

Bundschuh, R. (1998). *Magnetic Teaching.* Cincinnati, OH: Standard Publishing.

Campbell, L., Campbell, B., & Dickinson, D. (1996). *Teaching & Learning Through Multiple Intelligences.* Needham Heights, MA: Allyn & Bacon.

Center for Parent and Youth Understanding (2000, Spring). youthculture@2000 newsletter.

Center for Parent and Youth Understanding (2001, Fall). youthculture@2000 newsletter.

Cook Ministries. Retrieved August 22, 2002, from http://www.cookministries.com/curriculum/davidccook

Cully, I. (1983). *Planning and Selecting Curriculum for Christian Education.* Valley Forge: Judson.

Dewey, J. (1944). *Experience and Education.* New York: Macmillan.

Dockery, K. (1999). *The Youth Worker's Guide to Creative Bible Study, Revised and Expanded.* Nashville, TN: Broadman & Holdman Publishers.

Duckworth, J. (Ed.) (1989). *Hot Topics Youth Electives: School, Male & Female, Doubts.* Elgin, IL: David C. Cook Publishing Co.

Dunn, R. R. (2001). *Shaping the Spiritual Life of Students.* Downers Grove, IL: InterVarsity Press.

Dunn, R., & Dunn, K. (1979). Learning styles/teaching styles: Should they…can they…be matched? *Educational Leadership,* 36.

Engelkamp, J. (2001, Spring). *The American Journal of Psychology*; Urbana.

Erikson, E. (1959). Identity and the life cycle, *Psychological Issues*, 1, pp. 1-171.

Erikson, E. (1968). *Identity: Youth and crisis.,* New York: Norton.

Fields, D. (2002, March-April). Relational Basics, *Youthworker Journal,* Nashville, TN: CCM Communications, XVIII, 4.

Fowler, J. W. (1986). Faith and the structure of meaning. In Dykstra, C., & Parks, S. (Eds.), *Faith development and Fowler.* Birmingham, AL: Religious Education Press.

Gangel, K. (1974). *24 Ways to Improve Your Teaching.* Wheaton, IL: Victor Books.

Gardner, H. (1993) *Frames of Mind: The Theory of Multiple Intelligences* (10th Anniversary Edition). NY: Basic Books.

Graendorf, W. C. (1981). *Introduction to Biblical Christian Education.* Chicago: Moody Press.

Grasha, A. (1996). *Teaching with Style.* Pittsburg, PA: Alliance Press.

Harter, S. (1990). Identity and self development. In S. Freldman & G. Elliott (Eds.), *At the threshold: The developing adolescent.* Cambridge, MA: Harvard University Press, pp. 352-387.

Henderson, D. W. (1998). *Culture Shift.* Grand Rapids, MI: Baker.

Huebner, D. F. (1982, July-August). From theory to practice: Curriculum, *Religious Education,* 77.

Hunt, J. (1998). *Disciple-Making Teachers.* Loveland, CO: Vital Ministry.

Jessup, D., Musick, H., & Kirgiss, C. (2002). *Guys.* Grand Rapids, MI: Zondervan Publishing House.

Johnston, L. D., Bachman, J. G., O'Malley, P. M., & Schulenberg, J. (1996). *Monitoring the future: a continuing study of american youth* (8th- 10th- and 12th- grade surveys) [Computer file].

Junior Achievement (2002, May 21). Girls may make less money at summer jobs. Junior Achievement press release.

Koenig, L. (1995, March). Change in self-esteem from 8th to 10th grade :Effects of gender and disruptive life events. Paper presented at the biennial meetings of the Society for Research in Child Development, Indianapolis.

LeBar, L. E. (1964). Curriculum, in Hakes, J. E. (Ed.) *An Introduction to Evangelical Christian Education.* Chicago: Moody Press.

LeBar, L. E. (1981). In Graendorf, W. C. (Ed.). *Introduction to Biblical Christian Education.* Chicago: Moody.

LeBar, L. E. (1995). *Education that is Christian.* Colorado Springs, CO: Chariot Victor.

LeFever, M. D. (1995). *Learning Styles: Reaching Everyone God Gave You to Teach.* Colorado Springs, CO: David C. Cook Publishing Co.

Legislative Commission on the Economic Status of Women, Fact Sheet. Retrieved August 1, 2002, from http://www.commissions.leg.state.mn.us/lcesw/fs/marstat.pdf

Lynn, D. (2001). *Junior High – Middle School Talksheets.* Grand Rapids, MI: Zondervan Publishing House.

Marler, P. L., & Hadaway, C. K. (1999, Summer). Testing the attendance gap in a conservative church, *Sociology of Religion;* Washington.

McCarthy, B. (1987). *The 4MAT System: Teaching to Learning Styles with Right/Left Mode Techniques.* Barrington, IL: Excel, Inc.

Miel, A. (1946). *Changing the Curriculum: A Social Process.* New York: Appleton-Century-Crofts.

Mortimer, J., Finch, M., Ryu, S., Shanahan, M., & Call, K. (1996a). The effects of work intensity on adolescent mental health, achievement, and behavioral adjustment: New evidence from a prospective study. *Child Development, 67.*

Muuss, R. E. (1996, November 26). Theories of adolescence. *New York Times;* New York: McGraw Hill.

PBS *Frontline* (2002, January 31). Inside the Teenage Brain.

Pleuddeman, J. E. (1989). Metaphors in Christian Education, *Christian Education Journal 10:1.*

Quick Studies series (1992). Elgin, IL: David C. Cook Publishing Co.

Rice, F. P. (1987). *The Adolescent* (5th edition). Boston: Allyn and Bacon.

Richards, L. O., & Bredfeldt, G. J. (1998). *Creative Bible Teaching: Revised and Expanded.* Chicago: Moody Press.

RollingStone (2000, January 20). Issue 832.

RollingStone (2002, January 31). Issue 888.

RollingStone (2002, February 28). Issue 890.

RollingStone (2002, May 23). Issue 896.

RollingStone (2002, June 6). Issue 897.

RollingStone (2003, January 23). Issue 914.

RollingStone (2003, June 26). Issue 925.

RollingStone (2003, November 27). Issue 936.

Shelton, C. M. (1995). *Adolescent Spirituality.* New York: Crossroad.

Steinberg, L., & Cauffman, E. (1995). The impact of employment on adolescent development, in Vasta (Ed.), *Annals of Child Development* (Vol. 11). London: Jessica Kingsley Publishers.

Steinberg, L. (1999). *Adolescence* (Fifth Edition). New York: McGraw-Hill College.

Strauch, B. (2003). *The Primal Teen: What the New Discoveries About the Teenage Brain Tell Us About Our Kids.* New York: Bantam.

USA Today (2001, November 27).

Ward, P. (1999). *God at the Mall.* Peabody, MA: Hendrickson.

Warden, M. (1999). *What's Your Point?* Cincinnati, OH: Standard Publishing.

Wolfe, S., & Truxillo, C. (1996). *The relationship between decisional control, responsibility and positive and negative outcomes during early adolescence.* Paper presented at the biennial meeting of the Society for Research on Adolescence, Boston.